FIRSTFRUITS OF A NEW CREATION

ESSAYS IN HONOR OF JERRAM BARRS

Edited by
DOUG SERVEN

Published by White Blackbird Books, an imprint of Storied Publishing

Copyright ©2019 by Doug Serven

All rights reserved

No part of this book may be reproduced, stored in a retrieval system, or transmitted in any way by any means without permission from the publisher, with the exception of reviewers who may quote brief passages in a review.

Permission requests and other questions may be directed to the Contact page at www.storied.pub.

Unless otherwise indicated, Scripture quotations are from the ESV Bible (The Holy Bible, English Standard Version), copyright 2001 by Crossway, a publishing ministry of Good News Publishers. 2011 Text Edition. All rights reserved.

Printed in the United States of America

ISBN-13:978-1-7340181-0-3

Cover design by Sean Benesh

Painting reproduced on the cover by Paul Buxman, used by permission from Jerram Barrs

Edited by Claire Berger, Wes Martin, Kaitlin Martin, Doug Serven, Beth Vishanoff

Camille Halstrom's chapter is an expansion of material appearing in *Joyfully Spreading the Word: Sharing the Good News of Jesus*, edited by Kathleen Nielson and Gloria Furman (Crossway, 2018). Used by permission.

A significant portion "Evangelism and the Cultural Mandate" by William Edgar appears in another from in *Created and Creating: A Biblical Theology of Culture* (IVP Academic). © 2016 by William Edgar. Used by permission of InterVarsity Press, www.ivpress.com.

ALSO BY WHITE BLACKBIRD BOOKS

All Are Welcome: Toward a Multi-Everything Church

Birth of Joy: Philippians

Choosing a Church: A Biblical and Practical Guide

Ever Light and Dark: Telling Secrets, Telling the Truth

Everything Is Meaningless? Ecclesiastes

Heal Us, Emmanuel: A Call for Racial Reconciliation, Representation, and Unity in the Church

The Organized Pastor: Systems to Care for People Well

A Sometimes Stumbling Life: Making Sense of Our Struggles and God's Grace in the Journey of Faith

Urban Hinterlands: Planting the Gospel in Uncool Places

Follow whiteblackbirdbooks.pub for upcoming titles and releases.

PRAISE FOR FIRSTFRUITS OF A NEW CREATION

I first met Jerram at Covenant Seminary. I quickly realized we would not merely be talking about apologetics and evangelism. We would have it modeled for us in every class. Jerram lectured passionately, but he also listened to us patiently. He consistently provided compelling insights into God's Word, and he offered compelling insights into the human heart, including his own. My classroom notes cannot do justice to what I learned from him then or since. But this wonderful tribute to the man and his message comes awfully close.
Ryan Laughlin
Senior Pastor, The Covenant Presbyterian Church
St. Louis, MO

If it weren't for Jerram, I might not still be a Christian, and I definitely wouldn't be a minister. I know I'm not the only one to make that statement. God has given Jerram a gentleness and kindness which has broken through the walls of the most cynical of us. God has used Jerram to draw us closer to Christ. Jerram's caring love, patience, wisdom, and piercing questions have helped many to be more truly human. Jerram is a poet, scholar, evangelist, gardener, pastor, and even a tiny bit red dragon. This book incorporates many of those aspects of Jerram's teaching and influence on his students and friends. It shows how a fully orbed discipleship includes theology as well as aesthetics, deep cultural thought as well as practical response, and above all a love for God, his world, and all those made in his image. As you read you will be blessed and strengthened by those God has used Jerram to bless and strengthen.
Travis Scott
Senior Pastor, Grace & Peace Presbyterian Church
Pittsburgh, PA

Reading this book is like being invited to a retreat with Jerram and his friends and having the luxury of time to listen to the ways the Gospel continues to shape them. It is a delight to read these personal accounts of how the Scriptures and the life of Jerram pointed them faithfully to Christ, changing their heart orientation to others and God's world. Though their journeys are quite different from mine, in their writings I am drawn in close as a friend and fellow pilgrim. I was called to learn, examine, and reorder myself on the path of sharing Christ's love in similar ways with my neighbors. May you discover this rich feast, a refreshing engagement, a restoration of hope for yourself and others.
Susan DeAnn Harris
Member of the Covenant Seminary Advisory Board
Tulsa, OK

What a joy and privilege to read *Firstfruits of a New Creation*. I first heard Jerram speak in the early 1990s at a L'Abri conference in Kentucky. I was mesmerized listening to him connect a Biblical understanding of life to the issues of the day, and then he gently and carefully spoke to people in the Q&A time afterward. He communicated with such kindness, respect, compassion, and grace. It made a permanent impression. Almost a decade later, my husband and I were students in one of Jerram's apologetics classes at Covenant Seminary. He was the same as he had been at the conference, a great scholar who cared about people's lives. I filled several legal-sized notebooks trying to capture every important word of the lectures, and all the twists and turns they took in response to the student's questions. I remember Jerram saying, "The beauty of the Christian answer is that it enables us to cry and have hope at the same time." We weep with those who weep and never give cheap answers to people's doubts or suffering. As I've immersed myself in this essay collection from Jerram's colleagues, I'm reminded once again of a better way to be a Christian in the world. My gratitude runs deep.
Andi Ashworth
Author, *Real Love for Real Life*
Co-Founder Art House America
Nashville, TN

Reading through this collection reminded me of the excitement, joy, and challenge I felt sitting in Jerram's classes many years ago. Though I didn't understand it all at the time, I remember writing down everything he was saying, knowing it was changing my heart and mind forever. And I was not alone. These essays are a testimony to the far-reaching fruit of God's work through a humble servant. It's all here: a deep love for God, his truth, his image-bearers, and the culture they create. There is no replacement for the impish grin, the urgent tears, the wide-open-mouth laugh, and the gentle words of Jerram's presence, but this book is certainly a fitting tribute to his example. May it inspire a new generation to demonstrate and share the Lordship of Christ over all of life.
Robb Ludwick
International Chairman of L'Abri Fellowship
Eck en Wiel, The Netherlands

Of all the mentors who have had a profound, even life-altering impact upon me and my ministry, Jerram Barrs belongs at the top of the list. First as a young, green seminary student and now through almost twenty-five years of pastoral ministry, Jerram's notable combination of conviction and compassion have remained an anchor and lifeline. Of fathers in the faith, he is most certainly one of mine. I can think of no better person and no greater saint to honor with a series of excellent essays such as the ones contained in this volume.
Scott Sauls
Author, *Jesus Outside the Lines* and *Irresistible Faith*
Senior Pastor, Christ Presbyterian Church
Nashville, TN

In a solidified pluralistic society where the lack of the referential feeds the amoral, self-ethical and hopeless behavior so clearly portrayed in every layer of normal life, this book couldn't be more welcome. The authors of these essays represent the principles that Jerram Barrs so vividly portrayed and taught to the many people who visited English L'Abri, in his classes at Covenant Seminary, and in his lectures on

various topics. You will find deep insights that address real-life issues and questions. This book is a call to renew the mind, transform lives and impact surrounding cultures.
Luciano Pires
Co-Founder, Colloquium
Porto, Portugal

In the 1970s Francis Schaeffer was shedding light on how to think Christianly about animals and trees when few Christians were. Schaeffer and his wife, Edith, were trying to think Christianly about *everything*. Jerram Barrs was deeply influenced by the living out of that thinking in the L'Abri communities started by the Schaeffers. Barrs modeled this effort to understand the lordship of Christ over every feature of human existence. He taught classes not only on theology but also on the novels of Jane Austen, the plays of Shakespeare, and the magic in the *Harry Potter* series. That breadth of interest is reflected in this volume with thoughtful essays ranging from questions about the unequal measure of suffering God allows in his world, the influence of Oprah Winfrey on American culture, and what is revealed in the harmony of music. Pastors will be better pastors for reading this book with openness to its approach to the bruised and yet rich world we live in.
Ron Lutjens
Pastor Emeritus, Old Orchard Church
St. Louis, MO

I have been doubly blessed by the teaching and ministry of Jerram Barrs. The pastor who was instrumental to my own conversion as an adult was a recent student of Jerram Barrs. I realize now how beautifully this pastor implemented Barrs' heart and teaching on evangelism. Shortly after my baptism, I myself became a student of Jerram. He equipped me to reach out to others, and I started a ministry influenced based on the relational style he taught me. Now, by God's grace, people I am walking alongside are coming to faith in Jesus, and the Lord is growing their hearts to learn about relational outreach and apologetics.

I'm grateful for Barrs' teaching, and it is a delight to see the fruit of his ministry multiply.

Katherine Beim-Esche
Founder and Director, Fellowship of Former Christian Scientists
St. Louis, MO

Always and everywhere, we learn the deepest, truest lessons over the shoulder and through the heart. This collection of essays, *Firstfruits of a New Creation,* is born of a long love for Jerram Barrs, each one a way of honoring his heart and mind given for the Gospel of the kingdom to many students over many years, and I am one of them. When I made my way to the Manor House, the English L'Abri in Greatham, almost fifty years ago, it was its promise that drew me. I had no idea who worked there, but the possibility of my honest questions finding honest answers brought me to this centuries-old home in a village so small that the postal address was "near Liss." In my first days there, I met with Jerram, and his thoughtful kindness intrigued me. The more I read, the more we talked, and the more I learned from him. An honest humility, a deep knowledge of the world I wanted to understand, a surprising gentleness, an almost fierce commitment to the truth about God, about human beings, and about the universe all together made for a pedagogy that has formed me. I hope this book has a wide reading, both among those who know and love Jerram, but even more for those who are yet to be his students, learning from him about the things that matter most, over his shoulder and through his heart.

Steven Garber
Author, *Visions of Vocation* and *The Fabric of Faithfulness*
Professor of Marketplace Theology, Regent College
Vancouver, BC

In a time when spiritual authority is viewed with suspicion and apologetics is equated with an ideological competition, the legacy of Jerram Barrs' ministry is remarkable. Not only has he reawakened apologetics for many, but he has gripped their hearts with the authoritative claim of the Gospel. As his student I both trembled and cherished sitting under his teaching for the same reason: it would make me more like Christ.

This volume testifies to the Spirit of Christ in which Jerram has ministered to thousands through various accounts of those who experienced his salubrious presence, lingered over gracious conversation with him, and beheld his Christ-like manner. Read the stories and you will see a soul joyfully and soberly laboring to bring the shalom of Yahweh to a broken and hurting world.

Casey Petersen
Assistant Pastor, Main Street Church
St. Charles, MO

It's impossible to separate Jerram Barrs' teaching from his life. The authors in this volume demonstrate this reality effortlessly and with a variety of voices. I was introduced to Jerram's theological breadth and depth in 1992 when I attended a conference in Lancaster, PA, on spiritual warfare. Jerram shared the ticket with J. I. Packer. What struck me most about his teaching was an echo of holiness mixed with mercy, which I've come to appreciate as kindness. That was enough to send me and my family to Covenant Seminary in the summer of 1995 to study within the Francis A. Schaeffer Institute which he was heading up. Years later I'm back in Lancaster conducting a public-facing, culture-engaging outreach absolutely informed by Jerram's person. I read these chapters with familiarity and delight like the sounds of birdsong and cicadas. I found myself grateful, not only for a trail guide like Jerram, but also for the many folk he's influenced. The essays range from human origins (Collins) to epistemology (Meek) to worldview (Sung) and beyond. I especially appreciated the historical notes by Ronald Macaulay and Wade Bradshaw on his days at L'Abri and his "undeserved" physical suffering. You will meet Jerram Barrs in these writings, if you haven't already. Knowing Jerram, he'd prefer you meet up with Jesus, the forerunner of our faith.

Tom Becker
Author, *Good Posture*
Founder & Director, The Row House, Inc.
Lancaster, PA

Geerhardus Vos once claimed, "Jesus' method of teaching was not the philosophical one of defining a thing, but the popular parabolic one of describing and illustrating it." Countless Covenant Seminary students have been blessed by the teaching of Jerram Barrs, for he consistently teaches in the way of Jesus. Jerram passionately and personally draws people to a deeper understanding of God's Word and God's world by demonstrating the character of Christ. This fascinating collection of essays reveals and honors the work and spirit of Jerram, while doing so in a way that keeps our eyes fixed on Jesus. You will walk away longing to be more like Christ—which, I am confident, is exactly what Jerram would hope for you as well.

Stephanie O. Hubach
Author of *Same Lake, Different Boat*
Research Fellow in Disability Ministries, Covenant Theological Seminary
St. Louis, MO

This rich collection of essays is a testimony to Jerram Barrs' continuing impact. Many of the more personal essays paint a picture of Jerram that is easily recognized by those who know him—his irresistible passion for living out the love of Jesus, evident from a deep joy and both holy tears and holy anger, yet hopefully equally impacting and transforming for those who don't know him. Several of the more academic essays show the fertile ground that Jerram's thought provides for creative spin-off projects across various fields (from linguistics and epistemology to an analysis of Oprah's world). Just as learning from Jerram is being exposed to this beautiful mixture of a Christ-like compassion, a sanctified imagination and a deep personal challenge to one's character, so these essays written by several of Jerram's friends, colleagues and students, I am confident, will stretch and enrich anyone who reads them.

Arend J. Poelarends
Associate Professor of Physics and Astronomy, Wheaton College
Wheaton, IL

I first met Jerram and Vicki when we visited the English L'Abri in 1972. He was quiet and rather shy but welcomed us warmly. At the time I was a resident in psychiatry in Bristol, England, and we would often visit L'Abri for weekends. It was there that I found much help from Jerram and his colleagues in thinking through the relationship between medicine, psychiatry and theology. Later we were asked to join the L'Abri staff, and since then I have worked with and lived in Jerram's shadow for forty years, first at the English L'Abri and then at Covenant Seminary. This book is indeed a reflection of his life, character, and work. In the extraordinary diversity and depth of the subject matter of each essay, it beautifully demonstrates Jerram's concern for "the lordship of Christ over the whole of life." Each essay stands alone and needs to be read slowly, or the reader will suffer from indigestion with so much rich food. But each is tied to the whole with brief reflections from the authors on Jerram's thoughtfulness, care for individuals, gracious manner and his passion for truth. I am also amazed by the number of books he writes, his knowledge of great literature, speaking engagements he takes on all over the world, people he talks to, meals he cooks, bread that he bakes, trees, flowers, and bulbs he plants and tends, and chronic illnesses he endures with stoic courage and patience. Thank you, Jerram, for your faithful friendship, example, and companionship on this journey of life.

Richard Winter
Author, *Perfecting Ourselves to Death* and *Still Bored in a Culture of Entertainment*
Professor Emeritus of Counseling, Covenant Theological Seminary
St. Louis, MO

Jerram Barrs is my mentor in listening to hear. It's more than Jerram's teaching; it's more than his great books on evangelism; it's more than his captivating words when he speaks. It's his tears, his pause, a sense he is listening to my chaotic communications and can hear the core. Jerram was my Confessor, and in this volume I discern a similar empathy and give thanks for his gentle influence.

Allan Dayhoff
Author, *Church in a Blues Bar* and *The Genius in Your Wounds*
Founder and Executive Director, Evangelize Today Ministries
Fairfax Station, VA

I will forever be indebted to Jerram's gentle and holistic approach to life. As a young seminary student, his respectful and biblical outlook on creation, culture, and the issues of the human heart offered me an early glimpse of the loving yet firm nature of Jesus. His ability to listen, talk with people, and speak the truth in love allows room for the grace of God and the conviction of the Spirit, which has proven these last twenty-two years to be the most fruitful posture for me to take as a pastor, farmer, and curator of an agrarian study center. You have in your hands some of the best expressions of Jerram's vine-ripened life. Take your time with each author. Don't rush. Savor and enjoy!

Duane D. Otto
Farmer, Founding President of Ithaka Fellowship, Inc., and Lead Pastor of Christ Community Church
Chenoa, IL

One of Eric Liddell's acquaintances said about him, "It is rare indeed that a person has the good fortune to meet a saint, but he came as close to it as anyone I have ever known." Jerram Barrs has been a special and encouraging voice in my life, however little fortune was involved. He would not appreciate being thought of as a saint. The welcome he extends, the words of his mouth, and the meditations of his heart paint a vibrant and inviting picture of an honest and humble life lived before the face of God.

Each of the brilliant essays in the volume will prove to be a real help to us in our own welcome of others, our search for words, and our hearts' meditations as we, with Jerram, look for the return of the king.

Jack Harding
Researcher and Scriptorium Coordinator, Christian Heritage
Cambridge, UK

I, like so many others, have thought of Jerram as a mentor in the faith. I've learned from Jerram's teaching on Schaeffer's early and later years, his tremendous lectures, his Apologetics class at Covenant, his books, and an interview he so graciously gave when he sat down with me to talk about his life and the legacy of Francis Schaeffer. His personal conversion story and work are a tremendous and inspiring mark of God's providence. I am gratified to read more of the story of his work and life in these pages. Moreover, beyond the story, I appreciate and honor the very real human person that shines through by God's grace. Each time I have talked with Jerram, I am overwhelmed by his uniquely firm and yet gentle spirit and manner, and his deep love for truth, beauty, and the dignity of created persons. These attributes always shine through. They reflect both the heritage of his own direct mentor, Dr. Schaeffer, and, even more dynamically, the reflection of the image of Christ.

Dan Guinn
Founder and Developer, FrancisSchaefferStudies.org
Olathe, KS

I had few Christian resources in Hungary, so books by the Schaeffers were formative, and they led me to English L'Abri. After a week there, I found an intriguing person. The speaker's biblical wisdom, gentle and loving approach as he spoke to and about non-Christians reflected his empathy and ability to listen well. It melted me and helped me dare to be honest before God. I spent the remaining two months of study listening to this man Jerram Barrs because of the way he spoke about Jesus and taught me to love God and non-Christians more (and I learned a significant amount of English). Years later, Vicki and Jerram invited me for a dinner where I had the most delicious meal ever. It took me weeks of reflection to understand they had treated me as a most important guest. They made me feel like royalty! Being around the Barrs means experiencing the Gospel of Jesus and, in a similar way, perusing this volume inspired me afresh to follow Jesus and to love others.

Borbála Mikola
Assistant Pastor for Budapest-Külső-Kelenföldi Reformed Church
Budapest, Hungary

Jerram has left me with countless stories I remember about his example, counsel, love, or teaching. Decisions my wife and I make now are often formed by what Jerram taught or how he lived. He in part drew me to Covenant Seminary. He taught classes I took there, baptized my oldest, employed me briefly for his gardens, came to preach for my Pennsylvania ordination, and I have been privileged to count him a counselor and friend. Through this book, you will catch some helpful patterns that were part of Jerram's life: an abiding trust in Scripture, humble unapologetically intellectual faith, enjoying God's common grace in all of life, and living a whole life under the Lordship of Jesus Christ. Our painful polarization in society today has affected both world and church. Both need men and women like Jerram, who draws people by example to our savior, who came to dwell with us *"full of grace and truth"* (John 1:14). Take up and enjoy!

Jeff Zehnder
Senior Pastor
Fairview Reformed Presbyterian Church
Ohioville, Pennsylvania

CONTENTS

Foreword — 1

BEING HUMAN
Being (Even More) Human — 7
Undeserved Suffering — 27
Unexpected Encounters — 37
Christ and Character — 49

ENGAGING CULTURE
Welcome to Oprah's World — 67
Being Human at the Box Office — 81
Fittingness — 101
A Theater to the Cosmos — 113

SHARING CHRIST
A Man Who Told Me Everything I Have Ever Done! — 135
Love, the Final Epistemic (and Ontology Too) — 153
Turning My Eastern Worldview Upside Down — 171
Freedoms and Limitations — 185
Evangelism and the Cultural Mandate — 211
Apologetic Communication — 241

Short Stories About Jerram From His Students — 255

About White Blackbird Books — 267

FOREWORD

Mark Dalbey
President, Covenant Theological Seminary
St. Louis, MO

These essays were written in honor of Jerram Barrs' life, work, world of ideas, and his love for people. Those of us who know Jerram understand his desire to see those he teaches and disciples take his thoughts and ideas beyond where he himself could take them in their development and in their multiplying impact. His life and teaching are not about himself but about the God he serves, the people he equips, and the mission God invites us into to reach nations, generations, and the whole of life.

My life is one of many transformed by the way God has used my friend Jerram in a Gospel-shaping way to grow me into greater Christlikeness. My wife and our three children and their spouses have all experienced this blessing through Jerram as well. When I was a student in one of Jerram's Doctor of Ministry classes on worship, his presentation of the doctrine of grace became an experience of grace deep within my heart and life. Over the twenty-six years I have known Jerram, I have been his student, his colleague on the faculty of Covenant Seminary, his boss as vice president of academics and dean of faculty, and now his president. Though the relational roles have changed over the years, Jerram's manner of relating has been constant as he consistently treated me with dignity, respect, and love.

Jerram's impact on Covenant Seminary has also been profound over the twenty-eight years he has been with us. I have had the privilege of co-laboring alongside Jerram for eighteen of those years and can say without reservation that while he has been part of a team of people God has used to transform the seminary, without Jerram the transformation would have been significantly diminished. His primary role in that transformation process has enabled Covenant Seminary to become increasingly focused on and reflective of the grace, truth, and mission of the Gospel of the Kingdom of God's beloved Son. As a result, hundreds of students have been deeply changed in heart and mind not only through Jerram's classroom teaching, but also through his kind and mentoring presence in their lives. Since 1989, the faculty have become greater pastor-scholars even as they have grown as people through the influence of Jerram's words and manner.

The core principles of Jerram's life at L'Abri,[1] and as a professor at Covenant Seminary, a pastor, husband, and father all trace their way through the chapters that follow. His deep, uncompromising commitment to God's inspired and inerrant Word of grace and truth is foundational for everything else. His fervent commitment to the truth that people are made in God's image is expressed in a heart of grace and compassion toward everyone he encounters. His unwavering commitment to God's call to meaningful engagement with the presenting issues of the culture is an inspiration to many. And his commitment to the biblical vision of a coming new heavens and new earth, as well as to the present rule of King Jesus, helps us see how all of life and the breadth of vocational callings we engage in are meaningful and important to God and his mission.

The intersection of the story of Jerram's life with the story of Scripture and the mission of God make him a safe person with whom to talk about any issues of the mind or heart without fear of judgment and with the hope of finding answers. As the pages that follow will show, his sharing in God's image and living out that image in God's world, combined with the posture of a fellow sinner saved by grace, indwelt by the Holy Spirit, and empowered for a life of faithful stewardship and servanthood, have marked Jerram's life with the indelible stamp of God's own heart of love and mercy. Through him, I and many others have come to know and love our Lord a little better.

1. L'Abri (French for shelter) is a study center where individuals have the opportunity to seek answers to honest questions about God and the significance of human life. The first L'Abri community was founded in Switzerland in 1955 by Dr. Francis Schaeffer and his wife, Edith. From "Homepage," L'Abri International Fellowship, 2015, http://labri.org.

BEING HUMAN

BEING (EVEN MORE) HUMAN

Ranald Macaulay

MA, Cambridge University
Founder, Christian Heritage
Cambridge, England

By the time *Being Human* was published in 1978, Jerram and I and our respective families had been living in the Manor House, Greatham,[1] for seven years. The village lies about fifty miles southwest of London and is as hard to find in an atlas as L'Abri's birthplace, Huemoz, in Switzerland. In view of L'Abri's wide influence since, this obscurity may be significant, but more on that later. The Manor itself is mainly Victorian but a plaque on the front from 1789 confirms that some of it goes back to the French Revolution. Large rooms with typically high ceilings make it a gracious home, but nowhere is it what you would call sumptuous; impressive, yes, with a forty-foot oak staircase above the front hall, but not luxurious. And when we moved to the Manor, a tall cedar opposite the living room dominated the extensive lawns until it was shattered by gales later.

It was an idyllic situation: two young families living in a real Manor House surrounded by beautiful countryside just north of the Hampshire Downs. Sounds romantic, doesn't it? Few people in their thirties get that sort of break (and come to think of it, Jerram was probably still in his twenties). It was all pretty amazing. The trees, gardens, and outbuildings clustered about the big house provided a magical atmosphere. Children roamed in and out and climbed up and down without interruption. C. S. Lewis could hardly have devised better; indeed, *Narnia* via a door in the Well House seemed eminently feasible.

The romance, of course, hardly went beyond my description. Certainly, by comparison with what most people have at that age it couldn't have been better. We were happy. We loved being able to provide a shelter for those who came to stay. Our friendships were real. Our children got on well together. They particularly enjoyed the mixture of ages. When I led square dances, they joined in. And when it came time for their Sunday evening stories around the living room fire the adults got as much out of it as the children.

The Real Context

The truth remains, however, that life at the Manor in 1971 was far from romantic. Wherever we live, of course, we have to struggle with complications, yet the Manor did have its special strains. We were not simply restoring a dilapidated old house in the country; right there in the Manor, we were starting a L'Abri, and as the name implies we were creating a shelter for whomever showed up. This meant we had about twenty strangers to integrate into our family right from the start. They often arrived unannounced. Their backgrounds were diverse, and they didn't come through a selection process. Our task was to make them feel at home. Meals had to be cooked, studies supervised, supplies brought in from the shops. Budgets were tight. Basic expenses had to be taken care of first and salaries paid only if there was enough left over at the end of the month! As a faith mission L'Abri didn't have capital funds to fall back on—either then or now. So, when things needed fixing those of us living in the Manor had to fix them.

Our first week a storm flooded the basement and disabled the already hesitant boiler. There was nothing for it but to hand-haul buckets of water up through the entrance hall and dump them outside in the drive. Being January, of course, it was cold. Even when the basement was cleared the boiler wouldn't work, so we froze, and when the drainage problem was traced to its source we discovered the pipes were jammed solid with roots and soil. Then, too, the whole place had to be rewired which meant the floors were being taken up and the walls gouged out. Similarly, the old septic tanks were quickly swamped. Six-foot trenches had to be dug to connect to the mains beyond our boundary wall. In short, moving to the Manor in 1971 felt a bit like trying to settle in Outer Mongolia—and we had three small girls under the age of ten.

Into this melee of conflicting pleasures and pressures came Jerram and Vicki. By then the weather was warmer and a few of the teething problems taken care of. But even after our initial six months of settling, the challenges they faced were no less intense: it was simply L'Abri as usual. Home for them meant a small apartment called "the back flat" with a tiny kitchen and a dining room only slightly larger. Almost immediately they had to provide daily meals for the students. When Peter, their firstborn, arrived, they were really pushed for space. I mention all this to give you a better idea of the context within which *Being Human* was written, but there's more to it.

What we did not have to learn before embarking on the book was the content of *Being Human*. That was already clear to us, because we'd lived and worked with Francis and Edith Schaeffer at L'Abri in Switzerland. One of their common expressions was "the lordship of Christ over the whole of life" which sums up pretty well what we learned in this area. They also helped us to see what it looks like in real life. Edith, for example, took pains to make her dinner tables attractive. And "Fran" (as Edith called him) would invariably have a large art book open on his bed to savor whichever artist he was studying at the time.

It was a new and intriguing lifestyle for us and the more we examined their theology the less we could fault it. Hadn't Jesus said, *"Consider the lilies of the field.... Solomon in all his glory was not arrayed like one of these"* (Matt. 6:28–29)? Isn't the entire universe the work of God's hands? Why then would Christianity *not* be a glorious affirmation of life! The problem, we quickly saw, isn't human experience per se but sinful human experience. It was a huge relief. We basked in the freedom this refreshingly different vision of the Christian life afforded.

It had not been like this in Cambridge. As an undergraduate, an older Evangelical who later became a well-known preacher gently reproved me once for buying a few contemporary books like T. S. Eliot's *The Waste Land*! They would distract me, he felt, because they weren't spiritual. In the Schaeffer home such memories began to fade. I realized Christianity doesn't restrict our humanity, it restores it. These things, as I say, were clear to us. Our seven years at the Manor didn't add much to our intellectual grasp of the content for the book. We'd learned a lot of that already from the Schaeffers.

Misguided Alternatives

However as if to highlight what we'd already understood, our introductory years in the Manor provided us with many false alternatives. Almost every misrepresentation one could imagine could be found right there at L'Abri. Some of the students, for example, had the not-uncommon idea that the real point of becoming a Christian is to tell others about it.

This goes: "You've been saved so now you have to go and win others." They may not have been told this explicitly, but the message was clear. Since the need is urgent, nothing else should be allowed to get in the way. Social and cultural pursuits are merely distractions—like reading *The Waste Land*. All has to be set aside in favor of preaching the Gospel. Of course a proper emphasis on the urgency of evangelism is right. But is it the case that we need to "leave all" in this sense? Why go to college or take an ordinary job? Why get married? It was an emphasis, often accompanied by anti-intellectualism, that said, "The Bible doesn't need human reasoning, it just needs to be proclaimed. Getting to grips with the ideas of the culture is a waste of time." The development of a Christian mind was almost taboo even at university. The result was that few Christians had the faintest idea how to challenge the skepticism surrounding them.

Others had been involved in the charismatic movement, which was in full bloom just then. Michael Harper (who later ended up in the Greek Orthodox Church) had started the Fountain Trust,[2] and one of his conferences took place at Guildford Cathedral nearby. Thousands arrived for a heady cocktail of euphoria and hand-waving. Punters were confident that the charismatic approach to spirituality would turn things upside down. The Church would now be able "to march across the land" with a message of power. Once again, the sales pitch was simple and clear: "Your Christian experience is going to be unsatisfying and ineffective until you are baptized in (by) the Spirit"—in other words until you speak in tongues. It seemed plausible enough. The book of Acts says quite a bit about tongues-speaking so perhaps, after all, it is the sort of Christian experience we need?

The Anabaptist emphasis on peace-making through pacifism was also a draw. Even John Stott joined forces with the advocates of unilateral nuclear disarmament. His authority as an outstanding Evangelical leader carried considerable weight and his imprimatur seemed to guarantee the biblical integrity of this idea. We were less impressed. Jerram even went to Cambridge and London at John's invitation for a three-way debate with a leading British Mennonite. He basically showed that their view was far from biblical and was even dangerous. But nuclear disarmament sounded good at the time.

In a similar vein, left-leaning Mennonites in North America were championing the cause of a simple lifestyle. The socialist agenda wasn't hard to spot. Developing nations, it was said, would overcome famine and poverty best if we in the West lived more frugally and gave more generously. Jerram and I were, of course, sympathetic to this critique of western consumerism, and not simply because we were actually living the simple lifestyle. Our dislike of excessive consumption was as real as anyone's. But we were far from convinced that the Bible's remedy for social decline should be this. Were there not other factors maybe, like the absence of the rule of law and high levels of corruption? Or could poverty be related to idolatry? Compassionate spirituality, however, had an immense appeal, and many Evangelicals were drawn to it. The BBC and the pop idols of the day promoted it vigorously. Not to be active in support was to be heartless.

The catalogue of misleading models for a normal Christian life could be extended almost indefinitely. In fact the very phrase, "normal Christian life," can't help but remind the older ones among us of Watchman Nee's book of that title. Published in the 1950s, its title couldn't have been better: we do want a normal Christian experience, and some of the things Nee says are helpful.[3] Once again, however, his structure for spirituality is misguided. For one thing, he says the Bible teaches a tripartite view of the human self—body, soul, and spirit—which it is vital to accept in order to gain a proper understanding. But is it? Then he insists that our human minds, wills, and emotions belong not within the spirit but within the soul and as such can only be a hindrance. By contrast the soul, mind, and emotions need to be "put to death" in order that the human spirit may be released for its proper communion with God. The upshot is that most of our humanity has, somehow, to be jettisoned. This being so, it becomes difficult to see what Jesus means when he commands us to love God with our minds. Nee's writings, however, were a big influence in the post-war years, especially in the early charismatic movement.

As I've intimated, this entire range of alternative spiritualities, more or less representative of Evangelicalism then as now, was in fact confusion. Yet these were the sorts of things people were being taught. When tutoring at L'Abri, therefore, Jerram and I had to keep reminding people of the biblical basics. In many ways it was a sad enterprise, but we were learning how to argue the case for *Being Human* and to show what spirituality is and isn't. In that way, our preparation for the book had begun.

Pietism

It is, of course, entirely natural to wonder how such an array of misconceptions about the Christian life arose in the first place. Several historians have looked at this. Perhaps Mark Noll's *The Scandal of the Evangelical Mind* is the most well-known. He draws attention to Evangelicalism's neglect of intellectual engagement almost to the end of the twentieth century.[4] David Well's three or four titles, including *No Place for Truth*, add to this the decline of doctrinal teaching in Evangelical churches generally and its replacement, management, and technique.[5] Similarly, he draws attention to the promotion of consumer satisfaction rather than costly sacrifice. The subject is too big to broach meaningfully here, but a quick look at the background helps explain some of the reasons for our current confusion and thus the significance of what Jerram and I wrote about.

We need to go back to the early eighteenth century. Pietist leaders like Jakob Spener began a sincere and entirely laudable attempt to renew the German church. Sermons had become intellectual and wordy. It was hard for ordinary folk to see the connection between pulpit and everyday experience. They needed the Bible to be brought alive once again as in Luther's day. The movement became known as heart-felt religion. Small assemblies, or *collegia pietatis*, encouraged prayer, Bible reading, and fellowship and became active forces for change. Pastors began to preach more simply and to focus on devotional and experimental subjects rather than on doctrine. Caring for those in need was considered vital, as was mission to the lost. A stream of vibrant Christian experience spread quickly across Europe preparing the ground for revival both locally and abroad. The Wesley brothers and the Great Awakening echoed the new vitality. It was an impressive shift that had long-lasting results reaching to the present.

But there was a sting in the tail. A disinterest in the life of the mind and a lack of participation in the political institutions of the day weakened Evangelicalism irreparably. Piety of heart took precedence over piety of mind (as if the two are separable!), and though personal philanthropy became a pietist hallmark, it was at the expense of wider social engagement. These, too, were long-lasting results—unhappily.

But where was Truth in all this? Where, in particular, was a Christian mind? The consequences were disastrous, especially in terms of timing. The Enlightenment philosophers were gaining influence throughout the mid-eighteenth century. The French Revolution of 1789 reinforced their agenda. They unashamedly repudiated biblical revelation and morality. The intellectual and social challenges hadn't been more serious since the fall of Rome. Yet Evangelical believers were like Flotsam and Jetsam hardly knowing what was going on. The truth of the matter was they had deprived themselves of what they most needed in this unprecedented onslaught. Their neglect of public engagement had cost them their heritage without them even noticing it. Churches began to hemorrhage. The reversal of a Christian consensus in Europe was just a matter of time.

The Writing

So after seven years, Jerram and I were ready to put things down in black and white. On the one hand, we had been given ample evidence of how Christian spirituality can be misrepresented. On the other hand, we were satisfied about Christianity's intellectual credentials, though this appears in the book only as a footnote.[6] Conversations each day revolved around one of these topics and it was hard not to notice the pietist vacuum. As yet, though, the thought of writing a book hadn't occurred to us.

How that happened was almost incidental. Around 1976 an invitation came to speak at a L'Abri conference in Canada. We'd agreed in general terms to speak on the subject of spirituality but hadn't discussed the details. In a way we didn't need to. The topic was always in our minds. Only when we boarded the plane in England did we choose who should do what, and that too was fairly straightforward. We'd each developed our own interests and strengths and were able to give about half a dozen lectures between us.

The response was immediately encouraging. People were hungry for more. Our approach struck them as different. It seemed to them straightforward, common sense, biblical teaching without how-to gimmicks. They liked that.

That's when some suggested we put pen to paper.

It was easier said than done. We wondered if it was even feasible. Family responsibilities and a growing work meant we were already stretched. Typical L'Abri distractions hampered us, as I've indicated. Time for serious reading, let alone writing, was at a premium. In addition, a small Presbyterian congregation had formed in 1972, and Jerram and I were pastors there.[7] Writing a book seemed out of the question. However, a publisher had by now expressed interest. We knew the need was real. A decision had to be made. Our colleagues lent their support. So we took the plunge only too aware that we might not be able to do a very good job.

The Calgary Lectures were an immediate help. The subject divisions were there, and we only had to add a few more. Then we submitted the embryonic manuscript to IVP in the States. Jim Sires, the editor at the time, indicated that our styles would need to be smoothed out. That threw us a bit, but there was no turning back. We had a month's break from visitors, and Jerram and I set to work at a table in the living room. Looking across to the cedar tree, we took turns reading the text line by line. Finally a manuscript was ready to be sent off. Then Jim returned with it in person to finalize things. I don't think he ever forgave us for the Manor's unimaginable cold! But that was it. The book was published.

Weaknesses

Given what I've said about the misrepresentations at the time, my main reaction thirty years later is one of thankfulness—and no little surprise. I don't mean simply that I am glad the book was published and remains in print, though that is part of it. As a quite solid exercise in theology, the fact that it has stayed in print is no small achievement. It may even indicate its lasting significance because of its emphasis on the long-neglected teaching about God's image in man. God's defining statement about humankind in Genesis 1:26, we argued, provides an organizing principle for all that follows. Here was a new and critical addition to the discussion not because the doctrine had been neglected entirely, but because it had not been applied to this particular subject. *Being Human* recovered a timeless teaching on Christian experience.

Meanwhile, by 1978 other factors were at work toward the same end. The 1974 Lausanne Covenant, for example, was explicit: since Christianity is concerned with all human experience it can't be reduced merely to evangelism. Despite this, however, traditions were entrenched and the overall picture remains troubling.⁸ A contemporary illustration from the UK shows how deeply ingrained the older patterns remain. Key university churches are loud in their praise of Gospel ministry but still say little or nothing about the need to develop a Christian mind. It turns out their sole concern is evangelism. Though they say spirituality involves all of life, they deny it in practice. They simply regurgitate those teachings and attitudes which led to our decline in the first place, even in academic communities where we can least afford them.

Over against this reactionary influence, *Being Human* has helped some to stand their ground. One thing only, I think, makes it less effective than it might have been, and that is its failure to explore more fully the subject of sacrifice. Not that this should be exaggerated: Jerram and I had a modest agenda after all. We weren't trying to produce an all-encompassing manual or scale the heights nor plumb the depths of the Christian life. We simply wanted to get the right framework in place. Not that we were unaware of the problem. We even asked the publisher if we could add another chapter to say more about sacrifice. But he said the book was already too long. So we had to leave it: all of which stands behind the somewhat enigmatic title of my essay , "Being *Even More* Human."

Schaeffer's True Spirituality

Before launching into this, however, I need to do one more thing: I need to show the connection between what we wrote and what Schaeffer wrote if only to explain why we focussed on what we did. *True Spirituality* had been published a few years earlier, and Jerram and I had benefited from it. More than that, we knew the central place it held in Schaeffer's thinking. His introduction makes that clear. It was the basis for the work of L'Abri, he says, and for everything else he wrote. In this respect its general significance can hardly be exaggerated, even though its stylistic weaknesses are obvious.

The burden he wanted to share can be summed up by his expression "a moment-by-moment enjoyment of the living Christ."⁹ He'd had a period of questioning in Switzerland in the early 1950s which led him to review the basics of the Christian faith, which in turn led to a quite dramatic renewal experience. He was given a fresh insight into the biblical teaching about true spirituality. When we bow as sinners and enter a relationship with the living Christ, he saw, we are meant to enjoy him continually. Paul is similarly lyrical about this. He prays for his fellow believers, *"That you . . . may have strength to comprehend with all the saints what is the breadth and length and height and depth, and to know the love of Christ that surpasses knowledge, that you may be filled with all the fullness of God"* (Eph. 3:18–19). This was Schaeffer's burden. Despite the book's obvious stylistic weaknesses, as I said, it compares favorably with other great devotional literature from the past.

However, it has another weakness which is more serious. Where we were focusing on introduction and framework and not even attempting to cover the wider reaches of spirituality, Schaeffer was trying to do just that. He was exploring the journeys of the heart. That being the case and those being its strengths, what struck us was its inadequate framework. This may have been due to the fact that *True Spirituality* came out of an earlier manuscript. The original was a series of talks to denominational colleagues in the States in the early 1950s. So it was already some years before L'Abri started and a decade at least before the book came out. Possibly he felt that the framework issues were less important then (which I doubt) or he felt they would distract from the central thrust of his message (which is more likely). In any event, the absence of this complementary teaching created misunderstandings. We even found our L'Abri students getting confused. So we set out to provide a balance in *Being Human*.

On top of this, Schaeffer was using terminology related to the Keswick Convention[10] of the late nineteenth century. He had read the writings of Keswick speakers before L'Abri began. They had helped him during his uncertainties and he included their insights. Like them he stressed the need for faith in sanctification (as in justification) and the need to understand how, as believers, we have already died in Christ. The resemblance was more than superficial. However, in terms of their pietistic framework he was completely different. Yet this didn't come out in his book. We felt the vacuum needed to be redressed.

Ironically, then, both *True Spirituality* and *Being Human* suffered from the same weakness. Schaeffer was strong on experience. We were strong on framework. But each book left out something which would have made it better. In any event, because Jerram and I were responding to Schaeffer like this, we limited what we could achieve in *Being Human*. In providing a primer for spirituality only, we failed to say more about what being human really involves.

Being Even More Human

As with most things in our experience the nub of the issue involves the cross. We need to be clear not just about Christ's death but about our own also. First, we have to accept the fact that only Jesus can take away the guilt of our sin. Then we have to be clear that Jesus died for us not merely to reconcile us to the Father but to transform us into his likeness. As soon as we understand this, we realize that the height of Christian experience is not the forgiveness of our sins—though that is the indispensable "door" that Jesus speaks about (cf. John 10, Rev. 3). To be properly human we need first to accept this unique salvation and to hold onto it throughout our lives, for it is the rock upon which all else rests.

But what follows is equally important. Jesus says, *"You therefore must be perfect, as your heavenly Father is perfect"* (Matt. 5:48). Paul says, *Therefore be imitators of God, as beloved children. And walk in love, as Christ loved us* (Eph. 5:1–2). God welcomes us into his family not to provide us with rest and relaxation, but in order to change us into his likeness. Not that the rest isn't real, as Isaiah makes clear: *"in repentance and rest is your salvation"* (Isa. 30:15, NIV). We never work for our salvation the way man-made religions require. But alongside the rest comes our repentance. We commit ourselves to undergo, at God's hand, a process of gradual transformation, of continual repentance, of laying aside what is un-human so as to become properly human. On one hand this means becoming like Jesus in positive virtues, on the other it means being willing to die with him and to imitate his sufferings. He was kind, just, patient, generous, merciful, and all the rest. He was prepared to go to the cross. We have to become like that too, though always conscious of our shortcomings.

Knowing the importance of this theme of self-denial, Jerram and I devoted a whole chapter to it. It was partly what attracted us to L'Abri in the first place and certainly what we appreciated about *True Spirituality*. Schaeffer was insistent that we need to die not only to what is bad but to what is good—in other words to offer our lives to God without reservation, to become *"a living sacrifice"* as Paul puts it in Romans 12:1. But working within the limitations we had, our approach could be tangential only. The most we could do was try to offset the common impression that sacrifice means a denial of our humanity. In fact, it is our humanity's greatest affirmation. When Christians lay aside something for the sake of others they demonstrate God's eternal character—

and are most true to their own character as his image. When they resist sin, they give expression to human nature as it was made to be. Having been created in God's likeness they are restored to it by grace. Though sinful and in need of constant change until the end, self-sacrifice is the deepest affirmation of a believer's true (i.e., original) humanity.

My point is this: we were dealing with the subject of sacrifice only to defend it from misrepresentation. What we were unable to do was commend it for what it is in itself. The New Testament does just that—as did Schaeffer. Scripture doesn't just allow for sacrifice. It embraces it and urges it on us. I don't mean embrace as if it calls us to be ascetic, like a competition to see who can devise the most uncomfortable and difficult experiences possible. That is abhorrent in God's eyes. We don't artificially make the sacrificial situations (like some in the past who stood in freezing water up to their necks to show how spiritual they were!). We meet them as God leads us along. The servant is going to be treated like his master, and the student like his teacher according to Jesus (cf. Matt. 10:24–25). So difficulties and sufferings don't surprise us. They are par for the course.

Jesus couldn't have said this more clearly. The gospels are full of it. When Jesus anticipates his death in Jerusalem he immediately relates it to what his disciples must expect themselves. In fact, he goes further and insists that unless they are prepared to undergo a similar life—by taking up their own cross—they cannot be his disciples. In a sense it becomes the focus of John the Evangelist's whole presentation. At the final stage of Jesus' ministry, after Judas leaves to betray him, we read, *"When he [Judas] was gone, Jesus said, 'Now the Son of Man is glorified and God is glorified in him'"* (John 13:31). He focuses not merely upon Jesus' physical distress, great as that was, but upon what it reveals of God's nature. Christ's full glory, he says, the very nature of God in fact, is now going to become most evident in the world—by suffering.

The necessity of this kind of experience appears everywhere in the New Testament. Paul, too, is full of it. He underscores the point when writing about his thorn in the flesh"because it illustrates another aspect of the same principle (2 Cor. 12:7ff). Paul had heard about false teachers in Corinth who were impressive speakers and boasted about exceptional supernatural experiences. He cuts them down to size. He shows that he too has had remarkable supernatural experiences. But his main thrust is to draw out the reality of his sacrificial service to Christ. He lists all the trials as he travelled around—beaten up several times, hungry, living out of suitcases. And then he comes to his climax, not a climax of wonderful experiences, but of the opposite. He talks about his thorn in the flesh. Whatever it was it was a trial which finally drove him, in desperation, to beg for release: *"Three times I pleaded with the Lord to take it away from me,"* he says (2 Cor. 12:8). The intensity comes across in his emphasis on the three times (obviously not three times within the space of a few minutes but on three occasions when he felt he couldn't go on). It was a terrible experience. (Some, incidentally, on the basis of another text,[11] have inferred that Paul was suffering from an eye complaint because he goes on to say, *"You would have torn out your eyes for me"* Gal. 4:15.)

And what does God say to him in the midst of this trial? Far from releasing Paul, God tells him it is how his divine power is best revealed in the world. Weakness keeps Paul from becoming conceited and God uses it to show that what matters is not our success but our dependence. Again, we have to learn to be weak, to deny ourselves. Jesus did the same. He who had everything died for those who have nothing. He who was hated by sinners surrendered himself to their malice that they might see his love. As his image we are caught up within the same drama. We are made (and saved) to be like him. Paradoxically, the loss becomes our gain. Jesus is quite clear: *"Whoever loses his life for my sake will find it"* (Matt. 16:25).

Reformation and Renewal

This is why I went into some detail about our settling-in process at the Manor. It seemed an ideal situation as I said: two young families with no money, a large house and garden, lots of exciting things going on, and beautiful surroundings. The reality was different. I mentioned the cold, for instance. Were we living like that because we thought it more spiritual not to be warm? No. Should we have demanded better working conditions as our legal right? No. We had to make do with what we had. That's how God was preparing us for the book. The difficulties I outlined were our daily cross right there in the Manor. Yes, we could explain *Being Human* theologically, but we had to go through the process of learning to *become* more human. It was an indispensable lesson. In fact, it is the only really important lesson any believer has to learn.

Sadly, it is now the lesson western Evangelicalism has to re-learn, for our forefathers understood it well. To coin a phrase, we have had the dubious privilege of falling on easy, not hard, times. Consumerism has destroyed us. John Steinbeck's conclusion after traveling across the States near the end of his life was that our western lifestyle has made us soft—and a nation can't afford that, he said. He was merely echoing Moses before the Israelites crossed into the Promised Land, "When you become prosperous in your new surroundings realize how dangerous a situation you are in. Your comfort will tempt you to forget God. You will then lose everything. Your fate will be that of the peoples you are about to conquer: God himself will drive you out of your land" (Deut. 6–8 paraphrased).

That being the case, the American church faces a daunting challenge. If it is to escape the judgement of which the current financial and social crises are merely a preliminary, it needs to be reformed and renewed as never before. Since spirituality is more than "Gospel ministry only," the church has to affirm and encourage Christians to be engaged in art, commerce, music, invention, social action, and all the rest. We have to be restored to God's image in the totality of what he has made us to be. Pietism, in other words, can be tolerated no longer. A massive culture shift has to be implemented consciously and determinedly. Evangelicalism has to be returned to the model of her Reformation forbearers of the sixteenth and seventeenth centuries. She has to start by becoming salt and light within herself. Only then will she be able to renew the body politic. Truth is not best served if God's people vacate the public square. They need to enter and renew it. But truth is even less well served if, on entering, they know nothing of the reality of sacrifice. In short, the message of *Being Human* has to be infused with Schaeffer's insights in *True Spirituality*. They alone can energize the renewed vision which we outlined. Those engaged in the marketplace of ideas or commerce can afford to be no less dedicated than preachers, evangelists, or missionaries entering "Christian ministry."

This engagement was what made the Clapham Circle[12] in the early nineteenth century so powerful an instrument in God's hands. Charles Grant became the senior director of the British East India Company. Henry Thornton became the director of the Bank of England. William Wilberforce worked closely with England's youngest prime minister, Pitt, and was his closest friend after leaving Cambridge. Wealth and status were immaterial to them.[13] Whether successful or not, whether honored or reviled, their chief concern was to be faithful to God's calling. Their cry was the same as their master's, *"Not my will but yours"* (Matt. 26:36ff; Mark 14:32ff; Luke 22:41ff). This, and only this, is the sort of awakening which will suffice: a reformation and renewal marked by the biblical vision I've outlined is, I believe, our highest priority. We are truly human only to the degree we echo Christ's consecration. Anything less than this simply masks a new type of worldliness in which engagement in the world becomes an excuse for self-indulgence.

But what such a vision may lead the church to do in practice is not for us to say. As William Cowper memorably wrote, "God moves in a mysterious way his wonders to perform.... "[14] Renewal may come in unlikely ways and from a part of the church and a region of the world we don't expect. Within our own western churches, however, we must at the very least begin to address our own most glaring shortcomings. They are many and deeply entrenched as I've suggested. But the time for prevarication is long gone. We are weak now because we failed to face-up to our real weaknesses earlier. Three in particular need attention:

- our *lack of confrontation,*
- our *failure to develop true Christian character,*
- our *neglect of community.*

By *lack of confrontation* I mean our failure to mount an effective and public challenge to intellectual falsehood. Surrounded by agnosticism and atheism, the church must confront this rationalistic skepticism head on. The reason we have failed here is because Evangelicalism, as we saw, debilitated herself by withdrawing from the arena of ideas. She thought she was being spiritual, but she was in fact being faithless. Her failure to confront untruth was a dereliction of duty. These internal weaknesses are now exacerbated by seemingly invincible external pressures. Irrationalism, for one thing, has swept through western society in a way which is unparalleled in European history since before the Greeks. Many, on the basis of scientific materialism, have denied that God exists. Lacking a transcendent reference point, they are of necessity driven to treat everything, including intellectual ideas, as relative only. Therefore, the very concept of truth has died and life is rendered meaningless. Why talk about truth if truth is impossible?

Added to this, modern technology has simply reinforced the irrational trend. One writer likens the digital revolution to a "nuclear attack on the human mind."[15] Another compares its all encompassing embrace, particularly through television and the computer, to the totalitarian ideologies of the twentieth century:

> What is happening in America is not the design of an articulated ideology. No *Mein Kampf* or *Communist Manifesto*... [just] the unintended consequence of a dramatic change in our modes of public conversation. But it is an ideology nonetheless for it imposes a way of life... about which there has been no consensus, no discussion... only compliance. Public consciousness has not yet assimilated the point that technology is ideology. This in spite of the fact that before our very eyes technology has altered every aspect of life in America during the past 80 years....[16]

The end result is that Evangelicalism has to contend for truth within an intellectual climate inimical to truth. Far from enlightening the contemporary mind, technological advances have darkened it. Schools lament that children are able to attend so poorly. Concentration levels are universally in decline. People have been subjected—or rather have subjected themselves—to limitless distractions. They have been detached, as it were, from their own minds.[17] Image is everything. What a misguided philosophy produced in an earlier generation (a disinterest in ideas), technology has achieved mechanically in our own (an inability even to grasp ideas). And now an even more ominous threat has arisen. To philosophic and mechanical irrationalism must be added multicultural tolerance. Everyone is to tolerate everyone. All cultures, religions, and philosophies have to be seen as equal. None can claim preeminence. To believe otherwise is to be immoral and dangerous. Ironically, but not surprisingly, humanistic liberalism has unmasked her true self: those she tolerates are only those who ascribe to relative truth—her new absolute. It may even be a case of Robespierre *redivivus*. People must be made free when they resist. A reign of terror, in other words, may once again darken the skies of Europe. And where does this leave us as Evangelicals today? Our choice is stark and unpleasant, however we view it. If Christianity is true, we must stand up and be counted. We are ill-prepared for this. The public's patience with "fundamentalist bigots," as it calls us, is wearing thin. To confront falsehood in such a climate is to invite persecution. Widespread compromise, therefore, is not unthinkable.

Closely related to this is our softness as a result of western consumerism. When the need for *Christian character* is most acute, we realize that this is just what Evangelicalism has failed to develop. We have been closeted in ghettos, instead of pioneering ways of sacrificial living in the outside world (except perhaps through missionary activity to Africa or wherever!). Within an increasingly soft culture, church leaders have accommodated rather than challenged our desire for comfort. We have become as spineless as the rest. But the Apostle Paul envisages a very different kind of lifestyle: *"we rejoice in our sufferings,"* he says, *"because we know that suffering produces endurance, and endurance produces character, and character produces hope..."* (Rom. 5:3–4). On this account also, Evangelicalism faces a daunting challenge. As David Wells puts it:

> The choice for God now has to become one in which the church begins to form itself, by God's grace and truth, into an outcropping of countercultural spirituality. It is after all only when we see what the church is willing to give up by developing this antithesis that we see what it is actually for.... It must give up self-cultivation for surrender; entertainment for worship; intuition for truth; slick marketing for authentic witness; success for faithfulness; power for humility; a God bought on cheap terms for the God who calls us to costly obedience. It must in short be willing to do God's business on God's terms. As it happens that idea is... as old as the New Testament itself, but in today's world it is novel all over again.[18]

Lastly there is the absence of *community*. The same forces which militate against rational thought have reduced our experience of community. Those nations enjoying the greatest technological development are the ones enjoying the least community. A current survey in the United Kingdom is headlined "Love Thy Neighbour is Outdated in Britain."

Community spirit has almost disappeared with fewer people prepared to look out for their neighbors or ask them for help. It underlines the fears that the concept has become outdated, with only 6% of people agreeing that their neighborhood has a strong sense of community... 70 percent admit that they do not even know their neighbors' names.[19]

In a culture where even the family seems on the point of extinction, the church needs to shift gears dramatically. Everyone needs a family. Human well-being is related to the reality of human relationships, not to wealth and possessions.[20] People don't do well in massed groups—except to make themselves more easily the victims of manipulation.

They thrive best in communities where the individual is the principal concern. What then is the responsibility of the church? Clearly Evangelicals have to do something drastic both within their own constituency (how they carry out church) and within society at large (by creating vibrant communities open to all). People, not programs, have to become their central priority. And because larger and ever more homogenous congregations are opposed to this project, they must be downsized and personalized. More than that, the church has to apply its biblical insights and, by example, change the culture itself, holding out another ideal to emulate, offering a different idea of what community is actually like.

The Challenge

Given such weaknesses we could easily give up. That is both unhelpful and unnecessary. Our heritage by itself provides an antidote sufficient to dispel all hesitation. It reminds us that impossible situations can be reversed. Were our forefathers not similarly overwhelmed in their day? Did they not also wonder if the forces confronting them could be contained and conquered? Those who pioneered the development of New England, for example, faced animosity more severe than anything multiculturalism throws at us today. Political and economic developments in Europe were dire. The constitutional changes they longed for were denied them. The doors they hoped would stay open were slammed shut. The hopes they cherished were dashed.

What did they do? They determined first and foremost not to give in. They considered the options and chose to dare all. Putting their lives and the lives of those dependent on them in jeopardy, they sailed to a little-known land. Even as I write, another Thanksgiving Day commemorates their unsurpassed achievements. They gave rise to a nation whose freedoms and prosperity, for all its faults, has never been rivaled. Yet they are our direct forebears. It was through God that they prevailed. What they accomplished, sadly, has long been squandered. What inspired them is ridiculed. Yet the God in whom they trusted is our God also and his truth no less powerful four centuries later. God is not limited as we are. He made the heavens and the earth. He delights in his people. When he chooses to act in history, none can resist his will. Of course, withdrawal to another continent is no longer possible. No new world remains to be explored and settled. Yet in essence our challenge today is no different, and the courage and vision necessary no less exalted than theirs if we will but commit ourselves, regardless of the cost. No new *Mayflower* is needed. We don't have to go anywhere. But we do have to enable a new nation to rise in the ashes of what now surrounds us. Reformation and renewal can and must begin where we are. One inspiration will suffice to enable us to accomplish this, and only one—that we hear God's call to be *"even more* human" and respond without reservation.

---

1. The village is pronounced *gret-um*.
2. An ecumenical agency formed in the UK in 1964 to promote the charismatic renewal.
3. Watchman Nee, *The Normal Christian Life* (Carol Stream, IL: Tyndale House Publishers, 1957), 12.
4. Mark Noll, *The Scandal of the Evangelical Mind* (Grand Rapids: Eerdmans, 1994), 3–24.
5. David Wells, *No Place for Truth* (Grand Rapids: Eerdmans, 1993), 75.
6. Jerram Barrs and Ranald Macaulay, *Being Human* (Downers Grove, IL: IVP, 1978), 197–198.
7. The International Presbyterian Church—originally known as *The International Church: Presbyterian, Reformed*—was founded by the Schaeffers in Champery, Switzerland (a Catholic canton), before L'Abri began.
8. In addition to the *Lausanne Covenant* (1974) see the *Manila Manifesto* (1989) and the *Cape Town Commitment* (2010). See also my paper called "By the open statement of the Truth—Lausanne and the Polemical Imperative" at www.christianheritage.org.uk.
9. Francis Schaeffer, *True Spirituality* (London: Hodder & Stoughton, 1972), 24.
10. The Keswick Convention began in 1875 as a focal point for the Higher Life movement in the United Kingdom. The main idea of the Higher Life movement, also known as the Keswick movement, is that the Christian should move on from his initial conversion experience to also experience a second work of God in his life.
11. Galatians 4:15—Those who know Jerram will realize, of course, that I have deliberately chosen this example in 2 Corinthians 12 to honor his perseverance through a similar ear affliction. I honor Jerram by simply writing this essay but the truth of the matter is that no eulogy of mine can adequately express my indebtedness to him throughout my working life.
12. A group of Church of England social reformers based in Clapham, London, at the beginning of the nineteenth century (active 1780s–1840s). Charles Grant, Henry Thornton, and William Wilberforce were all members.
13. The Schaeffers founded L'Abri in an obscure village in Switzerland only because God led them there in dramatic circumstances (see Edith Schaeffer's *The L'Abri Story*). But their obscurity also underscored their dislike of American Evangelicalism's thraldom to business techniques, advertising, and big numbers.
14. William Cowper, "Conflict: Light Shining Out of Darkness," *Twenty-six Letters on Religious Subjects*, 1774.
15. Morris Berman, *The Twilight of American Culture* (New York City: Norton, 2000), 96.
16. Neil Postman, *Amusing Ourselves to Death* (London: Methuen, 1985), 162.
17. Postman, *Amusing Ourselves To Death,* 161.
18. David Wells, *God in the Wasteland* (Grand Rapids, MI: Eerdmans, 1995), 223–224.
19. Rob Cooper, "Love thy neighbour no more," *Daily Mail*, November 28, 2011, http://www.dailymail.co.uk/news/article-2067048/Community-spirit-disappeared-70-admitting-dont-know-neighbours-name.html.
20. See the work of the Relationships Foundation based in Cambridge, England.

UNDESERVED SUFFERING

Wade Bradshaw

DVM, Texas A&M University
Pastor for Discipleship & Director, The Ambrose Program
Trinity Presbyterian Church
Charlottesville, VA

All humans suffer, but they do not do so equally.

Both parts of this stark sentence have caused us to question the nature of our lives; but it is the second aspect, the inequity of our common circumstance of pain and sorrow, that I wish to consider briefly. Life not only presents itself to us as tragic; it also seems so *unfair* in the distribution of its tragedy. Everyone suffers, but some people have it comparatively harder. What are we to make of this? We might struggle a little less in our understanding if everyone encountered the same dose of sorrow. At least that way everything would be fair after a fashion. Why we are dealt a bad hand is a troubling question, but it is a different question from why some of us are dealt worse hands than others. For example, death might hint less insistently that life is absurd if each of us fell quietly and predictably into oblivion after blowing out the candles on our sixty-fourth birthday, surrounded by people who love us. But this is not the way of the world we live in. A few of us get to blow out many more candles that that; more of us than I care to admit never get a cake at all.

The question is just part of a much larger setting—the universal variety of lived-experience. If some of us are dealt comparatively worse hands, this also means that others of us are given better ones.

All of us suffer, but there is, of course, human experience besides suffering. There are happinesses and nobilities in the existence of men and women, and these good things produce in us the suspicion that life is deeply worthwhile and heavy with meaning: the joy at hearing my firstborn's first cry in a mission hospital in Kathmandu, the kindness and expertise of the Tibetan obstetrician who delivered him safely, the shared love of a husband and a wife that he so tangibly manifested. We rarely disquiet ourselves over the existence and experience of the true and the good and the beautiful. Certainly I didn't question these wonderful things in those first moments the same way that I questioned life's justice during the anxiety of the next forty-eight hours, a time during which my wife and I were concerned that he had been born with a heart defect and born miles and miles away from the kind of treatment that he would require. No, the good things—these are how we wish life to be—we even suspect that these are how things are meant to be. You may frown and ask yourself why a stranger is kind and lets you go ahead of them in traffic if you are used to drivers only being unfriendly. However, ordinarily we do not question the joyful and generous in the same way that we do the ugly and the spiteful. And these good things are also distributed unevenly. My son did not, in fact, have a heart defect, but I have a neighbor down the street whose son does. We consider it small-minded to envy someone their good fortune and yet most of us do not think it wrong to question our bad fortune. Surely, this hints at something about our situation.

Most of us go even further with our suspicions about life and we think that when we speak of things as true and good and beautiful we are saying something more profound than that these are merely what we desire and prefer. Most of us operate in life sensing that it is not our enjoying something that makes it good nor is something evil just because we do not like it. (This is why, though it can be a working model for public policy, utilitarianism can never be a real foundation for morality.) We know this because we have wrestled with our desires and preferences. And my struggle has not been merely between competing goods. I have at times had powerful cravings for things that I would say are not true but false, not beautiful but hideous, not good but bad. My instincts and desires cannot make the final decision about what I *ought* to do. I find that my loves are disordered. (This is why, though it has a great deal of explanatory power, sociobiology can never act as a foundation for human morality.) This friction between our loves is a great paradox about which the Bible has a great deal to say, and what it says is that we are dealing here with something much deeper than my preference for instant coffee over the really good stuff whipped up by a barista—my odd preference for bad coffee is the endless irritation of my friends.

Suffering exists—though periodically one bumps into well-meant attempts to deny its reality. Usually, in my experience, these efforts say that it is primarily a matter of perspective, that suffering is really only a secret good gone unrecognized. In this view, if we but had the proper prescription in our eyeglasses, suffering would either vanish as illusory or it would focus into something actually for our greater good. Sometimes this notion is held by religious people and sometimes by those who see no reason to be religious.

But I take suffering's existence as established and further find by observation that it is unevenly dealt abroad. In an episode of *Downton Abbey*, a young Turkish visitor to an English country home, himself just hours away from an unexpected death, proclaims at dinner that he would love to live in the past—so long as he could take the painless dentistry of the twentieth century back in time with him. The others around the dinner table titter appreciatively at his comment. But it is true: human suffering is uneven across time. Life-expectancy has varied enormously through the generations. In my own family tree, I have relatives who suffered the effects of diseases that are currently all but eradicated. And not merely across time, misery also varies widely across geography. My wife returned from our three years in Nepal troubled by her observations and wondered why life was so much harder there than in Chicago. More children in Asia died before their fifth birthday than children in Illinois, and even the survivors were statistically likely to die much younger. And it wasn't just death: health was worse, prospects of many sorts were worse, and it wasn't just because our friends in Nepal were lazy or less motivated or less "righteous" than the Americans. Perhaps one could spot reasons of sorts for these differences in terms of progress, technology, economics, or education, but these types of explanations do not do away with what appears as unfair. Living in what is called "late modernity," we can observe that technology, economics, and education do not automatically create human flourishing. And likewise, when these factors are comparatively highly advanced, we often find that suffering remains, but changes its form. I have known many people living happily in circumstances that I would have considered very, very uncomfortable. There is some cultural relativism here, but this does not render suffering only a matter of perspective or social construction.

Beyond the inequities of time and geography, anyone reading this article knows that suffering isn't equitable among the inhabitants of the same village in Nepal or the same neighborhood of America, among siblings in a family or colleagues in an office. You know this even if you have never visited Nepal or don't know which neighborhood, family, or office we are discussing. There is an unevenness about suffering between individuals occupying roughly the same place and time, culture and genome. The food chain requires a certain amount of suffering. This situation causes many of us to conclude that there is no transcendent reason at work, that our questions lose their meaning, and that this is just the nature of an environment that has occurred accidentally. We could wish things were otherwise, but that wishing changes nothing in the slightest. I am personally very sympathetic to this opinion, but I cannot rid myself of the suspicion that "it is nonsensical to ask for fairness from reality" is an answer that gives up too soon and begs a worthwhile question. I do not think that human dignity is a fairytale concept invented by nannies for the calming of nursery fears.

The unequal distribution of sorrow and pain among individuals might be less troubling if there was a clear cause and effect between the informed choices of individuals and the onset of suffering, a one-to-one relationship between what a person does and what pain they experience, some way that we could nod at their grief and whisper to our neighbors, "Yes, but she knew this is what would happen if she behaved that way. She has reaped only what she has sown." And sometimes—quite often in fact—we do bring suffering upon ourselves. Sometimes it is in ignorance, but far from always. Sometimes we play the odds, thinking that, though consequences might follow, surely, they will not follow for us. Not *us*—we are exceptional. A two pack a day habit can lead to emphysema, but not for me. Unsafe and indiscriminate sexual activity can have deadly consequences, but surely not for me. Because… well, because I'm *me*. At face value, we can see the foolishness of this strategy, but we cannot deny that we resort to it. Driving while intoxicated is heinously stupid and dangerous, but I have done it.

Now, being honest, we do often deceive ourselves. At least, I know that in a very irrational behavior *I* can lie to myself and pretend not to notice that I have done so. There are—what I experience as—layers to my self-conversation. But I do sometimes bring suffering on myself. Our choices are sometimes the clear cause of our afflictions. But a one-to-one cause and effect, our choice leading to an inevitable result, is not the way of our world, even if pretending to see it that way promises us mental comfort. No, not every smoker contracts lung cancer. Children have been infected with the AIDS virus from corneal transplants. And very often we are ignorant of the consequences of a choice that presents itself. Before we understood germ theory it was the dirty hands of a doctor that might turn a small problem into a much more serious situation. I didn't know it was loaded. I didn't know it was flammable. He was in my blind spot. I only turned my back for a second. I thought the power was off. Just this morning my wife backed our car over my foot, but fortunately it only caught the back of my new shoe rather than breaking my heel.

I made a choice, but I had no idea of all of the misery that it would cause. Human agency matters, even when the human agent is ignorant. The reality we inhabit is a fraught and dangerous affair. Later in the morning, my wife said that she never wanted to drive again. That's understandable—maybe it's all so dangerous and uncertain that it is best to participate in as little as possible. But as I type, she has reconsidered the good that she would forego to avoid the bad, and she is driving her mother to the doctor.

There are attempts to construct this one-to-one cause and effect of individual suffering, that is, to make what looks indiscriminate scrupulously fair, to make all suffering deserved. I can sympathize with this attempt also. It would not get rid of the unequal distribution of suffering, but it would provide the relief of everyone suffering to the extent that they, as responsible individuals, deserve. This is my understanding of karma—a very powerful doctrine believed by millions of reasonable and educated people. It may seem that I did not deserve what happened to me, but that is only because our perspective is limited to this current life. Again, the need for a different set of spectacles. If we were but able to see further around the wheel of existence, we would see that suffering is due to choices made, if not in this life, then in a previous incarnation of the individual. Karma is inexorable and enormously fair in a sense. No one can disprove this powerful explanation of suffering's inequality. It is very attractive to my sense of justice. The evil people always get it in the neck and always for what they did. Job's friends would have been right in assuming that Job was hiding some unrighteousness from them that was the cause of all of his grief. I cannot disprove karma, but I can say that I have seen a consequence of the belief in the idea that troubles me. The fairness of karma can rob people of the incentive to help alleviate the suffering around them, because if you stop the hurt, you are only postponing the inevitable, even postponing what is needful: the suffering person needs to work off their karma because it is the one-to-one ratio of suffering and deserving it—and we mustn't get in the way of that process grinding out moral justice by alleviating someone's hardship. They have to work it off or it remains an unpaid debt. This is an example of how an idea—in this case a religious idea—can bring tangible effects to the human environment. Often, the people who hold this idea do not let it go to this conclusion, but I have seen some who do.

The Bible, on the other hand, tells a tale as complicated as the world I find myself inhabiting. It reflects that we can bring suffering on ourselves. It also teaches that God as creator and ruler can afflict people for their evil and oppression in a direct and unmediated way. But it spends a greater amount of its pages, at least in my estimation, observing that there is not a one-to-one correspondence between our actions and our suffering. Not all suffering is deserved in this one-to-one cause and effect way. The Bible teaches that good people are often oppressed by bad people. It teaches that towers fall on people for reasons other than their own transgressions in this life—and there is only this one incarnation of life before the everlasting Resurrection. The Bible teaches that there was a fall of our first parents that affected all of reality as we experience it. It teaches that this fall brought a curse by the creator, and thus all of our world is subject to futility and frustration. The creation cannot be what it was intended, it groans—and this explains our sense that nothing is quite as it ought to be, including ourselves. Neither the fall nor the curse mean that we experience the longed-for one-to-one correspondence of my actions and my suffering. There is undeserved suffering, even in the world as described by the Bible. In point of fact, this notion is at the very center of the Bible's message—Jesus' suffering and death was wholly undeserved. And even some of his killers knew it.

I remember the day that Jerram Barrs came into my office from his own down the hall at the Francis Schaeffer Institute. He complained to me that he was having some discomfort in one of his ears: his hearing was peculiar and sound was causing him pain. I commiserated superficially, as we are wont to do. But the condition worsened alarmingly over a matter of weeks; the pain became intense. There was some question about the cause of his suffering, but it was largely agreed that he was afflicted with Meniere's disease.[1] His world became smaller as his symptoms worsened, until he could no longer tolerate the pain while listening to his wife play the piano beautifully. When he visited a church to speak—as he frequently did—he had to leave the sanctuary during the noise of glad worship. As his assistant, it became routine for me to go into a lecture hall before he taught a class at the seminary and tell the students to be as quiet as possible—certainly not to click their binders open while Jerram was in the room because of the agony that it caused him. As the disease progressed, he took to wearing the most effective and unsightly ear protectors as a normal piece of his wardrobe. The syndrome cuts people off from their environment, slowly forcing them into their own rooms where they can control the sound and the pain; most people with the affliction become seriously depressed, even suicidal. Thankfully—and remarkably—Jerram did not go this route. He continued a very busy schedule despite the pain he experienced. Perhaps most impressive to me personally was that, though I was privy to seeing how great his suffering was, he never lashed out impatiently at those of us around him.

The point I wish to make is that I watched Jerram suffer, that the pain—both physical and emotional—were real and not illusory, and that it was not an affliction that he deserved more than someone else because of things that he had done. Jerram, as an individual human, is a sinner and has not lived a life perfectly innocent of evil. (I wonder if a *Festschrift* in all of history has ever contained a statement such as that about the person it is meant to honor.) He is a person who is born into a fallen and cursed and frustrated creation. But these theological truths do not mean that he deserved this affliction. Nor is it as simple as God shall teach him through the experience. Suffering can bring some kinds of discernment and wisdom; the experience certainly requires deep faith that our Creator continues to love us steadfastly. But Jerram's suffering did not show that he had lessons to learn. Nor did my lack of suffering mean that I did not have things to learn and was therefore spared. True theology can show us that pain does not render life absurd, but it doesn't make our circumstances fair and equal, either. The scriptures teach that there is pain in childbirth because of the curse, but not all deliveries are of equal pain. Some faithful followers of

Jesus—for his sake—suffer persecution, some even suffer martyrdom. And others are not given the gift of suffering for his sake. Those who suffer for their faith are not necessarily more faithful than those who do not.

How are we then meant to react to this undeniable inequity?

I think that there are reactions all of us are meant to share, whatever our circumstances. We are not locked up alone in the room of our private experience. We acknowledge that suffering can be undeserved in the sense of it not being a one-to-one correspondence between our behavior and what follows. We are not responsible for our suffering in that way. This admission is not a threat to justice or the idea of God's governance of the world. We do not insist that our friend deserved pain more than we did—or that I must be worse than they are when I am the one afflicted. In fact, within the church we are meant to weep with one another and share each other's joys (Rom. 12:15). We empathize and do not cut the sufferer off as if they are unclean or contagious. This is not what Jesus did for us; he came and lived among us and shared our sorrows (Isa. 53:4).

And, in one of the great paradoxes of human existence, it is pleasing to God that we try and alleviate suffering. There is no karma to work off. Even if all pain and death ultimately are related to God's curse, this truth does not mean that we are to be passive. We do not have to accept any particular affliction as deserved in such a way that we cannot try to escape it or help others to do so.

We do not accept suffering as always for the purpose of teaching us lessons—and yet we do not deny that we are to learn to trust God whatever situation presents itself to us. Success in an endeavor is to help us grow in faith; but so also is failure and disappointment.

These, however, are coping in the moment; the long-term answer is that we await the Resurrection and the Judgment. There is no alternative to this waiting in Christianity. Jesus, the only innocent man, is now the firstborn of the Resurrection. He is ascended to his Father, but shall return. And when he returns it shall be for the restoration of all things. All that is evil shall be destroyed; all that is good shall be healed. We—who in ourselves are evil—have been made righteous with an innocence that is not our own. The oppressed, we are told because we do not yet see it, shall be vindicated. Many who in this current life seem despised and cursed shall be proven God's dear children. Conversely, many, who presently to our eyes look particularly blessed, shall go down into a hopeless darkness. This is the teaching of the prophets and the apostles. We are told that the creation itself is eagerly awaiting this revelation of the children of God, the setting of all things right. Only the Almighty God, who knows all things and sees all secrets is capable of this ultimate judgment and vindication. We are told to reserve judgment because we are so ignorant. We are told to postpone vengeance because this can only belong to God. Our generation has grown unsure and uncomfortable with the notion of God's judgment, but it is both our fear and our only source of hope. It is no coincidence that a generation which ignores the judgment is also a generation that has real questions about life having meaning and purpose.

We await the day of the Lord. I do not see how that day changes the fact that the distribution of suffering was inequitable, but we are promised that that day shall have a one-for-one correspondence between our responsibility and its outcome because we are to be judged according to our works, judged according to what we did with God's gift of the particular life we are given. He knows every mitigating circumstance. People who understand God's grace can sometimes downplay the importance which our obedience and actions and motivations are going to have when revealed at this judgment of Christ.

Now Jerram's example is, of course, very complex. I was there the first day that he began to suffer his awful affliction. But the years of pain went by, and we were separated by many miles. I was living in England and had the joy of baptizing two of his grandchildren. I began to hear strange rumors of good things, and then one day I received an email from the seminary where he taught. It was a very broad and very public announcement: Jerram had been healed. It was medically unaccountable.

I was thunderstruck—if such a term can be used for joy and gratitude.

This good outcome also is unequal. Not every follower of Jesus who wrestles beneath the serious trial of Meniere's disease finds deliverance in this shape. Certainly Jerram had suffered with a kind of courage and stamina I have very, very rarely observed. He never retreated into his room. He was tempted to depression but managed to live in hope. He continued to travel and to teach when both were excruciating. Just the attention caused by the ugly headphones wardrobe as he walked through America's busiest airports en route to teach at another conference would have been enough to make someone as vain as myself miserable and self-absorbed. But he didn't deserve deliverance because of this faith and courage. He was not responsible—at least so far as I can tell—for his restoration any more than he was for his trouble in the first instance.

But we have to await the day. Only God knows. Jerram's deliverance is a picture, though a very dim one, of what the ultimate deliverance shall be like, when that which is corruptible puts on immortality.

---

1. Meniere's Syndrome is characterized by recurrent episodes of vertigo, hearing loss and tinnitus; episodes may be accompanied by a headache and a feeling of fullness in the ears.

UNEXPECTED ENCOUNTERS

A (FORMATIVE) NEW BEGINNING

Michael Tymchak

PhD, *University of Manchester*
Professor of Education, *University of Regina*
Saskatchewan, Canada

Decisive moments in our lives are colored by their context, and really significant moments—those we might call turning points—can imprint us for life. As I reflect upon the fruitful life and ministry of my dear friend Jerram Barrs I cannot help but think how the context of his conversion to faith in Jesus Christ proved to be highly formative for the way he would live out that commitment. Having been privileged with a ringside seat during this period of his life, I thought it might be worth sharing my recollection of those days and these events for the benefit of our *Festschrift* readers. Many of you will know that at several points in his writing Jerram has himself offered brief vignettes of what happened. My hope here is simply to elaborate upon these accounts from the perspective of a not entirely innocent bystander.

The University of Manchester was a dynamic and exciting place for students in the mid 1960s: all of the social and intellectual forces that would so much shape the future of Britain and the West were very much at play. Doubts about modernity, the alienation manifested by existentialist literature (and the theatre of the absurd), excitement about technological innovation (Manchester's ATLAS computer was a game-changer for the computer sciences), not to mention the rhythm and beat of bands which at that very moment were being catapulted onto the world stage—the Beatles, Liverpool's "fab four" hailed from just down the Mersey River—were all very much part of the scene for undergraduate and graduate students alike.

For students with a Christian persuasion, Manchester University had another aspect, dare I say, equally dynamic and exciting. It was the academic home of one of the leading biblical scholars of the day, the redoubtable F. F. Bruce who, during this era, was the Rylands Professor of Biblical Studies. Other professors in the Department of Biblical Studies were also well known, such as Gordon Rupp, the Church Historian. The presence of scholars such as these, and many others, accounted for the fact that an unusually high proportion of graduate scholars from all over the world made their way to study at Manchester which was, by all accounts, Britain's leading provincial university. Keeping pace, InterVarsity Christian Fellowship's (IVF) student group, affectionately known as MIFCU (Manchester Inter-Faculty Christian Union), was large, lively, dynamic, and very outward looking: it frequently hosted leading Christian thinkers from all over Britain (and elsewhere) to give lectures and hold seminars—names like James Packer, Colin Brown, and Clark Pinnock were included on this roster. John Stott spoke at Swanick, IVF's national student convention attended by many MIFCUers. Speakers also included Michael Baughen, Rector of Holy Trinity Platt, just down the road from the University; he would later become Rector of All Souls, Langham Place (replacing John Stott). And, as we will note later in our story, Francis Schaeffer spoke in Manchester several times in the 1960s.

Not surprisingly, therefore, Manchester became an incubator for many young scholars who would eventually constitute the faculty of leading North American seminaries. Some came to study under Professor Bruce and others under one of the other world-class scholars of the day. People like Clark Pinnock (New Orleans Baptist Theological Seminary, TEDS, Regent College, and McMaster Divinity School), Ward Gasque (Regent College), Murray Harris (TEDS and Tyndale House), David Wells (TEDS and Gordon Conwell), and Donald Hagner (Fuller), to name only a few, came there to study. Before their books were published or their names had become well known, they could be found frequenting the library, attending or speaking at meetings, debating in seminars or simply sharing robust fellowship over coffee (and biscuits!) with friends. In addition, of course, there were many other circles of Christian students, from widely varying disciplines and diverse parts of the world, who met informally over coffee or at lunch, to solve the world's problems or just unwind at the end of a long day.

It was into this milieu that a young—dare I say unsuspecting—Jerram Barrs came to take his undergraduate studies in 1963. Jerram, quite oblivious to the theological undercurrents at Manchester University—much less God's larger plans for ambush!—came simply to study English and launch the next chapter of his adult life. I recall meeting him first in the autumn of 1965 as a visitor to our flat in West Didsbury. I shared the flat (apartment) with a young student destined for a medical career, named Richard Bibby. I was myself a student in philosophy and had come from Canada on a scholarship to pursue graduate studies. I can't quite recall how or where Richard and Jerram had met; I suspect it was playing racket-ball (squash). In any case, up the stairs bounded this lanky English undergraduate, just a little bigger than life. I recall being vividly impressed by Jerram's energy at that time and the unusual combination of warmth, friendliness, poetic sensitivity, keen mind, and athletic vigor that were all very evident. We quickly became very good friends—a troika!

Over time I would learn that coursing deep within Jerram's spirit was an undercurrent that was sometimes troubling, at times even a bit dark. It would surge over rocks and plunge down canyons in its search for direction and meaning; Jerram was not content with what was called the bourgeois life—getting a degree, a job, and buying a house with a picket fence along another row of boxes. Philosophers of the day called this search "angst"—it was a quest for meaning, purpose, and significance. Jerram put it this way:

> I wondered how any meaning and value can be given to human life. "Who am I, and is there any ultimate meaning to my life?" were questions that plagued my soul. I did not see any basis for being able to make a distinction between good and evil. I felt there was a difference, and I longed for there to be a difference, but I could find no reasons for such a difference.[1]

Most of the time Jerram presented a buoyant personality, a life marked by a multitude of interests and considerable vigor but on other occasions these deeper questions birthed an unsettled spirit, ranging over the earth in search of what, if anything, really mattered. It was pretty obvious that Jerram was deadly serious about his quest; he would play the game to the end. Just what that end might turn out to be was less than obvious in those early days. Thankfully a hand much greater than ours was at work—a hand with remarkable plans none of us could ever have dreamed, even in our wildest moment.

It's worth noting that Jerram's search was philosophical and theological. His strength of spirit and fundamental integrity were also evident, even at this early stage of his quest. For example, considering the pain he carried it is remarkable that he did not turn to any of the easy answers available from the pharmacology of his contemporaries so readily at hand. Again, he comments:

When I was a teenager growing up in England in the sixties, many of my friends struggled with such questions; but most of them attempted to drown their anxious thoughts with alcohol, drugs, or promiscuous sexual encounters, or to bury themselves in trying to find a life which would give them "personal peace and affluence" (to use Schaeffer's expressions). I found myself unwilling to take either of these routes.[2]

I do recall that at the time he watched a lot of movies. Perhaps he thought he might find some clues to follow in his quest for meaning. Perhaps they offered brief respite. Doubtless, also, as a student of English, they represented another genre for reflection and thought. The latter was pretty evident from our casual and informal conversations when he dropped by for chats as the weeks went by. What he did not know was that quite a different story would ultimately be told about his life. Another encounter awaited him.

During the year 1965–66 our flat at 30 Moorefield Rd. became something of a hub of thoughtful discussion and debate around the topic of the relevance of Christian faith for contemporary thought. That year my flatmate was Duncan Roper, a dynamic, outgoing PhD student in Mathematics from New Zealand. Another active participant in our circle was Irving Hexham, at the time a Gas Works technician; he would later attend the new University at Lancaster, study under Ninian Smart and eventually become a Professor of Religious Studies at the University of Calgary in Canada.

Occasionally we invited fellow Christians, but most often the meetings were wide open to a broad network of friends, acquaintances, and those who were just plain curious. Sometimes we played tapes of lectures; occasionally I would give a talk. By this time a small circle of us had become familiar with the work of an American theologian (then relatively unknown) who was domiciled in Switzerland; his name was Francis Schaeffer. We had also heard about his unusual study center named L'Abri in the remote Swiss village of Huemoz. Inspired by his tapes, we invited him to give a lecture at Manchester. I believe it was Irving who had come in contact with Ranald McAuley, Schaeffer's son-in-law, who was able to instigate this first visit. Immediately afterwards, in the summer of 1966, several of us travelled to Switzerland and became Farel House[3] students for a period of significant study: here, listening to Schaeffer lectures, augmented by a visit and more lectures by the Dutch Art historian, Professor Hans Rookmaker, one of Schaeffer's friends, our minds grew along with a vision for how we might share our newly acquired insights and learning. Momentum was building—plans and the message for our Sunday evening outreach coffee nights began to take clearer shape.

Our friendship with Jerram in the fall of that year naturally led to an invitation for him to join our Sunday evening coffee house discussions. "Coffee house" is a bit of a stretch—imagine a small third floor, low-ceilinged living room, with an even smaller kitchen adjacent. Into this we often managed to pack anywhere from six to twelve participants; the modest size of the group was more than made up for by their thoughtfulness and vigor. Jerram fell into the routine very quickly and with his usual gusto: when he wasn't engaging in questions and debate, he'd help with slinging coffee and cookies. Forty years later, many of the meetings fall victim to a memory blur, but some stand out vividly, as if they were only yesterday.

I recall one of those evenings particularly well. We expected some of the most serious and thoughtful seekers to be in attendance, so I'd decided to pull together a talk that melded the book of Ecclesiastes, Schaeffer insights, and some passages from Nietzsche, Camus, and Sartre that centered on the search for meaning and significance. Later I would learn that only two weeks prior to this meeting Jerram had taken a train out of the city to a well known outcropping of rock and cliffs in the Peak District of Derbyshire; his angst had reached the point of despair. As I have already said: Jerram was for real, he would play the game out to the end. Thankfully, that day he decided to give life another chance. He wrote, "I felt constrained to keep searching just a little longer before taking such a final step."[4]

He traveled back into the city and, as grace would have it, within a couple of weeks joined our coffee house discussion; the confluence of his personal search and the evening's discussion topic turned out to be the kind of thing that can only be orchestrated by a higher hand. I could sense that everyone was really engaged that evening. What I didn't know was just how significant it would prove to be for Jerram's life. "It pierced me to the heart, for here was a man, Mike, and here was a book, the Bible, that took my questions seriously and began to give them answers."[5] It was only the outset of a journey but by this time the journey was beginning to move in a definite direction.

Weeks and months went by. Many more Sunday evening discussion groups were held, not to mention casual visits and informal conversations during the week. At that time, for Sunday evenings we played portions of the tapes by Francis Schaeffer that would become the book, *He is There and He is Not Silent*. The seed planted was now about to burst into life. I well recall the moment during one of the coffee house evenings when Jerram asked to have a private chat with me. We left the living room and went to the kitchen: Jerram wanted to become a Christian; he'd made up his mind and was determined to know how. We knelt by a chair and prayed together. Jerram continued participating in the Sunday evenings, but now in a changed capacity: he went from seeker to one who had met the risen Lord, from bystander to disciple.

Every gardener or farmer knows, of course, that not all seeds planted and germinated survive and grow to maturity: there are birds, rocks, thorns, and thistles to be contended with. What was so clearly obvious, however, as I look back on those early days was Jerram's determination, his seriousness about discipleship (although I doubt that at the time he would have framed his decisions using terminology like that!). It was a step-by-step process.

The first test came rather quickly. Over the days of our early friendship and his attendance at the Sunday evening discussions—although quite separately from them—Jerram had developed something of a romantic attachment to a young lady. She was quite a pleasant person and she was warmly welcomed into our circle, but it was pretty obvious that she did not share Jerram's seriousness about the quest or the message. Her interests were elsewhere. In spite of the fact that their lives were headed in very different directions, however, the attachment was evidently growing. The issue was not one of moral compromise— the relationship was affectionate but entirely honorable—rather, it was a matter of wisdom, prudence and, dare I say, discipleship. I spoke to Jerram about the situation and tried to encourage his reflection on the relationship in light of his new-found identity. He didn't say a great deal; this was clearly a sensitive issue. Jerram is a very caring individual and possessed of strong emotions. I wondered about the outcome, and watched, not without apprehension.

At this point in the narrative I want to mention that I am very aware of the sensitivities around sharing an incident of this kind and do so, in part, only because many years have elapsed; but also, because those engaged in the intellectual side of coming to faith can sometimes underestimate, or even ignore, the vital role played by key decisions made in other areas of our lives. In this context, it may be instructive for those who know and admire Jerram's ministry, and have watched him survive many fiery trials, to become aware of how early on in his Christian life the mold was cast and the steel of obedience hardened. We are whole people, and in this case God was dealing with the whole man. The mind had been persuaded, the spirit enlivened, and now another step was required, another act of the will was called for—as it turned out, a step that would profoundly impact the rest of Jerram's life. Doors are closed and other doors are opened. But none of this was evident at the time. Then it was simply a matter of doing the right thing. At the time, of course, neither he, nor I, quite realized the significance of this choice—how it would set into motion the forging of a long obedience in the same direction.[6]

Again, I can recall the evening well: there was another beckoning for a private conversation beyond the reach of the noisy din of coffee room conversation. As usual we retreated to the kitchen and sat at the small table. Jerram spoke briefly and came to the point; he'd taken the step; the romantic side of the relationship was ended.

Weeks and months went by; graduation grew nearer. We talked about what he would do over the summer and beyond. The stories some of us told of the stimulating and profitable time we had spent as Farel House students at L'Abri were clearly appealing. Jerram determined to make his own journey and allow opportunity for his faith to become further nurtured and informed. As I recall, he left in summer— it was some time before August nineteenth for sure; he missed my wedding in Hull, Yorks to Beryl, a student of F. F. Bruce whom I had met at the University. But, of course, I was happy for him and knew he was doing the right thing. We kept in touch by letter (I guess we call it snail mail these days, but I seem to recall that the snails were much faster in those days!).

Picking up the thread of the story, relating especially to the difficult decision Jerram had had to make the previous year, I am reminded of another moment—this time in the small apartment Beryl and I had established on the first floor of 30 Moorefield Rd. in Didsbury (Manchester). Newly married friends (Trevor and Liz Watts) had taken over the third floor flat where the coffee evenings had been held; Beryl and I took up a flat on the ground floor for the beginning of our married life. At any rate, I was in the living room opening a letter received from Switzerland, from Jerram. He'd taken to L'Abri like a duck to water, all the while, of course, making himself very useful. In addition to his studies he'd become a Worker—he now planned to stay for a whole year—and he'd become Edith Schaeffer's gardener. Those of you who know Jerram will be aware of his multiple talents: beyond literature, poetry, and philosophy, and not any lower on the scale of importance, is his passion for gardening which he does with a flourish, adding his own signature. I think he calls it the "wild and natural style" (although my memory could be playing tricks on me here!). In any case, back to the letter, here Jerram the poet was quite evident: he told me that he had met the most marvelous and talented girl. She was Francis Schaeffer's secretary, her name was Vicki, and she was American. It was pretty obvious that in Jerram's mind there were simply not enough superlatives, even for someone who'd taken a degree in English, to do her justice!

Several years later as Jerram and Vicki stood on the steps of the little church beside our humble, small-town manse in the province of Saskatchewan, my own home town area of Canada, I couldn't help but marvel at all that had transpired. I'd taught Philosophy in Manchester for a year and then had taken a one-year appointment as a lay Minister with the United Church of Canada in a parish that encompassed my hometown of Edam. Jerram had stayed for a year at L'Abri in Switzerland, then he and Vicki married back in the States. They took up domicile in St. Louis so that Jerram could study at Covenant Seminary. Vicki, a qualified teacher, took up her profession again. They were full of stories; I invited Jerram to preach at the Sunday morning service, which he did happily and well. His text, as I recall very clearly, was taken from the first section of Psalm 40:

I waited patiently for the LORD;
he inclined to me and heard my cry.
He drew me up from the pit of destruction,
out of the miry bog,

and set my feet upon a rock,
making my steps secure.
He put a new song in my mouth,
a song of praise to our God.
Many will see and fear,
and put their trust in the LORD.
Psalm 40:1–3

Jerram spoke in the genre of a sermon rather than as a testimony, but the autobiographical origins and allusions were unmistakable: he was speaking from the heart, out of his own experience. And, as I reflect upon those words now, I can see how much the words spoken from the psalmist's testimony would be quite literally fulfilled in Jerram's own life: emanating from his life now established on a rock would come a new song, and *"Many will see and fear and put their trust in the LORD"* (Ps. 40:3).

So much had happened since we'd first met and little did we know how much yet lay ahead. None of us knew that Jerram and Vicki would eventually minister for a full decade with Ranald and Sue McAuley at the English L'Abri at Greatham, Liss in Hampshire; that Jerram would then be invited to become a professor at Covenant Seminary and eventually the founding director of the Francis Schaeffer Institute there; that Jerram would have a world-wide ministry in teaching, speaking, and writing; that they would raise three boys. Happily, neither did we know that Vicki would have to struggle with cancer, and (thankfully!) survive; that Jerram would have to persist in his ministry through much suffering, as he struggled with an extremely painful disease that afflicted his hearing for many years (hyperacusis), and recover—thankfully and miraculously! There are thorns in any bed of roses, as every gardener knows only too well, and this garden was no exception!

But on this beautiful spring day, our minds were simply in the moment. The sun shone; I got a great photo of Jerram and Vicki on the church steps. We walked over to the manse next door and then left on the twenty minute journey down the highway to the village of Edam so they could meet my mother, Johanna. My grandparents, Jan and Lena Vreke, had been immigrants from the Netherlands and were original founding settlers of the town in the first decade of the twentieth century. After a delicious meal, Vicki and my mom, both accomplished pianists (and both school teachers, albeit of widely differing ages!), regaled us with some marvellous pieces on the piano. Jerram and I sat back and enjoyed, as did Beryl. Doubtless, thoughts and images of third floor coffee house lectures and discussions—honest answers and honest questions—coupled with some difficult decisions and the wonderful grace of our heavenly Father were not far from our minds.

Little did we reflect on God's irony—though I do so years later—how much grandfather Vreke would have approved of Jerram's choice of seminary (Covenant Seminary) for he too was of a distinctly Reformed theological persuasion. Though himself a farmer who had not completed his full high school education (in Middleburgh, Holland), after his death, a copy of J. Gresham Machen's *Christianity and Liberalism* was found on his book shelves. Machen, now there's a name admired by the young Francis Schaeffer in his student days! It was my grandfather Vreke who had had such a formative impact on my own nascent theological thought—warning me to reflect carefully upon what was being preached from our local church pulpit (as he feared the drift toward liberalism had begun to set in). His thoughtful exchanges with the local ministers visiting his home were probably the first step toward our vigorous coffee house discussions many years later; for me they were a model of critical thinking and passion for the word of God! Wheels within wheels and ever God's grace triumphant, though the journey may be difficult and fraught with many a challenge—modern echoes of a pilgrim's progress. How fitting it seems to me now that Jerram should preach his first sermon in this heartland!

Postscript

In the providential grace of our Heavenly Father, the preparation and training phase of our lives is never far from his call; however, unlike doctrine, his designs and methods are never orthodox—they follow no simple pattern or formula. Left for another place and time are the stories of Jerrams' years prior to his arrival in Manchester, themselves a stepping stone: his parents and family, his love of good literature (including C. S. Lewis) and nature, the concatenation of forces, thoughts, and impressions that led to his decision to come to Manchester. Once there, was it merely the game of squash or a chance friendship encounter that led him to 30 Moorefield Rd?

Then there were the unusual circumstances that paved his pathway to faith: reflections on the writer to Ecclesiastes and his wrestling with the meaningless; taped lectures by an expatriate American pastor who, like Jerram, had himself striven with the deep questions of philosophical thought, literature, pop culture, and Christian faith; vigorous discussions, late into the night, open to very divergent perspectives, ideas, and argumentation—what kind of disciple would all of these learnings and experiences shape? Someone unlikely to be upset by the maelstrom of contemporary ideas; someone anxious to plot the connections between those ideas and faith, rather than leaving them in isolated compartments; someone who cares about teaching, not in the splendid isolation of an ivory tower, but with an eye to reaching out, climbing over walls, and bursting into well-fortified castles! And someone who, at the end of the day, cares about people and is willing to be inconvenienced by their needs, their demands, and their importunities—some call it being motivated by love.

Like Moses, who found himself in Pharaoh's court, fled, and was sent back again; like Joseph, born to a privileged position only to be sent through a wasteland of forgottenness before he was catapulted to the task prepared for him; like the rough-hewn fishermen, James and John—the Sons of Thunder (Mark 3:17)—not likely to be intimidated by the first sign of opposition; like the Apostle Paul, who studied under one of the leading scholars of his day only to be knocked off his saddle and blinded by the light of the Son; God has given us Jerram Barrs. Of course, we do not compare ourselves to these worthies, and neither would Jerram, but we are children of the same Father. And his call is the same: who will go for us? Jerram, like Isaiah of old, answers *hemani* (*"I will!"* Isa. 6:8). And the rest is history. *A deo Gloria!*

---

1. Jerram Barrs, "Francis Schaeffer: The Man and His Message," https://www.covenantseminary.edu/francis-schaeffer-the-man-and-his-message/.
2. Barrs, "Francis Schaeffer."
3. Part of L'Abri. See https://swisslabri.org/about-your-stay/work-and-study/.
4. Barrs, "Francis Schaeffer."
5. Barrs, "Francis Schaeffer."
6. To borrow from Eugene Peterson's book of the same title. Eugene Peterson, *A Long Obedience in the Same Direction*, (InterVarsity Press: Downers Grove, IL, 2000).

CHRIST AND CHARACTER

David Clyde Jones

ThD, Concordia Seminary
Professor Emeritus[1], Theology and Ethics
Covenant Theological Seminary
St. Louis, MO

I began teaching full-time at Covenant Theological Seminary in the fall of 1968 after an initial run as a part-time instructor and librarian's assistant, following the 1967 Summer of Love,[2] for which The Beatles provided the soundtrack with *Sgt. Pepper's Lonely Hearts Club Band,* and during which Arlo Guthrie tweaked the establishment with counter-cultural hilarity in *Alice's Restaurant.* I turned thirty that summer, which bought me a little time to live with the warning cliché not to trust anyone over thirty.

The summer of 1968 might well have been dubbed the Summer of Hate. Though there had been spasms of violence in America the previous year, it paled in comparison to the dramatic events of 1968. Martin Luther King Jr. was assassinated on Good Friday; student riots in Paris in May resulted in Bloody Monday. Senator Robert Kennedy was shot dead the night he won the Democratic Primary in June, and violence erupted between police and protesters at the Democratic National Convention in Chicago in August.

Fall classes began at the seminary in September.

Against this background, I taught my first MDiv course in systematic theology on the Doctrine of Scripture. In the entering class that year were several students from Bob Jones University and an equal number who had studied at L'Abri. It was not difficult to spot which was which—BJU students were used to coming to class in coats and ties. L'Abri alumni were more at home in sandals and jeans. We had our own seminary version of the establishment/counter-culture divide. I recall preaching a sermon in chapel that year titled "The Kingdom of Heaven is like a Great Net that Catches all Kinds of Fish!" Eventually mutual respect prevailed, and the two groups learned from each other, especially as they critiqued me from opposite directions.

It was my privilege to have Jerram Barrs in that first class. He had come from L'Abri with the idea of completing a one-year MA in theological studies to broaden his Christian worldview perspective in preparation for a career in teaching English literature. But during that year, he perceived his call to a ministerial vocation instead, and continued at the seminary for another two years to complete the MDiv degree. He and Vicki then settled in the UK to open the English branch of L'Abri in Greatham. Decades later I served with a group of Evangelical seminary professors that included Christine Pohl, professor of Christian social ethics at Asbury Theological Seminary and author of the widely acclaimed *Making Room: Recovering Hospitality as a Christian Tradition*. As we got acquainted, I learned that she was the first guest to arrive at the Greatham L'Abri, her faith "hanging by a thread". Jerram's ability to provide honest answers to honest questions in a hospitable environment was just the tonic she required, a seal on Jerram's decision to focus with Vicki on ministry.

When Jerram left the seminary after completing his course of study, the faculty was unanimous in hoping that he would someday return as a professor. Such was the impression he had made not only by his scholarship but also by his Christian character that was already well formed in such qualities as integrity, compassion, commitment, and moral courage. Of course, there was much growth to come through some severe testing, but even at this early stage the trajectory was clear.

When I became academic dean, I would approach Jerram from time to time to see whether he would consider a change of venue. The timing was never right until my last year in that position when Jerram contacted me with the news that he and Vicki had concluded that they would be open to making a move to St. Louis and seminary ministry. This was the capstone of my tenure as academic dean, and it made a nice bookend to my beginning with Jerram as a student and ending with him as a seminary colleague when I retired from full time teaching at Covenant Seminary after forty years.

Thus, I count it a high privilege to be asked to contribute to this volume in Jerram's honor, especially to write a chapter dealing with virtue ethics in relation to Jerram's exemplary life and ministry. A few years ago, when WWJD had become such a popular reference point in ethical decision-making, it was often transmuted on campus into "What would *Jerram* do?" So closely did Jerram's practice model that of Jesus that he could have said with Paul, but didn't for reasons of modesty, *"Be imitators of me, as I am of Christ"* (1 Cor. 11:1). It seemed to me that the best way to fulfill the assignment to write something on virtue ethics for this *Festschrift* would be to focus on "Christ and Character." There are a couple of reasons beyond its being such a key element in understanding Jerram.

First, the chapter title "Christ and Character" is intended as something of a counterweight to H. Richard Niebuhr's classic treatise on *Christ and Culture*, first published in 1951 and maintained continuously in print ever since. His five paradigms (opposition, accommodation, synthesis, dualism, and conversion) are now taken for granted as the indispensable starting point for developing a vision for Christian social ethics. The most recent example I know of is D. A. Carson, *Christ and Culture Revisited* (2008). Before that there was Glen Stassen et al., *Authentic Transformation: A New Vision of Christ and Culture* (1996). Right from the start it was observed, particularly by Anabaptist authors such as John Howard Yoder, whose early critique for his classes is included in *Authentic Transformation*, that Niebuhr's typologies point to a preferred conclusion: the conversion or transformation model. The enduring question is *how* Christians should act to achieve that goal.

When I first started teaching, I attended several conferences on the role of Christians in society. There were typically three types of strategies presented. Evangelicals such as Carl Henry emphasized individual regeneration. Anabaptists such as John Howard Yoder emphasized the church as a paradigmatic community, leading by resistance and example. Calvinists such as Nicholas Wolterstorff emphasized structural reform within the spheres God ordained for human flourishing. Properly understood, these are not mutually exclusive. I would say that cultural or social transformation involves three interdependent components: personal renewal, ecclesial practice, and structural reform. It is often assumed that this third component will issue in Christian triumphalism, but that does not necessarily follow. There are many ways of being "salt and light" in a fallen world without lording it over unbelievers. Non-triumphalistic transformation seems to be the point of the parable of the leaven (Matt. 13:33). The takeaway point is that Christian transformation of culture is rooted in Christian transformation of character.

The second reason for the focus on "Christ and Character" is that the subject of character formation is typically undertreated in Evangelical Protestant ethics, though there have been some notable Evangelical efforts to fill this gap recently, among them N. T. Wright, *After You Believe: Why Christian Character Matters* and Robert C. Roberts, *Spiritual Emotions: A Psychology of Christian Virtues*. Reformed theological ethics has historically been more attentive to the commandments than the virtues of the covenant way of life, but that imbalance is not likely to continue very far into the future. This chapter allows me to get in my two bits on Christian character while the pot is stirring. Bit one is what Christian character is; bit two is how it is developed.

Christian Character: What It Is

> O gracious God and most merciful Father,
> Who has [graciously given] us the rich and precious jewel
>   of thy holy word;
> Assist us with thy Spirit that it may be written in our
>   hearts to our everlasting comfort,
> To reform us,
> To renew us according to thine own image,
> To build us up into the perfect building of thy Christ,
> And to increase us in all heavenly virtues.
> Grant this, O heavenly Father, for the same Jesus Christ's
>   sake.
> Amen.
> —Preface to the Geneva Bible (1560)

In the most general sense, character refers to the qualities distinctive to an individual, as in the *Reader's Digest* series, "My Most Unforgettable Character." More specifically, it refers to the *moral* qualities of an individual, as in Martin Luther King Jr's famous line about not being judged by the color of our skin but the content of our character. In that sense, character usually carries with it the positive connotation of good. To speak of someone as "a person of character" is to make a positive moral judgment about that person. Central to the idea of character in the positive moral sense is "having the courage of your convictions." As James Davidson Hunter remarks, "Character is formed in relation to convictions and is manifested in the capacity to abide by those convictions even in, *especially in*, the face of temptation."[3]

Of course, to be truly good, one must act on *sound* moral convictions; they must be grounded in knowledge of the truth. While the Bible does not use the word *character*, it does have some important "character references" for God's people whose actions match the revelation of God's will. To cite just three, Noah was *"a righteous man, blameless in his generation"* (Gen. 6:9); Zechariah and Elizabeth were *"righteous before God, walking blamelessly in all the commandments and statutes of the Lord"* (Luke 1:6); and Tabitha (Dorcas) had the reputation of being *"full of good works and acts of charity"* (Acts 9:36). The individuals named are characterized by acting consistently with their convictions as the covenant people of God. Their character was formed in response to God's gracious initiative in calling them into a personal relationship with him to reflect his glory, particularly his attributes of justice, mercy, and faithfulness (Mic. 6:8, Matt. 23:23).

All approaches to moral character are, as we say, worldview dependent. They presuppose a basic framework that includes the origin of the cosmos, the nature of the human being, and the goal of history. Central to the question of moral character is a diagnosis of the human condition and its remedy. The biblical worldview is at its heart God's activity in history, aptly summarized under the rubric of Creation-Fall-Redemption-Consummation. The persons singled out above fall into this pattern: God reveals his covenant to his chosen friends who embrace the promise in divinely engendered faith. A distinctive way of life ensues leading ever onward to the fulfillment of God's glorious purpose in Christ. It is at the point of the Galatians' failure to grasp the essence of their calling that elicits Paul's most explicit definition of Christian character: *"My little children,"* he says, *"... I am again in the anguish of childbirth until Christ is formed in you"* (Gal. 4:19). For the apostle, the Galatians' lack of progress toward the goal of the Christian life means that he has to go into labor all over again to see them alive and growing properly.

In Paul's theology, union with Christ is the basic fact of salvation, and conformity to Christ is the progressively realized goal of salvation. Glorification consists in being made like Christ, the perfect image of God in human nature. The goal is finally realized in the age to come, but even now those whom God calls are being transformed into the Lord's likeness with ever-increasing glory (2 Cor. 3:18). To be renewed in the image of God (Eph. 4:24, Col. 3:10) is to be made like Christ, who not only is God but who also as a human being functioned in perfect harmony with the will of God. Christian character is essentially Christlikeness; the goal of the Christian life is to have Christ *formed in us*. The passive tense of the verb is significant. Classical moral philosophy regarded character as a human achievement, formed by repeated actions over time—like ironing pleats in a skirt or kilt until they take hold. That was apparently at the root of the Galatians' disastrous misunderstanding. *"What!"* says the apostle. *"Are you so foolish? After beginning with the Spirit, are you now trying to attain your goal by human effort?"* (Gal. 3:3). Becoming Christ-like is not a human achievement; it is rather a divine work, decisively begun in regeneration and progressively developed over the course of a believer's entire life.

Christian Character: How It Is Developed

> Creator Spirit, ... come from on high,
> Rich in thy sevenfold energy;
> Make us eternal truth receive,
> And practice all that we believe.
> —Veni Creator Spiritus, *trans. John Dryden (1693)*

The basic postulate of biblical ethics is that the Triune God has created beings in his image to know and to love him and to serve one another in love (Matt. 22:17–40, Gal. 5:13), and to participate in his righteous rule over the earth (Rev. 5:9–10). The idea of character in this worldview is epitomized as "Christlikeness." Just as this goal is manifestly distinctive, so are the means to it. In a famous passage on the Christian calling to become partakers of the divine nature *"through the knowledge of him who called us to his own glory and excellence* [arête, moral virtue]," Peter reminds his readers that the Lord *"has granted to us all things that pertain to life and godliness"* (2 Pet. 1:3–4). So, whatever it takes for Christ to be formed in us has been granted in keeping with his *"very great and precious promises."* Put in the form of a thesis, I would say that Christian character, or Christ-likeness, is the work of the Holy Spirit, through the means of grace, in the communion of the saints, by practice of the truth. What follows is a brief discussion of each of these components that I believe, when taken together, provide a comprehensive view of character formation according to God's purpose in Christ.

The Work of the Holy Spirit

The criticism of Evangelical Protestant ethics for its perceived lacuna when it comes to discussion of character formation and the virtues is somewhat offset when the classic Reformed doctrine of sanctification is taken into account. Sanctification is concisely defined as "the work of God's free grace, whereby we are renewed in the whole man after the image of God, and are enabled more and more to die unto sin, and live unto righteousness."[4] This is simply a different mode of expression for character formation, and while the language may be somewhat dated, it does have the advantage of being clear on the question of agency: it is the Holy Spirit who sanctifies, or alternatively, forms Christ in the believer. The difference between justification and sanctification, not always appreciated by either Roman Catholics or Evangelical Protestants, is that God in justification imputes the righteousness of Christ; in sanctification his Spirit infuses grace and enables the exercise thereof.[5]

It has become common in recent Reformed theology to distinguish between definitive and progressive sanctification, but the theological point, I believe, is better served by reserving sanctification for the progressive aspect of growth in grace, with the understanding that the definitive or decisive aspect is really equivalent to regeneration, which is properly defined as "that act of God by which the principle of the new life is implanted in man, and the governing disposition of the soul is made holy."[6] The theological term for "the governing disposition of the soul" is *habitus*. It should be obvious that such a radical change cannot be self-effected; as Jesus told Nicodemus, "You must be born again—from above!" It is a *monergistic* act of God, like effectual calling with which it is closely associated, and which I would define as "that mighty act of God by which we are united to Christ to become partakers of his grace and virtue." The *habitus* of grace consists of the great trio of virtues bestowed by the Holy Spirit in the application of redemption: faith, hope, and love (1 Cor. 13:13 et al).

While the inception of the Christian life excludes human cooperation, the same cannot be said of its maturation. As the old byword has it: passive in regeneration, active in sanctification. Without question, God is the agent of sanctification (1 Thess. 5:23); yet, as John Murray was careful to point out, "Our activity is enlisted to the fullest extent in the process."[7] The key to avoiding the impression that sanctification is the meritorious successor to justification is the recognition that it, too, is by grace through faith. The Holy Spirit not only regenerates, but also indwells and leads all those who by grace trust in Christ for salvation. By faith we realize our union with Christ, apprehend our victory over sin, appropriate the power of the Holy Spirit, and express our gratitude through a life of love. Christian character formation is described as living by faith (Gal. 2:20), walking by faith (2 Cor. 5:7), working by faith (Gal. 5:6), and overcoming by faith (1 John 5:4).

The active participation of believers in the process of character formation is expressed in the imperative to *"walk by the Spirit"* (Gal. 5:16), following the Spirit's leading (Gal. 5:18). The Holy Spirit leads people, not robots. It is not ours to resolve the mystery of grace and human responsibility. What is clear is that in dependence on the indwelling Spirit of Christ, we are to actively pursue Christ-likeness (1) in the power of the Spirit, with full recognition and self-conscious appropriation of salvation by grace (2) in the path of the Spirit, the way in which the Holy Spirit has traced out in the word and that Jesus has embodied in his life. We are called to practice the salvation that God has graciously bestowed upon us, precisely because *"it is God who works in you, both to will and to work for his good pleasure"* (Phil. 2:13).

Believing Use of the Means of Grace

As Jesus' analogy of the wind in his famous nighttime interview with Nicodemus implies, the work of the Holy Spirit is sovereign and mysterious, not open to human observation and analysis. Being the immediate creative work of God in the human soul, regeneration does not depend absolutely on external means; the Spirit works how, when, and where he pleases. Nevertheless, there are certain *outward and ordinary* means that Christ makes effective by his own presence and Spirit to impart to us the benefits of his redemption. These are, in the careful formulation of the Westminster divines, "all his ordinances; especially the Word, sacraments, and prayer."[8] While not limited to these three, they certainly deserve to be considered first as "means of grace" in developing a theology of character formation.[9] To counter the mistaken impression that "means of grace" implies that the ordinances are effective in and of themselves (*ex opere operato*) I have put "believing use" in the heading.

It is a commonplace of biblical theology that the Spirit works "by and with the Word," meaning the historical revelation of God in his Son (Heb. 1:1–2) that eventuates in the holy Scriptures, *"which are able to make you wise for salvation through faith in Christ Jesus"* (2 Tim. 3:15). Typical of believing appropriation of the inscripturated Word is the exhortation of James to *"receive with meekness the implanted word, which is able to save your souls"* (Jas. 2:21). This means attending to the Word, appropriating the vision of the coming of God's kingdom, bringing every thought captive to Christ, being shaped by the narrative of Scripture that centers on Christ.

"All Scripture," Paul says, *"is breathed out by God and profitable for teaching, for reproof, for correction, and for training in righteousness"* (2 Tim. 3:16). The reason why it is said that the Holy Spirit makes not simply "the reading but especially the preaching of the Word" an effectual means of grace[10] is because of the liability toward self-deception, particularly when it comes to the need for reproof and correction. Self-deception is explicitly addressed no less than six times in the New Testament. James in particular highlights this liability as it shows up in the gap between profession and practice: *"Be doers of the word, and not hearers only, deceiving yourselves"* (Jas. 1:22).[11] The preacher's role is to challenge those who hear in a way that might too easily be avoided by their personal Bible reading. This was the institutional role of the priests in the Old Testament, augmented by God's servants the prophets, especially in times of crisis. It was the purpose of the covenant with Levi that *"The lips of a priest should guard knowledge, and people should seek instruction from his mouth, for he is the messenger of the Lord of hosts"* (Mal. 2:7; cf. Deut. 33:10).

When the priests discharged this responsibility faithfully, the nation prospered. A good example is the priest Jehoiada, who engineered the rescue of the little Jehoash from the murderous attempt of Queen Athaliah, Jezebel's daughter, to eradicate the Davidic line. Jehoiada was married to Jehosheba, Jehoash's aunt; she kidnapped the one-year old royal seed and hid him in a backroom of the temple until he was old enough to be presented publicly as the rightful heir to the throne. The dramatic story is recorded in 2 Kings 11, after which we read: *"And Jehoash did what was right in the eyes of the Lord all his days, because Jehoiada the priest instructed him"* (2 Kgs. 12:2). That's the way it was supposed to be, but sadly for the most part was not (Mal. 2:8–9).

Looking back over the Old Testament revelation, Paul reminds Gentile believers that they had previously been *"strangers to the covenants of promise"* in which Christ was mediated to the Israelites (Eph. 2:12). Those promises were confirmed in outward signs, particularly circumcision and the Passover. Those who participated in them by faith were assured of the reality of the promises for them personally. The same principle is operative in the New Covenant of promise and its attendant sacraments, namely baptism and the Lord's supper. It is not necessary to understand how they work, only to receive them in faith that God is at work through them, though it may be below the level of consciousness and beyond rational explanation. All that is necessary to know is that the sacraments become effective means of growth in Christ-likeness "by the blessing of Christ and the working of his Holy Spirit in them that by faith receive them".[12]

Perhaps the best index to the coordination of the Word and prayer in Christian character formation is Psalm 119, which extolls the comprehensiveness of the holy Scriptures in twenty-two stanzas of eight verses, each beginning with a different letter of the Hebrew alphabet in succession, every one of which contains an explicit reference to the divine author. What is not as often recognized is that "every verse from 4 to the end is a prayer or affirmation addressed to Him."[13] These are often prayers for illumination: *"Open my eyes, that I may behold wondrous things out of your law"* (vs. 18); *"Make me understand the way of your precepts, and I will meditate on your wondrous works"* (vs. 27); *"Give me understanding, that I may keep your law and observe it with my whole heart"* (vs. 34). At other times the psalmist recognizes the need for divine enablement: *"I will run in the way of your commandments when you enlarge my heart"* (vs. 32); *"In your steadfast love give me life, that I may keep the testimonies of your mouth"* (vs. 88); *"Keep steady my steps according to your promise, and let no iniquity get dominion over me"* (vs. 133). Many other texts, of course, could be cited from this Psalm and others, some of which are clearly cut from the same cloth as the Apostle Paul's doctrine of the leading of the Spirit: *"Lead me in your truth and teach me, for you are the God of my salvation; for you I wait all the day long"* (Ps. 25:5).

In one of the great fourth century Trinitarian hymns, Ambrose of

Milan (339–397) offers a prayer for character formation in the image of Christ. The hymn in common use in English is the 1910 translation by Louis F. Benson, known by its first line "O splendor of God's glory bright." Not to quibble with Benson's fine work, but the first line would be more accurately rendered, "O splendor of *the Father's* glory bright," even if it does require an extra beat. The hymn begins in Latin *Splendor paternae glorie*; its opening stanzas are addressed to God the Son:

> O splendor of God's glory bright
> From light eternal bringing light
> Thou Light of light, light's living Spring
> True Day, all days illumining.
>
> Come, very Sun of Heaven's love
> In lasting radiance from above,
> And pour the Holy Spirit's ray
> On all we think or do today.

Having established the eternal relationship between the Father and the Son, and the Son's role in relation to the Spirit in the ongoing work of salvation, Ambrose makes specific requests for grace and virtue in living the Christian life:

> And now to Thee our pray'rs ascend,
> O Father glorious without end
> We plead with Sovereign Grace for pow'r
> To conquer in temptation's hour.
>
> Confirm our will to do the right
> And keep our hearts from envy's blight
> Let faith her eager fires renew
> And hate the false, and love the true.

I have made a point of reciting this hymn as an ethics class opener in recent years, but I can't recall ever having sung it in church. Maybe it needs a better tune. One would be hard put to find a more relevant prayer in song for divine illumination and character formation in living the Christian life.[14]

Active Participation in the Communion of the Saints

It shouldn't escape our notice that the petitions in Ambrose's great hymn are all in the first person *plural*: "And now to Thee *our* pray'rs ascend.... Confirm *our* will to do the right.... keep *our* hearts from envy's blight." That is how Jesus taught his disciples to pray, and it fits with the exposition of character formation in the epistles, which always assumes a corporate context. See, for example, the prayers of Paul in Philippians 1:9–11 and Ephesians 1:15–23. Plainly God's purpose is to unite believers to Christ and to one another in a temple indwelt by the Holy Spirit:

> *So then you are no longer strangers and aliens, but you are fellow citizens with the saints and members of the household of God, built on the foundation of the apostles and prophets, Christ Jesus himself being the cornerstone, in whom the whole structure, being joined together, grows into a holy temple in the Lord. In him you also are being built together into a dwelling place for God by the Spirit.*
> Eph. 2:19–22

Union with Christ means communion in the gifts and graces of the individual members of the body of Christ as *"grace was given to each one of us according to the measure of Christ's gift"* (Eph. 4:7). The role of apostles, prophets, evangelists, shepherds is *"to equip the saints for the work of ministry, for building up the body of Christ, until we all attain to the unity of the faith and of the knowledge of the Son of God, to mature manhood, to the measure of the stature of the fullness of Christ"* (Eph. 4:12–13). The goal is *"to grow up in every way into him who is the head, into Christ"* (Eph. 4:15). Peter makes the same point about the distribution of gifts being used to serve one another (1 Pet. 4:10–11). Components of active participation include ministry, discipline, community, and example as the body builds itself up in love.

The role of ecclesial example is especially prominent in Paul. Expecting a corporate response, he writes to the Philippians, *"Brothers, join* [together] *in imitating me, and keep your eyes on those who walk according to the example you have in us"* (Phil. 3:17). He is confident in his appeal to follow apostolic example inasmuch as it embodies concretely the character of Christ. This pattern is established early on in Paul's ministry. To the Thessalonians he writes, *"And you became imitators of us and of the Lord, for you received the word in much affliction, with the joy of the Holy Spirit, so that you became* [in turn] *an example to all the believers in*

Macedonia and Achaia" (1 Thess. 1:6–7). In the next chapter, he goes on to make the point that they, too, have benefited from ecclesial example, inasmuch as they *"became imitators of the churches of God in Christ Jesus that are in Judea"* (1 Thess. 2:14). Nowhere is this principle more dramatically illustrated than in Paul's second letter to the Corinthians, where the generosity of the joyful but poverty-stricken Macedonians is held up as a model of Christ-likeness for the Corinthians to follow (2 Cor. 8:1–7).

Practice of the Truth

In a remarkable passage that forms the climax of Paul's character-shaping appeal to the Philippians, he follows his exhortation to prayerful watchfulness with a tandem call to reflection and action that is essential to growth in the likeness of Christ. *"Finally, brothers, whatever is true, whatever is honorable, whatever is just, whatever is pure, whatever is lovely, whatever is commendable, if there is any excellence, if there is anything worthy of praise, think about these things* [tauta logizesthe] (Phil. 4:8). In mathematics, the literal sense of the verb *logizomai* is "to calculate." The metaphorical sense means something like "to reckon, take into account." In other words, the Christian mind is shaped by meditation on the virtues—the word translated "excellence" is actually a rare New Testament instance of *aretê*—perfectly embodied in the life of Christ. This is more than a futile mind game, however; in the true Christian life, contemplation is linked to practical activity. Paul continues, *"What you have learned and received and heard and seen in me—practice these things* [tauta prassete], *and the God of peace will be with you"* (Phil. 4:9). In short, Paul lived his message, and reminds believers that they have not only heard the truth but seen it in his own practice.

There is a similar construction in 2 Peter 1:8. Following an exhortation to pursue with zeal the virtues of faith—*aretê* again puts in an appearance in vs. 5—Peter remarks, *"For if these qualities* [i.e., virtues] *are yours and are increasing, they keep you from being ineffective or unfruitful in the knowledge of our Lord Jesus Christ."* Like Paul, Peter issues a call to diligent action: *"for if you practice these qualities* [i.e., the virtues associated with faith], *you will never fall"* (vs. 10). The ground of Peter's exhortation is the knowledge of God's full and free salvation in Christ and the high calling of reflecting his own glory and excellence (*aretê*). In answering this call, believers are engaged to the fullest extent, knowing that they may and must rely on God's power and *"precious and very great promises"* (vs. 4). Character, here provocatively presented as becoming *"partakers of the divine nature"* (vs. 4), is formed by diligent practice of the truth that is in Jesus.

In his great chapter in Ephesians on growth in the Christian life, Paul expressly grounds his appeal to believers on the proposition that *"the truth is in Jesus"* (Eph. 4:21), and that they are called to live accordingly. Their former practice of sensuality and every kind of impurity stands in stark contrast to the way they *"learned Christ"* (Eph. 4:20). When and how did that happen? First, we need to resolve a discrepancy in the English translation of verse 21 on which the major versions have differed from the beginning. Tyndale renders it: *"But ye have not so learned Christ, if so be ye have heard of him, and are taught in him, even as the truth is in Jesus."* The KJV, on the other hand, has: *"But ye have not so learned Christ; if so be that ye have heard him, and have been taught by him, as the truth is in Jesus."* The RSV revived Tyndale's rendering, and the NIV and ESV followed suit, while the NASB stayed with the KJV. What are we to make of this?

My wife and I have for some years been members of a small-group lay Bible study arranged through our local church. Over the years I've been impressed with the level of biblical understanding on the part of other members of the group, many of the women of which are leaders in Bible Study Fellowship. But occasionally I'm called upon for assistance when the question depends on some knowledge of Hebrew or Greek. I never know when I'm going to get one of these pop quizzes, and usually end up saying, "I'll have to get back to you on that." Since the group uses different translations, often someone wants to know which is more accurate. This text in Ephesians is a good example. Someone asked, "Why do some versions say, 'you have *heard about him,*' while others say, 'you have *heard him*'? What does the Greek say?" The first thing I found when I got home is that there is no equivalent for *about* in the Greek text, nor is there any textual variant that would explain an insertion. I can only surmise that it is an interpretive translation based on the historical fact that the Ephesian believers had not literally heard Jesus speaking or teaching. There are biblical-theological reasons, however, for a more straightforward reading of the text, namely, that the Ephesian believers, and indeed all believers today, have heard Jesus speaking through the apostles in the inscripturated word.

Here's what I mean. When the Lord revealed his covenant to Israel at Sinai, he literally spoke the Ten Commandments in the hearing of all the people. Then God called Moses up into the mount to receive further instructions, which Moses delivered orally to the people; and the people responded, *"All the words that the Lord has spoken we will do"* (Exod. 24:3). Then Moses wrote it all down in the Book of the Covenant which he read to the people; and the people responded, *"All that the Lord has spoken we will do"* (Exod. 24:7). Whether God speaks directly from the top of the mountain, or whether Moses delivers his word orally or in writing, there is no difference in authority. The proper response in each case is, "All that *the Lord* has spoken we will do." Turn now to the beginning of the book of Hebrews: *"Long ago, at many times and in many ways, God spoke to our fathers by the prophets, but in these last days he has spoken to us by his Son"* (Heb. 1:1–2). Fast forward to the description of the people of God under the New Covenant in chapter 12, at the conclusion of which we read, *"See that you do not refuse him who is speaking"* (Heb. 12:25). This coheres with the voice out of the cloud at the Transfiguration of Jesus: *"This is my Son, my chosen One; listen to him"* (Luke 9:35). Just as the Lord spoke through Moses, so the Apostle Paul can make the parallel claim that *"Christ is speaking in me"* (2 Cor. 13:3). Phillips, following the KJV reading of the Greek text, captures the sense admirably: *"But you have learned nothing like that from Christ, if you have really heard his voice and understood the truth that he has taught you."*

---

1. On Sunday, March 5, 2017, David Jones passed away after a battle with recurring cancer. He served Covenant Seminary as a professor from 1967–2017, and he was instrumental in bringing Jerram Barrs, his former student and good friend, to Covenant to teach and eventually establish the Francis A. Schaeffer Institute.
2. The Summer of Love was a social phenomenon that occurred during the summer of 1967, when as many as 100,000 people, mostly young people sporting hippie fashions of dress and behavior, converged in San Francisco's neighborhood of Haight-Ashbury.
3. James Davidson Hunter, *The Death of Character: Moral Education in an Age without Good or Evil* (New York: BasicBooks, 2000), xiii.
4. Westminster Shorter Catechism 35.
5. Westminster Larger Catechism 77.
6. L. Berkhof, *Systematic Theology*, 4th ed. (Carlisle, PA: Banner of Truth Trust, 1939), 469.
7. John Murray, *Redemption: Accomplished and Applied* (Grand Rapids, IL: Eerdmans, 1955), 147.
8. Westminster Larger Catechism 154.
9. The precise term "means of grace" actually occurs only once in the Westminster Standards. In the 6th petition of the Lord's Prayer we pray that God will "bestow and bless all means of grace" (Larger Catechism, q. 195). An alternative expression is "the ordinary means of salvation" (Larger Catechism, q. 63).
10. Westminster Shorter Catechism 89.

11. The other five references are Jas. 1:26 (*apataô*), 1 Cor. 3:18 (*exapataô*), Gal. 6:3 (*phrenapataô*), Titus 1:10 (*phrenapatês*), 1 John 1:8 (*planaô*). The verb in Jas. 1:22 is *paralogizomai*.
12. Westminster Shorter Catechism 91.
13. Derek Kidner, *Psalms 73–150* (Downers Grove, IL: IVP, 1975), 417.
14. For a practical and realistic contemporary treatise on prayer, see—wait for it— Jerram Barrs, *The Heart of Prayer: What Jesus Teaches Us* (Phillipsburg, NJ: P&R, 2008).

ENGAGING CULTURE

WELCOME TO OPRAH'S WORLD

A CURSORY GLANCE AT THE FORMER UNDISPUTED DAYTIME TALK SHOW QUEEN

Luke Bobo

PhD, University of Missouri-St.Louis
Director of Partner Engagement, Made to Flourish
Kansas City, MO
Visiting Instructor in Contemporary Culture
Covenant Theological Seminary
St. Louis, MO

Some Americans are such seismic history makers and have made such a deep and indelible mark on us that we need only to mention a word, phrase, or letter to refer to them in conversation. For example, mention the name "Magic" and fans of the Los Angeles Lakers basketball team will instantly know you are referring to the former prolific and effervescent point guard Ervin Johnson. Mention "The Donald" and fans will know that you are referring to billionaire President Donald Trump. Utter "J-Lo" and many will know you are referring to the Latin American actress, former *American Idol* judge, and recording artist, Jennifer Lopez. And if you mention the letter "O," fans and admirers will know that you are referring neither to The Big "O" (Oscar Robertson) nor to

President Barack Obama, but rather to the former daytime TV talk show queen Oprah Winfrey.

To say that Oprah's influence is ubiquitous would be a gross understatement! Her nationally syndicated *Oprah Winfrey Show* aired for 25 seasons. And before the undisputed daytime talk show queen's final show in 2011, she wielded unequivocal influence on American culture. Consider these few examples:

Youth lexicon

In 1993 *Jet* magazine reported that the word "Oprah" had become part of the youth lexicon, meaning "to engage in persistent, intimate questioning with the intention of obtaining a confession; usually used by men of women, as in 'I wasn't going to tell her, but after a few drinks, she *Oprah-ed* it out of me.'"

"Oprah's Crash" of 1996

In 1996 Howard Lyman, head of the Humane Society's "Eating with Conscience" campaign, described cattle feeding procedures in the United States that, conceivably, could lead to the spread of mad cow disease (or the dreaded bovine spongiform encephalopathy). After hearing this, Oprah blurted out on live TV, "[Knowing this] has just stopped me cold from eating another hamburger."[1] After the show, cattle prices plummeted and kept falling for two weeks in what beef traders dubbed the "Oprah crash" of 1996

Oprah's Book Club

When a book was selected for the coveted Oprah's Book Club, that book typically sold an additional 500,000 to 700,000 copies! Because of this phenomenon, the publisher of *The Road* by Cormac McCarthy printed 950,000 copies.

In *Science of Mind,* Zuniga writes, in an article entitled "The Higher Power of Oprah Winfrey," that Oprah "has become a spiritual guru, counselor, and best girlfriend to an audience of more than 49 million viewers each week in the US and to an international audience in 121 countries. More than 2.6 million people read O magazine each month."[2]

Probing Question

The question is: why does Oprah wield so much influence in our global culture? Why does she have such an enormous throng of followers? I certainly have some opinions based on my personal research and observations. However, since Oprah is such a public figure and cultural icon, I surveyed several family members, friends, seminarians, and colleagues for their opinions too. Specifically, the people and groups I surveyed included:

- Approximately 200 seminarians at Covenant Theological Seminary (St. Louis, MO).
- The executive board of the Center for Bioethics and Culture Missouri (CBC-MO), which was composed of health care professionals, professors, clergy, and lawyers.
- "The Village," which is how I refer to a group of very close personal friends. Including my wife and myself, there are four couples in all, and of the other seven adults, I went to high school with three of them. Five of us attended college together and all the men are members of the same fraternity. Members of "The Village" have taken vacations together and shared many joys and sorrows.
- Cobra parents. Cobra was the name of my son's basketball team in the Rockwood School District in St. Louis, MO. I asked the parents of my son's teammates to respond to my survey.
- A host of family members and friends
- University of Kansas Black Alumni chapter. All graduates of KU, these men and women are lawyers, social workers, administrators, and engineers.
- Several leaders of First Baptist Church of Chesterfield (Chesterfield, MO).
- A hair stylist at Great Clips (St. Louis, MO).

I asked two basic questions of my survey participants:

1. Do you watch *The Oprah Winfrey Show*? If yes, briefly explain why. If no, do you know someone who does? Explain why that person watches if you can.
2. Why do you think Oprah's voice is so influential?

I will interact with a few of these survey results throughout this chapter and will attempt to answer my original question about why Oprah wields such enormous influence in our global culture using three Ms: *medium, messenger,* and *message*.

Medium—TV

Unquestionably, the medium of television has tremendous influence. I believe there are at least two reasons for TV's influence: first, the credibility of the messenger (more about this later) and second, "media as epistemology." This latter phrase is taken from Neil Postman's book *Amusing Ourselves to Death*. Postman asserts that TV has become our primary means or way of knowing what is true about the world and ourselves. Postman writes, "Television has achieved the status of 'meta-medium'—an instrument that directs not only our knowledge of the world but our knowledge of *ways of knowing* as well."[3]

In general, our culture is obsessed with TV celebrities. To put it bluntly, we are enamored with celebrities. For example, I spotted former St. Louis Cardinals' center fielder Jim Edmonds at a local eatery and I was very tempted to hound him for an autograph. Some would say that many celebrities have a cult-like following, much like the former leader of the Branch Davidians, David Koresh, had a following. And as one Covenant Seminary professor put it, "We like famous people to tell us what to believe." And because we are easily enamored with celebrities, we are tempted to follow the celebrity "if they live a compelling enough narrative."[4] Gabler adds, "Like all art, the best of them (celebrities) resonate with us because they provide us with life lessons or because they capture the cultural moment or because they give us a glimpse of transcendence or because they stimulate the imagination."[5]

So, when we couple our obsession with celebrities as credible messengers of knowledge with the inherent influence of the television medium, we are figuratively swept away by the medium of TV's current. As Postman writes:

> The credibility of the teller [or messenger] is the ultimate test of the truth of a proposition. "Credibility" does not refer to the past record of the teller or messenger but... rather credibility refers to the impression of sincerity, authenticity, vulnerability or attractiveness... conveyed by

the actor/reporter [or in our case, Oprah, the undisputed daytime talk show queen].[6]

If you watch and listen to Oprah long enough, you'll quickly agree that she is indeed transparent, sincere, and authentic.

Oprah is influential because she communicates through a medium that holds so much dominance in our culture and, most importantly, because of her credibility as a celebrity. That brings us to the messenger. There are several qualities about Oprah that make her attractive as a messenger and these attributes also contribute to her influence.

Messenger

As a messenger, I believe Oprah is influential because she is: a) authentic or transparent, b) a good steward of her affluence, c) a good steward of her influence, d) sincere and compassionate, and e) a real inspirational hero.

Authentic/Transparent

Of all the talk show hosts—past or present—it is not a stretch to say that we know more about Oprah's personal life because, as Janet Lowe writes in her book *Oprah Winfrey Speaks*, "Oprah is the Queen of Confession."[7] In other words, Oprah is the queen of authenticity.

We know quite a bit about Oprah's early years before *The Oprah Winfrey Show*. For example, most of us know about Oprah being born to Vernon and Vernita out of wedlock. Most of us know that when Oprah was fourteen years old she ran away, stole money from her mother, and had sex with older boys to win their approval and affection. Most of us know that Oprah lived with her mother in Milwaukee and excelled in school even as she was unruly at home. She was so wild that her mother attempted to put young Oprah in a juvenile hall but was turned away because there were no available beds. Most of us know that Oprah got pregnant when she was fourteen years old and gave birth to a premature baby boy who soon died. Most of us know that Oprah used crack cocaine in hopes that the shared experience would bring her closer to a man she was dating. Some of us might know that Oprah once wrote a suicide note because she was so distraught over a relational breakup.

How do we know so much about Oprah? Because she has shared her story openly with us either in print or on the air. For instance, on January 13, 1995, Oprah told her TV audience about her crack cocaine use. Her childhood story, her relational woes with Stedman, and her woes with overeating are also well-known to us. This transparency enabled Oprah to connect with her audience, especially women. With her vulnerability, Oprah "carefully establishes herself as both the paradigm and [also] the exception of racial lessons."[8] As the paradigm, Oprah is an example of all Americans who can transcend their circumstances no matter how egregious. Oprah's vulnerability made her one with her audience. Oprah once said, "I am every one of [my audience], and they are me."[9]

Her vulnerability has created as one sociologist has called it, "parasocial relationships, in which a crowd of strangers have the illusion of a face-to-face, intimate relationship with the star of the show."[10] Oprah has made herself known to us to such a degree that we get a sense that we know her. She projects the aura of "being a common person" as one male respondent to my survey put it. Another sixty-year-old Caucasian male respondent said, "Oprah has the aura of 'common folk.'"

Maryaan Koehl, a fan who waited in line for Oprah's show, said Oprah "is like the one friend you trust, the one you know has good taste. You stick with a girlfriend like that."[11] Oprah comes across as truly *one of us*. In other words, we often see her broken humanity in living color. It's her authenticity (her willingness to show us her brokenness and her struggles) that makes her so human and attractive. Oprah's authenticity is not only attractive but very powerful. And this authenticity or realness pays great dividends.

Consider these words from marketing expert John Grace, director of New-York-based *Interbrand*, who says Oprah is "a very important brand in our culture. Her presence as a brand is embodied by trust, human-to-human connections and realness. Her audience comes to believe Oprah is real and she is telling the truth."[12] In fact, a sixty-year-old African American male respondent to my survey corroborated this sentiment when he said Oprah's "warmth of personality and her ability to be real" make her so accessible and influential.

Generous/Steward of Affluence

Another reason why Oprah is influential is because of her generosity. She was once quoted as saying, "With all this fame and money, I have to do something more than buy shoes."[13] And she certainly has!

I heard pastor Rick Warren, author of the bestseller *The Purpose Driven Life,* speak while he was in St. Louis several years ago. He used the phrase "being a steward of affluence," by which he means using one's affluence unselfishly for the good of others. Oprah has certainly been a good steward of her wealth for the well-being of others. Consider these few examples:

- In 1986 Oprah became involved in the Big Sisters program at the Cabrini Green Housing project in Chicago. She invited the young girls to her home for pizza and slumber parties. And Oprah took these young girls on shopping sprees and a ski trip.
- In January 1998 the weather was frigid in Chicago and the heat was out in the Robert Taylor Homes—an impoverished housing development. Destitute mothers were huddled close to the open doors of their ovens, trying to warm themselves. While filming a segment of her show at a local Walmart, Oprah got wind of this horrible plight. She soon made a deal with Walmart and purchased 500 space heaters for the residents at the Robert Taylor Homes housing development.[14]
- On her December 26, 2006 show, Oprah told the story of a young couple who bought a fixer-upper home. The wife became pregnant. The husband developed gangrene in his right leg, which was eventually amputated below the knee. He was fitted with a prosthetic and was unable to finish the renovations. Oprah discovered this couple's misfortune and funded the completion of the renovations in time for the arrival of the couple's baby.
- After six years and $40 million dollars, the construction of the Leadership Academy, an all-girls school in South Africa, was opened in 2007. Winfrey, who has donated millions of dollars to education in America through the Oprah Winfrey Scholars program, said she decided to build the academy in South Africa rather than the United States out of love and respect for Mandela and because of her own African roots.[15]

There are countless others who have benefited from her wealth and generosity. Several respondents to my survey mentioned Oprah's generosity as a major reason she is so influential. One will suffice here:

a thirty-year-old African American male respondent quipped that Oprah "speaks for the common person, has humble roots, and is *generous with her wealth.*"

Steward of Influence

Oprah's voice is like the commercial jingle years ago that said, "When EF Hutton speaks, people listen." Many people listen to Oprah. She has ascended to a position of power in our culture. To illustrate her influence and power, let me borrow the phrase "steward of influence," also coined by Rick Warren. Another reason why Oprah carries so much influence is because she has used it to help others. It's truly Oprah's aim in life to serve or minister to others. This is the reason why Kathryn Lofton refers to Oprah as "Preacher Queen"[16] and titled one of her book chapters accordingly. This preacher label is not new. When six white kids were about to beat her up when she was in the first grade, Oprah told them about Jesus of Nazareth and what happened to people who tried to stone him. After this incident, the kids called her "Preacher."[17] So it is no coincidence that Oprah considered her show a ministry. She even told the Academy of Achievement, "I always wanted to be a minister, preach, and be a missionary. And then for a while a teacher. I feel my show is ministry; we just don't take up a collection."[18] She used her show as a platform to do good and to address controversial societal issues. A forty-year-old African American female respondent said, "Oprah is not afraid to address issues that others are unwilling to discuss."

Consider these few examples of societal issues broached on her show.

- On her August 15, 2006 show, Oprah showed the pictures of eight child predators on the loose. She offered $100,000 reward to anyone who provided information leading to the capture and arrest of any one of these child predators.
- In the first year her show was nationally syndicated, Oprah picked up her crew and moved production to Forsyth County, Georgia to do a show on race. She asked a group of local citizens why, for more than 75 years, they had not allowed a black person to live in the county. One bearded man said, "if blacks moved back to Forsyth County, it would be a rat-infested slum ... because blacks don't care." I am

happy to report that "some [other] white residents of Forsyth County in the audience booed at the man's comments."[19] It is reported that after the show, Oprah left because she did not feel comfortable.
- The Oprah Bill. Because of her heart and passion for kids, in 1991 Oprah initiated the National Child Protection Act and testified before the US Senate to encourage members to pass a law establishing a national database of convicted child abusers. In 1993 she watched as President Clinton signed the national "Oprah bill" into law.
- On other shows, Oprah has not shied away from dicey, difficult issues. For instance, she addressed issues such as what to do in an emergency, finding lost relatives, and taking a stand against guns. She has also aired shows on deadbeat dads, the Ku Klux Klan, Native American anger, and mothers who fought to protect their children from drugs and violence.
- On a lighter note, Oprah used her show to showcase everyday American heroes. I remember one show where she celebrated the heroic act of a sixteen-year-old girl who discovered her mother being attacked by a bear in their home; the daughter's quick thinking and action saved her mother's life. Oprah has used her show to showcase some extraordinary people. These shows gave you a warm fuzzy feeling. I must admit I was a sucker for these human-interest accounts.

Sincere and Compassionate

Oprah is both sincere and compassionate. One newspaper reporter said, "Oprah *out-sinceres* [her early mentor] Phil (Donohue)."[20] Consider these responses from my survey participants who also vouch for Oprah's sincerity and compassion:

- A thirty-year-old Caucasian female respondent said, "Oprah is compassionate, caring about [the] topic and people...."
- A forty-year-old Caucasian female respondent to the survey said Oprah is so influential and has a high profile because "she is honest and sincere."
- A thirty-year-old African American female said, "Oprah seems to be truly empathetic with her guests and to those in need."

- A thirty-year-old Korean American male respondent said Oprah "tugs on the heart, is empathetic, and is empowering."

Oprah was certainly sincere and compassionate to her television show guests, but her sincerity and compassion are also evident in our society (and the world). As one example of her public display of sincerity and compassion, consider this story:

After meeting Kalvin, a thirteen-year-old living in the Westside Chicago Projects—who she considered taking into her own home until boyfriend Stedman pointed out that Oprah would have to take in Kalvin's whole family—Oprah started a program called Families for a Better Life. Kalvin's family became the pilot project in a $6 million program that helps welfare families improve their situations. Oprah tutored Kalvin, paid for his school supplies while Kalvin's mother earned her GED, and eventually was able to move her family out of the projects to a safe home. Kalvin's mother says her problems are still a long way from over. She works long hours and her children miss their old friends, but at least she now has hope for their future.[21]

Indeed, we see Oprah's sincerity and compassion have "hands and feet" both inside her studio and in the public arena.

A Real Inspirational Hero

Oprah's story is truly a rags-to-riches story. Considering her background—born out of wedlock, substance abuse, and being raised in abject poverty conditions—the underdog has won! In Mississippi, where Oprah lived with her grandmother, they had their own water well but no indoor plumbing. It was Oprah's daily task to bring in water. When she moved north to live with her mother who cleaned houses for a living, they were not just poor, according to Lowe, "they were achingly poor."[22]

When we consider Oprah's bouts with low self-esteem, family dysfunction, being molested, being a sexually active teenager, and being a black woman in the United States (or as one respondent put it, "being a 'double minority'"), the odds were stacked heavily against her. Yet Oprah has truly beaten the odds; her story is truly inspiring to many, including me. As an African American, I am extremely proud of Oprah's success! She has transcended class, gender, and poverty to become the first African American female billionaire in history!

For one lady, Oprah had so inspired her that she said, "Oprah is me.

We're both black, we're both the same age, we treat people the same way. That could be me."[23] A forty-year-old Caucasian female respondent said Oprah is so influential because "her inspirational success story [makes her] influential among women."

Because Oprah has risen so far from her humble and meager beginnings, people are eager to listen to her. A fifty-year-old African American female respondent agreed, saying Oprah's "rise to fame from poverty, rape, etc. makes her voice so influential." People are eager to learn how she overcame so many obstacles. Her rise from abject poverty to her position of power and prestige has earned her the right to be the nation's spiritual advisor and therapist. Folks are eager to sit at her feet and learn from Oprah's tutelage.

Finally, another reason why Oprah is so powerful is because of her message.

Message

Before discussing Oprah's message, let me say something about our current spiritual milieu. We live in a time in which:

- There is "an easy [and uncritical] acceptance of all things mysterious."[24]
- The individual self is the center of the universe.
- We have all seen and/or experienced the breakdown of the family.
- We are encouraged to pursue what satisfies our spiritual longings. In other words, when it comes to spiritual matters, "it is a virtual free-for-all."
- We are encouraged to be both parishioner and our own pastor/priest.
- Tolerance of other views is not only celebrated, but is considered the highest truth.

Given our current spiritual landscape, Oprah's message finds itching and attentive ears willing to listen. "Writer Fran Lebowitz says that not only is O the greatest media influence on the adult population but she has almost become a religion."[25] I would argue that Oprah is the incarnation or embodiment of her religion, and she preached her message on her show, on her website, and in her magazine.

Tenets of Oprah's Message

The tenets of Oprah's message resonate with many given the spiritual milieu described above. These tenets include:

- *Follow your own truth.* Every person is his or her own authority when it comes to what is true. However, if all fails, follow Oprah's truth as one follower endeavored to do every single day.[26]
- *Seek self-improvement (or self-actualization).* In Oprah's world, "you make your world, you make your beauty, you make your accessories, and *you make your composite self* (italics mine)."[27]
- *Believe in yourself.* We hear these words everywhere in America, especially at middle- and high-school graduation ceremonies. These words mean to believe in your own abilities, willpower, and cognitive abilities to prosper. It is unfettered optimism in the inner capacity of the human spirit.
- *Draw upon the strength inside.* Oprah would call this the "inner voice" or "God force" in all of us.
- *Seek your own personal happiness.*
- *Tolerate other religious views.* In Oprah's world, no one can say they have and know true truth absolutely; to do so would be insensitive, intolerant, and absurd. Thus, believing and purporting a passage like John 14:6 (Jesus saying, *"I am the way, and the truth, and the life. No one comes to the Father except through me."*) is reprehensible in Oprah's world.

Oprah's message begins and ends with the self. Her message of seeking your personal happiness goes over well in our self-consumed and self-absorbed culture. It's all about the individual—take time for yourself, follow your passions and wants. Who doesn't want to hear that, especially from an authoritative messenger like Oprah?

Oprah was eager to preach this message of seeking one's happiness. For instance, during a 2001 *Live Your Best Life Now* tour, "a single, thirty-six-year-old explains that, pressured by her family, she recently moved back from Hong Kong but longs to return to Asia. Oprah says, 'Bye!', and adds that if she should have a change of heart, 'just click your heels and come back home.'"[28] In Oprah's world, every dilemma has a ready and simple solution. For instance, Cheryl Richardson, a lifestyle makeover expert (and colleague of Oprah's who often appeared on her show), gave this advice to a woman who was feeling guilty for not wanting to spend so much time with her elderly parents. "Richardson tells her to take time for herself, that 'happiness neutralizes guilt.'"[29]

Oprah's message of tolerance is another reason why she has a large following. In her world, everyone is right (except rappers who degrade women); there is no one universal truth. Oprah would say: follow your own truth, listen to your inner voice, or follow your gut, which in her opinion is never wrong. This message is readily and uncritically accepted in a culture that emphasizes the autonomy of the individual. Oprah's message finds traction in our religiously pluralistic society in which all views are accepted, equally credible and equally true. Incidentally, Oprah's acceptance of all views or tolerance is the reason one twenty-year-old white female respondent believes Oprah is influential, remarking that "Oprah is accepting of all views."

Oprah would support a buffet-style view of spirituality. In other words, she would agree with the idea of designing your own spirituality. You can pick and choose from a vast menu of options to connect with the divine or transcendent, whether that be self, the universe, or nature. Smolowe and Steptoe described Oprah's blend of spirituality as an "inspirational mix of New Age, New Testament, and down-home wisdom."[30] No wonder we find on the cover of *Science of Mind*, "Oprah: a *Matinee* Ministry (italics mine)." Oprah offers something for everyone and encourages each person to design his or her own truth and then tenaciously pursue and live by it.

We might say it this way, Oprah's message is very postmodern, nonsectarian, and focuses on the individual self as his or her own authority on all things that matter. Indeed, this message is still very popular in our culture.

It's the medium (of TV), the messenger, and the message that I believe affords Oprah a position of enormous influence in our global culture.

---

1. Lowe, *Oprah Winfrey Speaks*, 135–136.
2. Marielena Zuniga, "The Higher Power of Oprah Winfrey," *Science of Mind*,.
3. Neil Postman, *Amusing Ourselves to Death* (New York: Penguin, 1985), 78–79.
4. Neal Gabler, "Celebrity: The Greatest Show on Earth," *Newsweek*, December 21, 2009, 64.
5. Gabler, "Celebrity," 66.
6. Postman, *Amusing Ourselves to Death*, 101–102.
7. Lowe, *Oprah Winfrey Speaks*, 40.

8. Kathryn Lofton, *Oprah: The Gospel of an Icon* (Berkeley, CA: University of California Press, 2011), 126.
9. Lofton, *Oprah*, 126.
10. Lowe, *Oprah Winfrey Speaks*, 38.
11. Lowe, *Oprah Winfrey Speaks*, 37.
12. Lowe, *Oprah Winfrey Speaks*, 34.
13. Lowe, *Oprah Winfrey Speaks*, 86.
14. Kate Maver, "Oprah Winfrey and Her Self-Help Saviors: Making the New Age Normal", *Christian Research Journal* 23, no. 4 (December 2001): 12.
15. See www.eurweb.com/story/eur30607.cfm.
16. Lofton, *Oprah*, 118.
17. Lofton, *Oprah*, 129.
18. Zuniga, "Higher Power of Oprah", 84.
19. Lowe, *Oprah Winfrey Speaks*, 47–48.
20. Lowe, *Oprah Winfrey Speaks*, 36.
21. Lowe, *Oprah Winfrey Speaks*, 146–147.
22. Lowe, *Oprah Winfrey Speaks*, xv.
23. Lowe, *Oprah Winfrey Speaks*, 39.
24. Edith M. Humphrey, "It's Not About Us," *Christianity Today*, April 2, 2001, 67.
25. Lowe, *Oprah Winfrey Speaks*, 1.
26. Jessica Grose, "Life in the Time of Oprah," *The New York Times* (2008).
27. Lofton, *Oprah*, 125.
28. Jill Smolowe and Sonja Steptoe, "O On the Go," *People Magazine*, (2001): 54.
29. Smolow and Steptoe, "O on the Go," 54.
30. Smolow and Steptoe, "O on the Go," 52.

BEING HUMAN AT THE BOX OFFICE

RESPONDING TO THE STORIES OF A BROKEN WORLD IN FILM

Denis D. Haack

MATS, Covenant Theological Seminary
Founder/Director, Ransom Fellowship
Savage, MN

I've never gone to the theater with Jerram Barrs or set aside an evening to watch a movie with him. I do not remember ever hearing a lecture by him that was explicitly about engaging film as Christians. I know he has often assigned *Babette's Feast* to his students, a Danish film that speaks powerfully to the themes of hospitality, creativity, and the possibility of redemptive relationships in human community. I have heard Jerram mention films in lectures, and we've talked together about various movies, very brief conversations I wish could have been more frequent and more leisurely.

Nevertheless every time I walk into a theater, his influence is not far away. A primary theme in his teaching, preaching, and writing has been to expound what the Scriptures reveal about living faithfully as a follower of Christ in a fallen world. In doing so he has informed the significance I place on the cinema as a form of cultural dialogue, showed me why I can love movies without guilt, shaped the way I view and respond to them, and motivated me to find creative and winsome ways for God's people to be biblically discerning with film rather than reactionary and defensive. I am always aware when I teach Film & Theology at Covenant Seminary that everything I say to my students is in some way a development of what I have learned from him. It is a debt I am eager to acknowledge and for which I am profoundly grateful. So grateful, in fact, that Margie and I named our son after him. This chapter is a brief summary of what I learned from Jerram and what I've gone on to teach my students and the people in churches where I have been invited to lecture and teach.

Yet what Jerram teaches was so radical to me when I first heard it that I struggled hard and long to make sense of it. It was so antithetical to what I had been taught to believe about living as a Christian that I couldn't see how he could possibly be right.

On Being Spiritual Not Worldly

I grew up as the son of missionaries. Dad and Mom were successful church planters in the Philippine Islands in a province named Pampanga about forty-five miles north of Manila on the main island of Luzon. We were part of the Plymouth Brethren, a fundamentalist movement that began in the mid-nineteenth century when a clergyman named John Nelson Darby (1800–1882) left the Church of Ireland to join a group of Christians who met together regularly for the breaking of bread (communion) outside any denominational structure or church authority. As his ministry of Bible teaching expanded in succeeding years, Darby expounded a novel system of theology that became known as Dispensationalism. He was particularly interested in what the Bible said about prophecy and the end times, and he popularized the idea of a divided return of Christ. In this view, Christ would return to rapture the church into heaven and then later return a second time to judge the world and establish his millennial kingdom. Darby's views on the end times became popular among American Christians especially with the 1909 publication of a reference Bible by C. I. Scofield (1843–1921) in which Scofield's study notes interpreted the text along dispensational lines.

Now here is where it gets interesting and applies to my topic, the cinema. At the heart of classic dispensationalism is a sharp divide between the New Testament and the Old, between two peoples of God (the church and Israel), between the heavenly and the worldly.[1] The

Brethren are also pietistic, meaning they see experiencing a warmly personal, quietly heartfelt relationship with God and an inner assurance of salvation as central to Christian faith and life. These two doctrinal emphases—along with other influences such as the legacy of American revivalism, the embrace of a spiritualized theology of teachers like Watchman Nee, a separatist ecclesiology, and more—caused the Brethren to see life as divided into two sharply distinguished spheres, the sacred and the secular.

Although they emphasized their distinctiveness from other fundamentalists, the Brethren movement in which I grew up shared this sacred/secular dichotomy with most other American fundamentalists. The idea of the dichotomy is very simple and very appealing. Think of it this way—everyday experience for the Christian falls into two categories, the spiritual and the physical. We spend time in prayer, talking to a God we are convinced is real yet is invisible, a distinctly spiritual act involving an unseen spiritual sphere of reality. Then we say, "Amen," and engage in a decidedly physical act such as making breakfast, or painting a wall, or weeding a garden. We involve a physical sphere of reality we can see, touch, smell, hear, and taste. So as ordinary experience confirms, life before God is ultimately divided into two spheres, a spiritual sphere that is heavenly, perfect, and eternal, and a physical sphere that is earthly, fallen, and temporary. The spiritual is of more lasting significance, more deeply pleasing to God, and more essential than the merely physical. After all the realm of the spiritual partakes of the things of God while the physical is secular, partaking of the things of the world. So the sacred/secular dichotomy not only described reality for us, it provided guidance in how to live as a Christian. We desired to be spiritual and to avoid worldliness. Thus a few things in life—like worship, prayer, and evangelism—are spiritual and pleasing to God.

Everything else, though perhaps not sinful per se, is at best secondary, and becoming too engrossed with it was being worldly. Because it was so basic to Brethren belief and practice, I remember this notion of a sacred/secular, spiritual/worldly division was explicitly applied to every aspect of our lives as Christians. It was central to my understanding of the faith as I was growing up. I could not imagine Christian faith apart from it.

No place was this division between spiritual and worldly more sharply defined than when it came to the world of cinema. Movies were part of a world that was destined to be burned in the fire of God's judgment after his people had been raptured out of it. The same was true of all art, all of human culture, everything of the physical or secular sphere. Only what was spiritual would endure. Everything that is of the earth will be annihilated.

To use Darby's own version of the Bible, *"The day of the Lord will come as a thief, in which the heavens will pass away with a rushing noise, and the elements, burning with heat, shall be dissolved, and the earth and the works in it shall be burnt up"* (2 Pet. 3:10). The world and all that is in it is temporary, of no eternal value, so caring for it was likened in sermons to arranging deck chairs on the Titanic.

A spiritually minded person must *"not love the world or the things in the world. If anyone loves the world, love for the Father is not in him"* (1 John 2:15). Worldly Christians ruined their testimony before non-Christians by going to the theater, becoming associated with a decadent Hollywood. Even if the movies we watched weren't bad it was impossible to reconcile spiritual concerns with worldly entertainment.

> *If then you have been raised with Christ, seek the things that are above, where Christ is, seated at the right hand of God. Set your minds on things that are above, not on things that are on earth. For you have died, and your life is hidden with Christ in God.* Col. 3:1–3

I want to be clear that I am grateful for any number of things the Brethren bequeathed to me, especially the conviction that the Scriptures are trustworthy. My years in Sunday school taught me the Bible. And I am grateful for the fine biblical scholarship of F. F. Bruce (1910–1990) who was part of the movement and whose books remain helpful additions to my library. I left the Brethren years ago but gladly acknowledge that I share an Evangelical faith with them.

Still, by the time I got to college in the sixties, my confidence in this dichotomized faith was tipping toward unbelief. For one thing, I found the pressure to focus on spiritual activities, especially witnessing, more than I could tolerate. It was disheartening to fail so badly so much of the time. Besides succeeding in being spiritual all the time was frankly unappealing, since it meant having to insert something spiritual—usually witnessing—into every conceivable activity. For another, trying to thread my way between ordinary life and what was deemed worldliness seemed like an impossible quest. The sacred/secular dichotomy seemed clear in sermons but hopelessly blurred in practice. Another problem was that I seemed to be curious about all the wrong things and constantly attracted to worldly concerns. When I raised questions about the arts or philosophy, a discomfort seemed to descend on the room like a chilly fog. Regardless of the subject I raised, the conversation always quickly circled around to whether my devotional life was regular or whether I had an assurance of salvation. Was I perhaps ashamed of Christ and his Gospel? More and more it became clear that the Christianity I had been taught had nothing to say to art and culture, except to insist that caring about them was a sign of worldliness.

Finally I decided I was left with two possibilities. One was that Christianity was not true, and so must be rejected. It did not live up to its claims to be the answer to all of life's questions, to address all of life's issues. The other possibility was to acquiesce to living a dichotomized life, embracing a privatized faith for the sake of getting to heaven but for the sake of sanity living day by day immersed in what I knew to be worldliness, contrary to God's will and dishonoring to Christ. My conscience never allowed me to accept the second possibility—it seemed hypocritical and dishonest. Yet try as I might I could not stop believing in Christ.

The Sacred/Secular Dichotomy Is Worldly

The year was 1968. Someone gave me a copy of a just-published book, *The God Who is There* by Francis Schaeffer. I had never heard of him.

It was highly confusing. He talked about culture, the arts—even specific films—with thoughtfulness and respect, yet he did not appear in the least worldly. Quite the opposite. I had never heard such a bracing, substantial, and compelling presentation of Christian faith. I could not comprehend how he could reconcile his interest in film with what the Bible taught.

Over the next few years, I endured an inner wrestling match that often left my soul feeling raw and unsettled. I have occasionally heard Christians talk about someone changing their convictions or beliefs about something as if such transformations happen relatively easily—hear the truth, change your mind, problem solved. The reality is just the opposite. Giving up something you have heard taught for years and believed for years for something you've been sternly warned against time and time again can be a wrenching experience. Even if you want to believe or want to assume the new perspective is correct, there is a fear that if you make the change then everything else making up your life and worldview might collapse as well.

I read *The God Who is There* again. I remained confused.

Slowly I came to see that the notion that life is divided into two distinct spheres, spiritual (meaning significant) and physical (less significant to God) has been read *into* the Bible rather than taught *by* it.

As Jerram Barrs and Ranald Macaulay showed in *Being Human: The Nature of Spiritual Experience* (1978) this sacred/secular dichotomy is actually an ancient heresy smuggled into Christian thought from a pagan source (from Greek neoplatonic philosophy). There is *no* sacred/secular dichotomy taught in the Bible, and the division should not be reflected in how we think and live. It was a simple, yet utterly transformative idea.

Now read the Bible *without* assuming beforehand that life is divided into sacred and secular spheres. Read from the beginning. As we do, we discover a perspective on life, culture, and creativity—including the arts, like film—that is as breathtaking and as practical as it is liberating.

Art—Including Film—Is a Good Gift of God

The opening pages of the Bible reveal that human creativity and culture are rooted in creation. This means they are good gifts of God, an expression of his image in humankind, and pleasing to him. In the creation narrative we find the essential kernels of human creativity that have blossomed into science (Gen. 2:19–20), practical skills and crafts of all types (Gen. 2:15), and the arts (Gen. 2:23). Culture, creativity and art are not to be dismissed, disdained, or relegated to insignificance by God's people because they are essential to the Creator's plan for us, his creatures. After God had called all things into existence he determined what he had made was "very good" (Gen. 1:31). Christians may mean well when they look down on physical things as "less spiritual," but in doing so they are substituting their own evaluation for God's. Seen in this light, the sacred/secular dichotomy brings us perilously close to the sin of blasphemy.

At creation God told our first parents he intended them to be involved in the world he had made, *"to work it and keep it"* (Gen. 2:15). To "keep it" means remembering it remains his, so that we must steward the creation, caring for it tenderly so that it is properly used, and never abused. The term used for "work it" is often translated "to cultivate," which is related in turn to the idea of culture.

Art and culture—and by extension the cinema, an art form and cultural artifact birthed in our technological age—are not a surprise or interruption to God. They are essential to what he ordained for us and created us for. He made human beings to be creative and so the results and products of that creativity seen in culture are part of his gracious plan for us. For many Christians this simple statement is radical or would be if they really thought about it. Yes, it is a fallen world and art, like Aaron's sculpted golden calf, can be perverted for evil ends (Exod. 32). But that does not make art and culture wrong or less significant or worldly. Sculpture can also be used to God's glory (Exod. 25:17–22, 31–40, Ez. 4:1–3).

The cinema, a part of human culture, is not simply a fluke of history, or worse a result of the fall, and therefore a product of human sinfulness. It is a good gift of God and an expression of his image in us.

The Centrality of Story

In our reading of the Bible we discover that, though the story begins with creation, the narrative continues to unfold. The Scriptures reveal an unfolding story in four parts: Creation, Fall, Redemption, and Restoration. Each part is essential to the entire plot and each part propels the story onward to its appointed end. As human beings we live in and take part in this drama, for blessing or for curse. It can be no other way, for this is the story of history, the narrative of reality, not a matter of choice.

No one can say one day, "I think from now on I'll live outside the story." There is no outside for those who are called into existence by the word of God. God, as author and sustainer of the story who knows the end from the beginning and dwells in the eternal now, is outside. We can know that, but we will never share it because though we partake in his image we will never share his infinity. So we will always be inside the story and the story, shaped and defined by God's word, will always define us and the reality in which we move and have our being. The story is the drama in which we play a role,[2] the theory of everything that forms our worldview.[3]

Each of the four parts of the story provides answers to questions absolutely critical to the story.

Creation tells us who and where the characters in the story are, where they came from, what they are like, and what things were like originally.

Fall tells us what went wrong, why tension and brokenness have occurred, how bad the problem is, and how this brokenness has disrupted the way things were originally.

Redemption reveals the solution to the problem, the cost of that solution, rules out insufficient solutions, and defines what is needed to heal the brokenness and restore the relationships that have been so badly fragmented.

Finally, *Restoration* tells us where the story is ultimately headed, what the end will be and whether the characters in the story have reason to hope for something better. The biblical story is centered in Christ as Creator, Judge, Savior, and King. It presents itself as *The Story* that defines all of life and history. This is why Christianity has something significant to say to every part of culture and reality. It is not merely a narrow religious message speaking only to "spiritual" issues and a life to come. Creation, Fall, Redemption, and Restoration provide, John Stott says, a "true perspective from which to view the unfolding process between two eternities, the vision of God working out his purposes. It gives us a framework in which to fit everything, a way of integrating our understanding, the possibility of thinking straight, even about the most complex issues."[4]

The very existence of this biblical narrative forming the outline of Scripture, the flow of history and the structure of reality should help us realize why story is so important to our lives and thinking. When we meet someone new, for example, we ask them to tell us the story of their background. When a friend returns from a hiking vacation in the Alps, we want to hear the story of their adventures. As we tell our stories we come to know each other and to see what values, ideas, fears, and dreams animate us.

Each generation, culture, and community have stories—historical and mythical—that embody the things we hold dear. "Storytelling of all kinds," Roy Anker says, "cinematic and otherwise, stimulates people with the vital questions of what the world is like, what is likely to happen next, and why what happens does happen. Everyone wants to know the answers to those questions."[5]

If we want to know a culture then we need to listen carefully to its stories. And since all human narratives take place within the more grounded biblical story of creation, fall, redemption, and restoration, good human stories tend to follow the same pattern. A classic western, for example, lets us see life in the isolated town (Creation), then the oppression and pain when the thugs take over (Fall), the arrival of the mysterious figure on a white horse and his suffering in his effort to stop the thugs (Redemption), and finally, at least a hint of the relief in the town as he rides away into the sunset (Restoration).

Not every story, or film, has all four chapters, of course, nor do they all tell the story in the same order, but the basic elements remain. Daniel Doriani correctly identifies the relationship between human stories and the biblical narrative:

> Biblical dramas do not follow the patterns of literary dramas because someone 'massaged' the stories to make them fit. Rather, God has structured human nature and creation so that certain elements are present in all stories worth telling. If biblical dramas have the same structure as fiction, it is because art imitates life, not because the Bible imitates art.[6]

The reason the stories told in the movies make such an impression and foster so much conversation over coffee is that they touch on the deepest questions human beings can possibly ask. "In short," Roy Anker observes:

> Despite its reputation as a mindless, soul-less diversion, cinema regularly wrestles with the central deep mysteries about origins, meaning, purpose, intimacy, destiny, morality, and the possibility of God —those domains of human inquiry to which philosophy, theology, and the arts have traditionally devoted themselves.[7]

Stories are fragile and precious things, even though they are so commonplace it is easy to forget that. In the midst of all the clamor and busyness, we can all remember the stories that transfixed us, sobered or delighted us, and suddenly brought a bit of clarity. It is a rare event, all things considered, but when life is brought a bit more into focus by a good story, and the bigger questions about meaning, significance, and hope are made clearer, we feel suddenly very alive. We can also feel very threatened since the big questions in life are truly that, Big, and tend to shatter our complacency. This is why the Bible is full of stories, why Jesus told them so passionately, and why he repeatedly warned his listeners that it is possible to have ears that listen but fail to really hear.[8]

Every generation has stories, some new and some ancient, told by storytellers and poets gifted at relating the events of the moment to the things that do not pass away. Not only is it unsurprising that children love stories, the very fabric of life in time suggests we cannot flourish apart from a story that weaves together the transitory moments of existence into a coherent whole. The technological media that dominate our world has not removed the need for story—it has produced new forms for story to take. Film is storytelling. And today the movies are perhaps the single most vital form of storytelling that exists in our postmodern world.

It is a tragic misunderstanding to imagine that the cinema is merely a form of entertainment. Yes, movies are made to be entertaining, just as my wife and I wanted the bedtime stories we told and read to our children to be entertaining. Our real goal, however, was to pass on to them visions of virtue and wickedness, purpose and meaning, things that were worth living for and dying for. The movies are a strategic form of cultural dialogue in our world, evoking a lively conversation about the things that matter most. "There is a conversation going on in popular culture that the church is not engaged in and is often unaware of," Craig Detweiler and Barry Taylor insist:

> The marketplace includes more than business and the routine of everyday life. Ideas are exchanged in the marketplace. The dramas of life, lived between the wedding song and the funeral march, are played out in the marketplace. It is where humans face the challenges of living and dying, in ways not adequately addressed by stock, religious propositions. The belly of messy culture is also the place where questions of ultimate existence and reality are posed in naked, stripped-down fashion, devoid of the religious language of etiquette and propriety.[9]

This is a conversation I believe we Christians cannot afford to miss.

I did not have the words in the sixties to name this cultural dialogue, but I found myself in the middle of it. At the time I still understood Christian faith only in terms of a sacred/secular divide where the cinema was worldly and unworthy of a spiritual person's serious attention. To my surprise it was not the witnessing of Christians but film that was sparking regular, lively discussions among students about the meaning of life and death, the possibility of redemption, and the relevance of hope. Theaters that showed Ingmar Bergman's brooding, provocative films like *The Silence* (1963), *Persona* (1966), and *The Passion of Anna* (1969) were crowded with students, who discussed late into the night about how life could be meaningful and whether it was possible to know. I felt out of place, guilty for being at the theater at all, and yet stimulated by the discussion in far deeper ways than I had ever experienced in church. Never did I meet the fabled unbeliever who would reject the faith because my testimony had been fatally compromised by the worldliness of watching movies. Instead my non-Christian friends expressed astonishment that I never had seen Bergman's classic, *The Seventh Seal* (1957). They wondered just how seriously I took the questions I claimed were addressed by the Christian Gospel if I would not take that film into account.

Joining the Conversation

As Donald Drew showed in his groundbreaking book *Images of Man* (1974), movies both reflect our globalized culture and help to shape it. This means that for the Christian, movies can serve as both a window of insight into our post-Christian world and a point of contact to talk about the things that matter most.

Usually when someone sees a film, the first thing friends ask is "Did you like it?" It's not an inappropriate question. Art by its nature engages our imaginations and sensitivities, and so our personal response is as essential to its design as is our response to a delicate flower growing out of a tiny crack in a boulder high in the Rockies. I would argue, however, that though the question of whether we liked it is not inappropriate; it is not the most important question for the faithful Christian. The question with which we must be even more concerned is "Did I get it?" Why are people resonating with this film? Why do they identify with these characters or that plot? What have they seen and heard and why does it strike them as important?

There are far too many movies to see, and many movies are of no interest to me. I have friends skilled in reading the culture whose recommendations I trust. Some films, like *The Tree of Life* (2011) promised to be influential even while still in production. And occasionally after I have decided to skip some movie, I arrive at the coffee shop near my home and discover that the baristas are all discussing it or find the young adults at my church have all seen it and are talking about it, so I make plans to see it. *Lars and the Real Girl* (2007), a quirky yet profoundly human mediation on relationships, is one I saw that way.

To be part of this conversation about the things that matter most, we will have to follow Christ into the world. In a brief video made under the auspices of Covenant Seminary, Jerram Barrs was asked to reflect on what animates his life and teaching. He said:

My passion is to teach our students and people in our churches to be in the world as Jesus was in the world, because that is what Jesus prayed on the night before he died. That we would be sent into the world as he was and what that means for us is that he calls us to give ourselves to be friends to the people around us; unbelievers, no matter what they believe, no matter what they worship, and no matter what they do or how disobedient they are to God's commandments. Jesus sets us a wonderful example by going to the home of a man like Zacchaeus who was corrupt and greedy, scandalizing his contemporaries when he did so. But that is exactly what Jesus calls us to do, to give ourselves to the same type of close personal relationships with people no matter what they think, no matter what they believe, no matter what they worship, no matter how they live—to treat them with the same wonderful dignity and respect that the Lord treats us and to love them not simply despite their sin, but because they are sinners, and in great need of the Lord's mercy. So that's my passion: that we be in the world as Jesus was.[10]

Being in and loving the world in this sense is not just pleasing to God, it is central to our faithfulness as Christians and echoes God's own love for the world (John 3:16). When St. John warns us not to love the world (1 John 2:15), he is not telling us to disdain art and culture. He is not denying what God's Word already taught in creation. By "world" he means all those systems, institutions, and structures of a fallen humanity that, like the building of the ancient ziggurat in Babel (Gen. 11:1–9), trusted in human ingenuity and ability alone, thus arraying themselves against the reign and word of God.

What St. John rightly warns against here are the schemes and organizations of worldly power that vandalize God's shalom, carelessly destroy or thoughtlessly misuse his good creation, or oppress and dehumanize those Christ came to save. The Gospel is centered on a cross that promises salvation not just for souls but "far as the curse is found."[11] The fire in the earth's future that St Peter speaks of is not one of annihilation but of purification.

The Lord has not given up on his creation, the earth is his and someday by grace will be renewed.[12] We are not destined to be raptured from a planet that will be burnt out of existence, but to live forever in a renewed earth where our creativity as God's image bearers will flourish unhampered by the fall.[13] When St Paul instructs us not to be earthly minded, he relates this explicitly to Christ's enthronement at the Father's side (Col. 3:1–3).

Thus, a mind set on things above views all things within the perspective of Christ's Lordship. It means living as if we really do trust his providential care and believe his word rather than acting as if we were autonomous creatures able to make it on our own if we just get better organized or more productive or efficient. It is why a "devotion to Christ and a reality of prayer as we live in daily dependence on the Lord"[14] is one of the commitments Jerram Barrs set when he formed the Schaeffer Institute.

It is in accepting the truth that our neighbors are truly made in God's image that we can join the conversation already going on. One difficulty is that many Christians start at the wrong point.

The first question we ask often tends to be "What's wrong here? What did the movie get incorrect?" Don't misunderstand: I am not suggesting that we should fail to disagree when and where it is appropriate. Many stories, many films, in a fallen world make claims that are contrary to truth. What I am arguing is simply that beginning with disagreement makes us seem... well, rather disagreeable. Most of us have experienced this in reverse and know how it kills any desire for conversation. We finish a project, or make a speech, or show something we've done, only to have the moment squashed by someone immediately pointing out the flaws, saying it was all wrong, and making certain everyone knows they know better. It may turn out that they are correct, but it's still a discussion killer. And if we are disagreeable often enough, people will find others to talk to, especially about the things that matter most to them.

There is a better way to begin, a way that embodies our conviction that our neighbors bear God's likeness and should be treated with dignity. It is to listen to their stories. Or, as another Schaeffer Institute commitment expresses it, taking care to "understand the culture in which we live."[15] Understanding follows hearing.

The Reality of the Fall

Yet we live in a fallen and sinful world, which means we must be discerning about life, including the movies (Rom. 12:1–2). Some Christians, eager to distance themselves from the legalism of previous generations act as if no rules apply. They consume movies like everyone else does. We must never forget that after Creation in the biblical story comes the Fall. Though there is no sacred/secular dichotomy for the Christian, there is a dichotomy—and it is not minor. The division identified in the Scriptures holds eternal death in the balance, and if we have eyes to see we will realize that history is littered with the remains of those who took it lightly.

God created the work. He called things into existence in Genesis 1 and 2.

If we understand reality in terms of a sacred/secular dichotomy, then we create a hierarchy. A few things are spiritual while the rest is physical. Under this rubric, the spiritual aspects of life are most pleasing to God, and everything below the gap is less pleasing, of no lasting or eternal significance. Living in such a reality involves constant juggling, trying to bring some of the things on top down to justify the things that are below. Spending weeks weaving a rug by hand, or running a 5K, or raising a flower garden is below the gap, and prayer is above, so filling the time doing them with prayer somehow justifies the task.

However, we should consider how the Bible describes where we live, in a world that is fallen, sinful, and broken. And the brokenness reaches into every nook and cranny of my existence. Nothing is exempt.

The Bible even identifies some of the specific ways fallenness extends into art. In Exodus 32 we read the story of how Aaron led the Israelites astray when he sculpted a calf of gold for them when they feared Moses would never return from the smoke and lightning that had engulfed the mountain. That piece of art became an idol (Exod. 32:1–4), a substitute for God and his word.

Film can do the same, becoming a love that causes us to be insensitive to sin or an activity that begins to define how we use our time. The golden calf was Aaron's excuse to pander to the Israelites' baser desires (Exod. 32:21–24) just as film directors insert bad language or nudity not because the story requires it but to increase box office receipts. Through the calf Aaron propagated lies, untruths about God and the Israelites' own history (Exod. 32:4) just as many films present stories that do not reflect life as it truly is. And there is even a passage that shows how art can be trivialized (Amos 6:1, 4–5) so that it distracts us from faithfulness and wastes precious time and resources we were meant to steward and use for God's glory.

Taking sin seriously means we will be aware of such perversions in art—and film—and be in accountable relationships with godly friends so that our faithfulness can be enhanced as we grow over time. It means that if there are scenes in a film that will tempt us to sin in an area where we are weak and prone to fail, we will choose to see other films instead. Walking blindly into a theater to see some film when we know we are vulnerable is both foolish and inexcusable. There are plenty of ways to vet which movies to watch ahead of time.

On the other hand, I should realize that my weakness may not be yours, so I must be careful not to transform my standard for an acceptable film into a rule for all believers. And we must be careful to define sin biblically. It is not sinful to see a naked person, or to recognize hat person's beauty, or even a sexual dimension involved. God made us that way. What is forbidden is lust—using my imagination to touch that person or undress him or her or to take anything for which I am not entitled. Still, as John Frame argues, that does not mean that I must, for righteousness' sake withdraw from all instances of sin in culture.

I would not go to a film for the purpose of watching an actor and actress in a nude sex scene (thus I will not see XXX movies) any more than I would take a walk in the park to spy on kids making love behind the bushes. On the other hand, I would not stay away from the park out of fear that I might happen to observe some illicit sex. Similarly, if film actors wish to commit sin before the camera, that is their responsibility. I don't believe I commit sin when I, in the normal course of my cultural pursuits, observe what they, without consulting me, have chosen to do in public.[16]

Being Discerning with Film

Learning to listen with care to the culture's stories in film involves reflecting on a series of simple yet probing questions. Together these questions become a way to process the film thoughtfully—as a window of insight into our world and a point of contact for discussion with friends in that world. They are a way to be discerning as a Christian, to engage cinema faithfully and creatively.

First, what is the film saying? Because it is a story, answering this naturally involves answering questions that take the nature of story seriously. Who are the characters? What happens? Why? How do things resolve? In the end, what is the message(s) the film communicates, implicitly and explicitly? These questions are not difficult. They are the questions children ask of stories when we read to them. They are not difficult yet they are probing enough that they can be used for a graduate seminar to unpack the many layers of meaning in a work of fiction.

Second, what does the film make attractive? The way characters are depicted, the way the dialogue progresses, the way the plot develops always highlights some point of view. Film like all art is communication, a conversation begun by the artist and inviting a response from the viewer. What is delightful about the craft of the cinema is that often the point of view is framed subtly, with color or lighting or musical background or editing. If every time a character is on screen they are accompanied by somber, dark music and deep shadows around their eyes, that will affect our view of them. It's supposed to do so.

What is the film saying? What is made attractive?

The third question I will propose reminds us that when we respond to a film we are responding to a piece of art. The question is this: *How does the film work as art?*

Just becoming aware of the various aspects of cinematic art can begin the process of our being more sensitive to them. It includes something like this: In what ways were the techniques of film-making (casting, direction, lighting, script, music and sound, sets, action, cinematography, editing, etc.) used to get the film's story across, or to draw us in to make it plausible or compelling? In what ways were these aspects of filmmaking ineffective or misused? Think and talk about such things with humility—an explicit eagerness to learn, a willingness to be corrected, a properly tentative tone for non-filmmakers with an opinion—and we will be far better learners, and more like Christ in the process.

Discernment begins with observation. What is the film saying? What does the film make attractive? How does it work as art? If we intend to truly hear our neighbors' stories, we must answer these questions as objectively as possible.

We've probably all known times when people have not listened carefully to us and then trivialized our ideas. It's demeaning and if nothing else is proof that they are not taking us seriously as persons. Our ideas are not treated with respect but rather dismissed as inconsequential, as they promulgate their own ideas instead. There is no reason for people to listen to us if we do not listen to them.

The test with observing film objectively is this: when we identify what the film is saying, what it makes attractive, and how it works as art, the film's director should be able to agree. It's a good exercise to imagine the director sitting nearby listening to our reflections.

As I have already suggested, Christians tend to be poor listeners. Convinced we have the truth, we are often so eager to speak that truth that we skip listening. Convinced we know God's law for good and evil we quickly identify what people have gotten wrong in order to straighten them out. I am not suggesting that we fail to share that truth or argue for morality and justice. I am suggesting that listening first will allow meaningful communication. Listening shows people that we love them. Listening shows we treat them and their art with dignity rather than run roughshod over them and their convictions. And listening allows us to identify what aspects of truth, morality, and justice they might be ready to consider.

The fourth question is this: *Where do we agree, and why?* Common grace refers to the fact that fallen people living in God's world are capable of truth, morality, and beauty even though they may not be Christian. St. Paul tells us that a great deal can be known about God and creation, even apart from what is revealed in his word in Christ and Scripture (Rom. 1:19–20). We should therefore expect to learn from films, and to find much with which we will agree.

The Shawshank Redemption (1994) is about hardened criminals in a brutal penitentiary and is a brilliant exposition of the power and necessity of hope.

Lost in Translation (2003) is about two hopelessly jet-lagged travelers in Japan, It captures what it means to yearn desperately for home. When I saw it in the theater I sat through the credits stunned, realizing it was a moving study of what the Bible calls being "lost" (Luke 15:24).

Saying where we agree naturally offers bridges to further discussion. In this we can be like Jesus who used intriguing statements (Mark 4:1–9) to identify who wanted to actually talk further (Mark 4:13–20) and on a deeper level (Mark 4:10–12). It is easy to become nervous about a conversation because we aren't in control. It is a practical exercise in trusting God, believing that God's Spirit is at work in ways we have no way to see or know. A good conversationalist does not turn a conversation into a presentation.

What is the film saying? What does it make attractive? How does it work as art? Where do we agree?

With these four questions we have entered a conversation, and we have taken the first four steps in being discerning about film. These four questions allow us a way to respond to films without defensiveness and without being reactionary. This alone will speak well of the Gospel. Many non-Christians wonder why, if Christianity is really true, it breeds so many followers who tend to be judgmental and negative, quick to disagree and eager to correct everyone around them. Even if we are not in an actual conversation at the moment these questions provide a solid way to begin reflecting on a film. Good films, like all good stories need to be processed thoughtfully and to do that we need to begin by making certain we are hearing objectively and sympathetically.

The next question is the one with which too many Christians begin, but should not. Until we have observed with care, we are not in a position to disagree and we have not earned the right to do so. But now we are ready to consider what we would wish to challenge: *With what do we disagree and would like to question?*

I don't know that it is often argued that disagreement is a tender and precious skill that can be brutal and ungodly if misused, but I wish to suggest that here. To disagree can save a person from death, but to disagree callously can cut someone so deeply they stop listening to the way of life.

If we are in conversation with non-Christians who agree with what the film presents, this is a wonderful chance to ask them some questions. It is a chance to learn while we gently push our friend about their beliefs. Why are you convinced this is true? What difference does it make in your life? Are you so convinced that you would recommend I believe it? How would it improve my life?

Our willingness to disagree, to question or challenge some idea, should be thoughtful, complete, and with respectful reasons (1 Pet. 3:15). If we don't know something we should admit it, which is far better than reacting. Anne Lamott correctly warns us against being the sort of Christian who gets angry that others don't believe.

Think of it as a series of intimately interrelated questions: With what do we disagree and so would like to question? Why? And how can our disagreement be stated winsomely and creatively so that the non-Christians in our pluralistic world might be able to understand? Here's a hint: if we would say it that way in a Sunday school class, it probably won't be understood or appreciated by our non-Christian friends.

Conclusion

Considering film as God's gift means we can appreciate it for the lively art form it is without feeling guilty. I am not suggesting we must all enjoy the cinema equally. God has made us to respond to beauty with greater fullness and individuality than that, and it's a good thing since human art is far richer than any one of us can fully apprehend. The range of human taste and sensitivity to beauty mirrors the amazing diversity of God's creation. What I am suggesting is that being drawn to finely crafted films is not forbidden or somehow suspect of true spirituality. My love for film is instead an extension of my love for God and his glory in creation that is reflected—dimly at times in a fallen world, but still reflected—in human art. Film is able to do things no other art form can accomplish. It is a profoundly communal art, requiring the cooperation of so many different people with so many different skills it is a wonder that any movie comes together well, yet many do.

A biblical view of the cinema, rooted in the creation and in God's image in us, means we can expect films to reflect glimmers of the glory of God. Glimmers can even be glimpsed when the filmmakers did not intend them. This is one of the most deliciously subversive ideas implicit in the biblical understanding that culture and creativity are good gifts of God. Even a film that in its dialogue denies the Creator's existence shows in its own ingenuity and craft a glimpse, even if through a glass very darkly, of the creativity that is part of that Creator's image. Yes there are bad films, perverse films, poorly crafted films, exploitative films—but I am not talking about that here. Because human beings are made in God's image, and because that image is not erased by the fall, our creativity always reflects something of the likeness of God implanted in our nature as his creatures. Which is why beauty can be seen in the work of godless people, and why light sometimes breaks out in work produced by those who intentionally choose to delight in the darkness.

As Christians, we can approach film gratefully rather than apprehensively. Yes we live in a fallen world. Still this is our Father's world, and his good gifts to us in creation and culture are reasons to be grateful. Sometimes it seems that the children of light are better able to notice and comment on the darkness than to be grateful for the light. That should not be so. Yes we must be discerning, but any sense of discernment that does not flow from a deep well of gratefulness will always be less than fully Christian.

It is why Jerram Barrs, in establishing the Schaeffer Institute as a part of Covenant Seminary, listed as one of its commitments, "Appreciation of God's gifts in all of life."[17] Taking the reality of the fall seriously —another Institute commitment—should never be allowed to smother our gratefulness to God for his grace.

Gratefulness is an essential aspect of our calling before God. It's why St. Paul, in the midst of giving a series of commands to the believers at

Colossae, says simply, *"Be thankful"* (Col. 3:15). He doesn't identify what we should be thankful for but insists instead that gratefulness should be a characteristic that helps define our identity as God's people. Our engagement with art (or anything else, for that matter) in a fallen world will be effectively shaped by the attitude we bring to it. Perhaps one of the reasons so many Christians react so defensively to movies is that they approach the topic of the cinema and the experience of film feeling apprehensive rather than grateful. Gratefulness allows our apprehension of God's grace to take center stage in our view of things, reminding us that even in a fallen, secularized, postmodern society the tomb remains empty and so we have nothing to fear.

God calls us to demonstrate what it means to be human, even at the box office.

---

1. O. Palmer Robertson, *The Christ of the Covenants* (Phillipsburg, PA: Presbyterian & Reformed Publishing, 1980), 226.
2. Kevin J. Vanhoozer, *The Drama of Doctrine: A Canonical-Linguistic Approach to Christian Theology* (Louisville, Kentucky: Westminster John Knox Press; 2005), 366–97.
3. Ellis Potter, *3 Theories of Everything* (Destinée Media; 2012).
4. John R. W. Stott, *Involvement: Being a Responsible Christian in a Non-Christian Society*, 1 (Grand Rapids, MI: Fleming H Revell; 1985), 61.
5. Roy M. Anker, *Catching Light: Looking for God in the movies* (Grand Rapids, MI: Eerdmans; 2004), 4.
6. Daniel M. Doriani, *Getting the Message: A Plan for Interpreting and Applying the Bible* (Phillipsburg, NJ: P&R Publishing; 1996), 64.
7. Anker, *Catching Light: Looking for God in the Movies*, 5.
8. See for example, Matthew 11:15; 13:9, 43.
9. Craig Detweiler and Barry Taylor, *A Matrix of Meanings: Finding God in Pop Culture* (Grand Rapids, MI: Baker; 2003), 23, 27.
10. Transcribed by the author April 3, 2012 from "Faculty Video of Jerram Barrs," uploaded by Covenant Seminary on Sep 17, 2010 (http://www.youtube.com/watch?v=wh1ZPeMa6CA).
11. Michael D. Williams, *As Far as the Curse is Found: The Covenant Story of Redemption* (Phillipsburg, PA: P&R Publishing, 2005).
12. Wim Rietkirk, *Millennium Fever and the Future of this Earth* (Savage, MN: Ransom Fellowship Publications, 2008).
13. Rietkerk, *Millennium Fever.*
14. http://www.covenantseminary.edu/academics/institutesinitiatives/francisaschaefferinstitute/
15. http://www.covenantseminary.edu/academics/institutesinitiatives/francisaschaefferinstitute/
16. John M. Frame, *The Doctrine of the Christian Life: A theology of Lordship* (Phillipsburg, PA: P & R Publishing; 2008), 893–897.
17. http://www.covenantseminary.edu/academics/institutesinitiatives/francisaschaefferinstitute/

FITTINGNESS

ON THE NATURE OF HARMONY

John Mason Hodges

*MM, Orchestral and Opera Conducting, Indiana University
Founder/Director, The Center for Western Studies
Memphis, TN*

OK, I admit it started out because of a girl in grad school. Isn't it always about a girl? I thought, how was I ever going to be able to put a relationship together? But my broken heart just opened my eyes to the fact that I had a bigger problem. How were the elements of life supposed to fit together? Love, family, career, significance, and most of all truth, goodness, and beauty? I found I couldn't make things fit, and when some dear Christian friends led me to Jesus, I began to see that my longing for the parts of the world to fit together was not a dream of my own doing. God had placed the desire in me and used it to lead me to him. My world changed forever.

    Just knowing that things fit together gave me hope, but I still had the problem of figuring how they did. If all things were to orbit around Jesus, anything that would not fit needed to be transformed or jettisoned. I had lived my life for my music since the second grade, first playing the piano then the trumpet in bands and orchestras, then going off to university and graduate school to train to conduct orchestras on stage and in the opera pit. Now however, I needed to either place this musical world into proper orbit around my Lord or give it up altogether.

One of the reasons Christianity had held so little interest to me until my twenty-fifth year was that it seemed to be so anti-intellectual. It seemed impossible to give up the beautiful and varied world of reason and art in order to live by faith. Fortunately when I received this gift of faith, I also received some books by great Christian thinkers that helped. My first book was C. S. Lewis' *Mere Christianity*, and the second was Francis Schaeffer's *Escape from Reason*, in which he began to connect the dots of the philosophy classes I had taken.

Perhaps one didn't have to park his mind at the door of the church after all! For this (and many other insights) I will always be grateful for Dr. Schaeffer's work. Though I never met Dr. Schaeffer, his books led me eventually to study at English L'abri, later to speak at many of the conferences, and to become friends with Mrs. Schaeffer and with many of the next generation of L'abri workers, including my dear friend and wise older brother Jerram.

Still the question remained, What about my love of music in particular? Was there a way to put that love in its proper place under my newly established first love? If not, music simply had to go, and that thought gave me a deep ache. I was sure there had to be a way to fit them properly together. What role did music play in the mind of the Creator? I seemed to have two experiences of music. The first gave me a means of expression for my teenage emotions. The second gave me a glimpse of worlds I had never imagined. As a teen I listened to popular music and played in rock bands beginning in seventh grade, which gave me an inexplicable emotional catharsis. But I found I got a similar experience listening to Copland's "Fanfare for the Common Man" or the slow build up and climax of Saint-Saens' "Organ Symphony."

However there was a second kind of musical experience, far deeper, more profound and more mysterious, that I found through Mozart's Horn Concertos, or the slow movement of Khatchaturian's "Piano Concerto," or the opening of Sibelius' "First Symphony." These experiences were so profound that when I became a Christian I knew there had to be something God was doing through the beauty I found there. I began to study aesthetics, to pursue what was considered beautiful and why.

> The books or the music in which we thought the
> beauty was located will betray us if we trust to them;
> it was not in them, it only came through them,
> and what came through them was longing.
> —C. S. Lewis

I wrote my graduate thesis on the role that the conductor could play in the philosophical realms of beauty and art. Looking to establish definitions for such lofty words, beauty, and art, I was led to Plato, Kant, Schopenhauer, and Susanne Langer, who worked to connect meaning with artistic expression. Except for Plato, everyone I read came after Descartes and the Enlightenment, and dealt mainly with a personalized experience of beauty: the sensation I knew so well of joy and ache felt upon hearing a beautiful melody, or sensing a beautiful form. I always thought I fit right in with the nineteenth-century Romantics. But now I was after was something that would go beyond that personal, sensational world and address what I found in my second experience.

I found, as most of us do, that when I experienced this beauty, I longed to share the experience with someone else. It was personal, but it longed to be communal.

Why was that? Could it be that the experience of musical beauty is not only a matter of personal preference? If the experience of beauty was purely of personal significance, why would we desire to share it with others? Could it be that we treat it the way the scientist treats a new finding? That we want a sort of peer review of our assessment? The scientist wants to prove that his experiment was valid and true. Could it be that I wanted the same sort of support when I would play a recording for a fellow student in my dorm room? Was I looking for corroboration?

Perhaps we want to know that our discoveries and delights are indeed worthy of being called beautiful. But if that is the case, there must be some sort of standard outside myself we all can relate to. Sometimes when I played my latest discoveries to my fellows, they would share my enthusiasm which would double my joy. Sometimes one would show me how another composer had "done it better"—an extra turn of phrase here, a deeper understanding of form there, a subtle change of harmony that returns in the finale to change the meaning of the whole work.

Through these discussions I realized something else had happened. Not only was my knowledge of the available repertoire increasing, but my loves themselves were being honed, sharpened, adjusted. While I still loved the cathartic emotional expression I found in my favorite rock music or in various Tchaikovsky and Strauss tone poems, the second kind of experience ultimately moved me in a different and more profound way. There was something in the exquisite gem cut of a Mozart aria, or the complicated interplay of lines in a Bach fugue, or the soaring gravity of a Brahms slow movement that reached further into my heart to speak of something I had never considered before. It might be said that the former works gave cathartic voice and expression to something that was already in me, but the latter works opened my eyes to things that were *not* in me, and once the lack was revealed, my longing for those things increased.

What was this longing? Why was I, like Lewis, pained by it but simultaneously desirous of it? I found that it drove my conducting. I worked in rehearsals to get at the right tempo, dynamics, articulations, timing, etc. precisely so that I could get closer to the experience and expression of that experience that the music revealed to me.

...for God is beauty itself, in itself....
—Etienne Gilson

I began to think there was more going on in our appreciation of music than simply finding works that attracted us. There had to be two variables in this equation to find beauty, not one. There is the work itself, which can be good or not, but there is also our internal sensibilities themselves which are honed to perceive beauty in a work or not. Thus if a work is not called beautiful, it may be because it lacks internal excellence, but it also could be because the listener didn't know what to make of it.

I remembered Thomas Aquinas had described beauty as the conjunction of two events: the qualities of the object (unity, proportion, and clarity) and the response of the subject (that beauty is that which pleases upon being perceived). There is no doubt that the Fall can affect our ability to create beauty in music, but it seems it has also had an effect on how we perceive it as well. In other words, our apprehension of the beautiful in music (or in anything) is a variable just as the choices of music vary.

I realized that if we were to understand just what goes on in the appreciation of music, we were going to have to consider that both the piece of music and the listener are parts of a bigger pattern. Instead of thinking that the listener's preferences are unchanging, sacrosanct, and the highest criteria in musical judgment, it seems that there is an exterior criteria that is applied both to the composer at the time of the composition and to the listener at the time of apprehension. It is as though each of them is trying to get at something beyond the music and using the music as a medium of communication with it. The composer is inspired by an idea, a feeling, a vision that he wants to communicate by way of the language of music. To paraphrase Hamlet, there are more things in heaven and earth than are dreamt of in our language of words, and some of those need expression by way of melody and harmony. So, the composer composes to the best of his or her abilities, even honing those abilities and increasing that musical vocabulary through study, in hopes of getting close to the expression of the vision. The listener also looks to learn the language of music to apprehend the vision that has inspired the composer. In the performance, the composer speaks to the listener in the language of music about things beyond words.

The soul is weighed in the balance by what delights her.
Delight or enjoyment sets the soul in her ordered place.
"Where your treasure is, there your heart will be also."
—St. Augustine

Christopher Dawson has written that our present society seems to have taken shape as one that "will acknowledge no hierarchy of values, no intellectual authority, and no social or religious tradition, but will live for the moment in a chaos of pure sensation."[1] In our culture, we assume that the listener is a sort of consumer with his own preferences and that those preferences are not to be questioned, making the success or failure of a piece of music a matter settled by its popularity. If enough consumers consume it, it is a success. However this overlooks something of great importance. The human being is not ultimately a consumer; he is a worshiper. By worshiper, I mean the human attaches their heart to things they love, and what we love matters to God. Jesus said, *"Where your treasure is, there your heart is also"* (Matt 6:21).

To become a consumer of music is not only to reduce the music to a commodity, which misses much of the point of music, but to abandon human beings to a sort of slavery to our limited preferences. To never question our preferences is to lift them to the ultimate authority and make an idol of ourselves. This is the assumption, for the most part, that I found in the Church whenever I heard Christians discussing music, and I longed to be able to express to believers what I had found music could be and had been for many Christians in the past.

What would happen to our experience of music if we reintroduced God into the equation? Don't Christians need to start with God when addressing aesthetics just as we do in ethics and epistemology? It is easy to see how we can't understand moral goodness without allowing God's self-revelation to guide us. It is easy too to see how there is no truth unless it begins with God's words. But where could we begin when we consider beauty? What if God's intention were to reveal himself through beauty just as he does through goodness and truth? It is easy to see how moral behavior or speaking the truth can reflect the glory of God, but what about beauty? The gracefulness of the blossoming rose, the soaring Rocky Mountains, and the fireworks in a well-cut diamond move us even if we don't know how to explain them in words. What is going on?

I assumed the answer had to lie in the revelation God had given us in the Bible. Does the Bible offer a standard for beauty like it does for truth and goodness? I could find verses about what we should call true and good. But it was much harder to find those verses about what we should call beautiful.

But I did find them. Before addressing beauty, the other two transcendentals (truth and goodness) are found in the Word himself, the person of Jesus. The Word incarnate is what the truth actually is (John 14:6), so the words he sends by way of the Holy Spirit's inspiration through the prophets and apostles is completely reliable and inerrant. Likewise the example of goodness we have is the person of God (Exod. 33:19). He is what goodness is. Yes his characteristics are described in Holy Scripture, but it is his character on display. There is no standard of truth or goodness behind or above God that he refers to. He himself is what those things are. I say this because while there is truth and goodness described in the words of the Bible, the perfect manifestation of these attributes is to be found in the person of God, and they cannot be fully encapsulated by any list we might draw on our own from the pages of the Bible. It is this God, who is truth and goodness, who created all things, became flesh and dwelt among us, and who now is loosed among us in the person of the Holy Spirit, and the one in whom we live and have our being.

Given that truth and goodness are fully manifest in God, it should not be too hard a stretch to theorize that God is also what beauty is. It is true that the incarnated Son of God had no superficial beauty to draw us to him (predicted in Isa. 53:2), but there was something profoundly beautiful about Jesus' character in this world that did indeed draw people to him. But it isn't just superficial majesty. There are two ways the Bible offers us a glimpse of what this beauty of God is.

First there are indirect ways. The Bible speaks of beauty in Psalm 27 as a characteristic of God, greatly to be desired. In fact, David says that to *"gaze on the beauty of the Lord"* is the one and only thing he really desires (Ps. 27:4). In another hint, the first example of God filling someone with his Spirit comes about in Exodus 31 when men are filled with God's Spirit in order to create beautiful things for the tabernacle. A third indirect reference is when the Bible speaks of the beauty of creation and how that beauty reflects the glory of God (Ps. 19:1). These may not give us a Ten Commandments of beauty (always do this, never do that; blue is beautiful, green is not; straight lines are more beautiful than curved ones; or similar nonsense), but what these examples do is require us to consider the nature of beauty because the Scriptures teach that God is to be the fulfillment of our desire for beauty. God intends and empowers us to make beautiful things, and his glory is reflected in the beauty of his own handiwork, giving us a model to follow as men and women created in his image.

But there is a more direct way that the Bible informs us about beauty. Not so much in didactic statements of revelation (as above) but in the forms of that revelation. God's revelation to us in the Bible is in words. Those words are in sentences; those sentences in paragraphs; and those paragraphs in chapters and books. What is more, those words have sounds (in the original languages), and those sounds have rhythms, rhymes, and they can be formed into acrostics, metaphors, similes, and puns. Most of all, they are formed into stories—stories about how God interacts with people; stories about how individuals embody human characteristics, sing songs, make choices; stories about how God too embodies personality. God loves and hates, he acts, and he has patience.

In other words the revelation of God is in literary form, and that form is part of the revelation itself. Why did God write it in this form and not another? The very choice of words themselves creates a form or medium by which he reveals himself. Could the form affect, even participate in the content of the revelation? God chose to reveal himself this way, and we must believe that since he is God he could have chosen any of a number of ways to reveal himself. The fact that he chose to make most of his revelation literary—that is, in story form (Genesis and Exodus, for example), poetry and song (Psalms), parables (in the gospels), theater (prophets), and metaphor (i.e. *"I am the bread"* or *"I am the vine"*)—rather than only in didactic teaching—that is, lists (Ten Commandments), bullet points (Leviticus), or commands (Gen. 2:16)—is important. Why?

Perhaps there are some things that are better understood by way of poetry than prose. If so, it means that beauty plays a significant part in God's revelation of himself to us. The *form* of the revelation may be a part of the revelation itself. For example, chapter 28 in the book of Job takes twenty-eight verses to get to its point. Those who skip over the first twenty-seven verses to memorize the twenty eighth (and most worthy of memorization it is: *"The fear of the Lord, that is wisdom"*), will miss out on the depth of the meaning of that final verse. It requires the first twenty-seven verses to draw the heart away from its misguided attachments and to prepare its soil for the seed of verse 28. So it is the very form of the chapter that the Holy Spirit uses to prepare us for the revelation. The form of the chapter itself is beautiful. It begins where we are, then, through word pictures, metaphors, and repeated questions that give the chapter rhythm, we come to the point of embodying and experiencing awe of the Lord before he gives us the didactic verse. We find that we are in a position of awe before we are told that our very position is what wisdom is.

So it is through the harmonic beauty of the combination of form and content that the Bible reveals the character of God. This is at least one way the Bible teaches us about beauty. To pick up on this, however, requires the exercise and honing of our God-given gift of the imagination, which creates new things but also sees relationships between what already exists. It requires an imagination to see the relation of the two sides of a metaphor. Jesus taught in parables and metaphors, and when the disciples needed them interpreted, he gently chided them saying,

"*Don't you understand this parable? How then will you understand any parable?*" (Mark 4:13) Whatever he meant to do to hide the truth from the unbelievers, he certainly intended believers to know these truths about the kingdom, and that knowledge could and would be communicated through poetic devices and understood by the exercise of our imaginations.

Metaphors are the relation of two disparate things (Juliet and the sun, Jesus and the vine), and the ability to perceive the relation of those things requires a poetic imagination. Musical harmony turns out to be also a relation of two or more disparate things. Harmony requires the relation of differing pitches. You cannot have harmony with unisons or octaves. So musical harmony is literally a manifestation of the harmony of the Trinity, made up of disparate Persons, all making one God. Jeremy Begbie has spoken about this, writing that hearing can better discern the nature of the Trinity than sight (I recommend his book *Theology, Music, and Time* for a full explanation).

> It came as a surprise that so dry a question as "what is a sound?" should lead at last to a philosophy of modern culture. Had I thought more about the Pythagorean cosmology, and the true meaning of harmonia I should perhaps have known beforehand, that the ordering of sound as music is an ordering of the soul.
> —Roger Scruton

The apprehension of music's beauty has the effect of a certain "ordering of the soul,"[2] (what Augustine refers to as *ordo amoris*) and that ordering leads to further and deeper appreciation. Roger Scruton refers here to Pythagoras' understanding of harmony as the rational relation of physical pitches to one another. Plato also wrote about how important it was to introduce young children to beautiful music before they were able to reason because the heart attaches itself to beauty. Then, as maturity grows, the child looks for harmony in other things as well, such as the harmony of visual art, good business transactions, the harmonious marriage, and eventually in the application of justice in the city. Justice is the harmonious relation of reward and penalty to a citizen's action.

Jonathan Edwards wrote an essay entitled *On the Nature of True Virtue* that described what he called "primary beauty"[3] as the beauty of the goodness of God. The idea is that in God himself all the qualities of truth, goodness, and beauty come together. The Trinity, with his interlocking three persons, each fully God, and each in complete union with the other two, is the source of everything right, loving, just, fine, beautiful, and graceful. Edwards then shows how God made the world to reflect God's primary beauty in the physical world. "Secondary beauty,"[4] Edwards said, included harmony in music as another one of the ways God's beauty was manifest in the world. Here's a quote from Chapter 3:

> Why such analogy in God's works pleased him, it is not needful now to inquire. It is sufficient that he makes an agreement of different things, in their form, manner, measure, etc. to appear beautiful, because here is some image of an higher kind of agreement and consent of spiritual beings. It has pleased him to establish a law of nature, by virtue of which the uniformity and mutual correspondence of a beautiful plant, and the respect which the various parts of a regular building seem to have one to another, and their agreement and union, and the consent or concord of the various notes of a melodious tune, should appear beautiful; because therein is some image of the consent of mind, of the different members of a society or system of intelligent beings, sweetly united in a benevolent agreement of heart.... And here by the way I would further observe, probably it is with regard to this image or resemblance which secondary beauty has of true spiritual beauty, that God has so constituted nature, that the presenting of this inferior beauty, especially in those kinds of it which have the greatest resemblance of the primary beauty, as the harmony of sounds and the beauties of nature, have a tendency to assist those whose hearts are under the influence of a truly virtuous temper to dispose them to the exercises of divine love, and enliven in them a sense of spiritual beauty.[5]

So the connection I was looking for had become clearer to me. God himself is internally harmonious, in that he is one God and three distinct and diverse Persons, and his love for "being in general,"[6] as Edwards puts it, is a harmonious relation that is beautiful. God created the world that reflects the harmony of his nature and love, which includes such non-musical harmonies as marriage, the union of two (very) different persons; fruit, the union of soil and seed; well-composed visual art, consisting of unity and diversity together in the same frame; and music itself (at its vibrating source), the harmony of varied pitches working together to generate scales and chords which become the building blocks of millions of compositions in hundreds of styles. The question that began with God's design for music led me to see and appreciate more of his design in other areas of his creation.

This has become a life-long study inspired by Dr. Schaeffer's work, and by extension, the work of Jerram Barrs. For that, I am, and will be for all eternity will be, grateful.

---

1. Christopher Dawson, *Progress and Religion: An Historical Inquiry*, (The Catholic University of America Press; Reprint edition, 2001), 176.
2. Roger Scrunton, *Aesthetics of Music* (Oxford: Clarendon Press, 1999), pg#?.
3. Jonathan Edwards, *On the Nature of True Virtue*, 13, https://www.earlymoderntexts.com/assets/pdfs/edwards1765.pdf.
4. Edwards, *True Virtue*, 13.
5. Edwards, *True Virtue*, 14.
6. Edwards, *True Virtue*, 17.

A THEATER TO THE COSMOS

DRAMATIC INCARNATION FOR A POSTMODERN WORLD

Camille J. Hallstrom

MATS, Covenant Seminary
MFA, University of Pittsburgh
Professor of Theater, Covenant College
Lookout Mountain, TN

This chapter is an expansion of material appearing in *Joyfully Spreading the Word: Sharing the Good News of Jesus*, edited by Kathleen Nielson and Gloria Furman (Crossway, 2018).

"God has put us on display...
we have become a theater to the cosmos,
to angels, and to men."[1]
1 Corinthians 4:9

Because of Jerram Barrs I discovered the central metaphor that has informed much of my thinking and writing about Christian approaches to dramatic art: theater is incarnation.[2] As a seminary student searching for material on how to think about and do drama Christianly, I was frustrated that much of church history has been vociferously anti-theatrical.[3]

Furthermore, contemporary Evangelical writers have tended to produce theologically and/or artistically weak treatments of theater (assuming they aren't ignoring it altogether). "Well if you're working with Jerram," a fellow student encouraged me, "he can surely point you to something good!" And though I had my doubts such material could be found anywhere in North America, lo! there it was, just gathering dust in Jerram's office—an unbound galley proof of Max Harris' *Theater and Incarnation*.[4]

Drawing a useful parallel between what takes place when the words of a dramatic text are staged (or *put on* by actors) and what took place when the pre-existent Word *put on* flesh, the book's correlation of theater and the Incarnation has helped me firm up what I see as the inherent goodness of dramatic presentation (together with the peculiar power it may have for evil). Furthermore Harris' analogy has helped me envision a two-pronged model for doing dramatic work in a Christian way. Not only is 1) the *end* of dramatic production (the final enacted performance) incarnational in nature, but we who serve the Lord in theater and film must also make sure that 2) the *means* of production (how we treat our fellow workers, audiences, etc.) is incarnational as well. In what follows, I hope to elaborate somewhat on both ideas, concluding with two stories of attempts at incarnational production practice.[5]

Dramatic Performance Is Incarnational

When actors perform, according to Harris' analogy, the words of a script are *enfleshed* in a fashion not unlike what took place when the divine Word put on flesh. If, in the world of philosophical discourse, it can be claimed that "ideas have legs," in the world of dramatic art ideas have not only legs, but hands, mouths, loves, hatreds, good deeds, and evil. Who for example is not aware that parents—Christian and otherwise (even Hollywood parents according to one *L. A. Times* poll[6])—are often concerned about the potentially negative impact watching TV and film may have on their children? Kids are hard-wired to learn through observation of their environments–being "audiences"—and mimicking those around them—being "actors." Language, physical gesture, cultural, and gender norms are learned as children play house, store, *Star Wars*, or *Harry Potter*. "Let's pretend" is a kind of apprenticeship for adult life.

But adults learn this way too. That is part of why the Word became flesh. We needed a model who could demonstrate for us what it is to be, in every way, *"tempted as we are, yet without sin."* (Heb. 4:15). Here then is also a model for the goodness of dramatic incarnation. Our neighbors need examples of how people can fully-yet-righteously experience and rejoice in God's good-yet-fallen creation. Because we often aren't creative enough to figure it out on our own, we need fully-fleshed models of how it is possible to have hope in a world of suffering, or how to *"abhor what is evil"* yet *"hold fast to what is good"* (Rom. 12:9). Paul wrote, *"Be imitators [mimētai; μιμηται]*[7] *of me, as I am of Christ"* (1 Cor. 11:1) not presumably because he was vain. Rather he was meeting a real human need. A theater of righteous, imaginative, and hopeful incarnation could meet that need too.

Dramatic Production Practices Should Incarnate Christ for Others

Dramatic art, as a collaborative art form shared as a collective experience with audiences, is involved at every turn with human relationships. And just as the Word put on flesh for us, now we are to incarnate the Word for others. *"Now you,"* wrote Paul, *"are the body of Christ"* (1 Cor. 12:27). How we interact with our brothers and neighbors is a large portion of our witness and calling in the world. We are *"to be imitators [μιμηται] of God"* (Eph. 5:1), for *"God chose to make known... this mystery: which is Christ in you, the hope of glory"* (Col. 1:27).

In our production practices—such as our consideration of 1) the impact our production choices will have on those who see them, 2) how we treat each other onstage and backstage, and 3) how we handle business dealings with the wider profession—Christians must always keep the call to love foremost in our theory, practice, and prayers. The second Great Commandment is to love our neighbors as ourselves (Matt. 22:39), and Jesus said it's when we love, people will know we are his disciples (John 13:35). We must pray God enables us, through loving artistic, interpersonal, and business practices, to incarnate Christ for those we encounter in every area of theater and film production.

Paul said God had put his ambassadors on display as a *theater* to the cosmos (Cf. Heb. 11:39–12:1). The word in 1 Corinthians 4:9, frequently translated "spectacle," is actually the word for "theater" (*theatron*; θεατρον). While the designation might be applied to the church generally,[8] it is my prayer that this verse moves the church to prepare some of her members to become missionaries to the people group of dramatic professionals who are not likely to be reached by outsiders. The dramatic arts are arguably today's most influential mode of cultural communication. We are fools if we neglect proclaiming God's kingdom in this vital marketplace.

Incarnating Words—What It Doesn't Necessarily Mean

It likely isn't news to many readers that contemporary Christian artwork, dramatic or otherwise, tends to suffer from too much message. We are, after all, Evangelicals—naming ourselves after the activity of spreading good news. When we aren't getting out the message, we start to feel uneasy. Likewise if a given drama doesn't contain a clear Gospel presentation, or a strategy for saving one's marriage, or surviving the apocalypse, we aren't quite certain we've made godly use of our time. Unfortunately this tendency to make message-heavy art often means we produce work which is neither especially good art nor contains a good message. Besides such work likely will only be viewed by those already in our camp; we end up preaching to the choir, and none too well at that. Peck and Strohmer write:

> [Art] is not propaganda.... The artist has had an experience... [and] wants you to enter into the experience yourself... she creates the barest outline of a situation... just enough clues for you, almost unconsciously, to work out the rest for yourself. (One sees the process clearly in biblical parables).... This is why artistic activity does not appear to offer a "clear message." If it does, its cover is blown, its power is gone.... Art, therefore, can be the means whereby the outsiders can, for themselves, taste something of what life under God in Christ is like.... They are not having ideas imposed on them, and they are left free to make the discovery in their own way.[9]

David Fetcho posits real art as that which serves to remedy a condition he dubs "stasis of perception."[10] Art, he says, works to reorient perception, either away from or back to the ordinary, so the ordinary can be truly experienced. It re-patterns perception so as to create the conditions for a new way of seeing, a new epistemology. Art is more often about the seeing than about what is seen. It does not seek to displace the functions of other forms of human communication (e.g., sermons, lectures, etc.), nor should it be expected to function as they do.

Fetcho writes:

> The intent of art is to confront the stasis of perception, which is itself both emblematic and reinforcing of moral and spiritual stasis. And such epistemological stasis, or complacency, is the most effective buffer to Jesus' call to *metanoia* or conversion.[11]

Scripture frowns on those *"who have eyes, but see not, who have ears, but hear not"* (Jer. 5:21). Similarly if we prefer artwork which tells us what we want to hear, as opposed to helping us see what is actually there, such work may actually constitute *"itching ears [gathering] teachers to suit their own passions"* (2 Tim. 4:3). If our preferred art only tells us what we already know and does not challenge us to see what we never before perceived, it will not only fail to develop in us ears to hear, it may actually deepen our (culpable) deafness.

If we find, as just one example, that our tastes run toward sentimentality,[12] we may be guilty of desiring what Wolfe calls "the luxury of an emotion without paying for it."[13] Wolfe points out what painter Thomas Kinkade's says about his own paintings:

> [Kincade says,] "I like to portray a world without the Fall." [Wolfe continues,] I have yet to encounter any evidence that Kinkade cites scriptural or other warrant for this modus operandi. The Bible, as a narrative, seems fairly explicit about there being a Before and an After. Moreover, Christ's message was not to pretend the world isn't fallen but to take up our crosses and follow him through suffering and sacrifice. To create a body of work illustrating a world without the Fall is... to render Christ superfluous.... Kinkade's apologetic seems to fit the definition of sentimentality as the "misrepresentation of the world in order to indulge certain emotional states." That he is tapping into a deep human need seems unquestionable. But the response... to that need is both inadequate and dangerous.[14]

Forty years ago Francis Schaeffer gave a related warning. The Christian worldview can be divided into what he called its major and minor themes. The minor theme is the brokenness of the fallen world. The major theme is the meaning and purposefulness of life. The art of

Christians, Schaeffer said, does have a place for the minor theme. However, insofar as modernist art of non-Christians tended to emphasize only the minor theme, Christians must take care not to so major on the minor that we end up being equally unbiblical. Schaeffer provided the reverse warning too, one which the Kincaide quote above demonstrates has not been fully heeded: "If our Christian art only emphasizes the major theme, then it is not fully Christian but simply romantic."[15]

Lack of Theological Aesthetics, or Trying to Stand on a Two-legged Stool

Might we lay some more fruitful theoretical foundation for our incarnations of words? One likely root cause of our producing message-laden or romantic art is, to quote T. Chris Crain, that "Evangelical systematic theology is beastly."[16] Meaning what? He writes:

> Simply [that] it has neglected one aspect of the triumvirate of transcendentals: truth, goodness and beauty. Evangelicals have done well in defending the *truths* of the faith–the inerrancy of Scripture, the Virgin Birth.... Evangelicals have also excelled in touting what is *good* about the faith and what *goods* the evangelical should pursue.... But when it comes to speaking about *beauty* in a systematic, theological manner, evangelicals are silent. And this silence renders, by default, evangelical theology beastly... [as] absence of goodness implies evil, so does a lack of beauty imply ugliness.[17]

Crain reminds us that historic systematic theology did not suffer from this deficiency. Nor do contemporary non-Evangelical systematic theologies. Crain cites Catholics Richard Viladesau and Hans urs Von Balthasar, and Protestants Karl Barth, Edward Farley, and Frank Burch Brown.

> In the history of Christian theology, beauty has often been discussed by leading theologians. Augustine, Gregory of Nyssa, Anselm, Bonaventure, Aquinas... to name but a few, all spoke of the beauty of God and Christ. ... Beauty is the dazzling display of the truth and goodness of God as reflected in the glory and holiness of his person and works.... Probably the greatest exemplar of a theologian utilizing the concept of beauty is Jonathan Edwards [who wrote].... "God is God, and distinguished from

all other beings, and exalted above 'em, chiefly by his divine beauty, which is infinitely diverse from all other beauty."[18]

Our beauty-less theological roots can issue forth in a fairly pragmatic value system. As mentioned above, we have even named ourselves based on one practical, measurable activity: getting out the good news.[19] But are God's values equally pragmatic? What if God really did set beauty on par with truth and goodness? Has our more utilitarian approach given us a skewed perspective on God and Christian duty?

Once when I was in seminary in St. Louis, some of us visited the Roman Catholic Basilica in town. It was gorgeous, majestic, and awe-inspiring.

Afterward we discussed our reactions to it.

I said, "I hadn't been expecting it, but just walking up and down the aisles, looking at those magnificent mosaics and columns got me thinking about the glory of God. I caught myself singing hallelujahs." Another person, who had been a missionary in a poor country said, "I just kept thinking 'How many people could you feed with all the money it took to build this place?'" And then I felt guilty and selfish and worldly. Why hadn't I thought about feeding poor people?

But then I had another thought, which I shared with him, and when I did, I could see a happy "Yeah…" dawning on his face. I said, "You know, in Scripture, God told Israel to care for the poor. But he also directed them to build a magnificent tabernacle and temple, which he himself designed. Maybe in God's economy it's possible and proper to do both."

Respected dramaturg Morgan Jenness relates once learning a similar lesson:

> I had been… wondering what my life in the theater was really about. I decided it was all nonsense and that I really wanted to do something more meaningful with my life. So, I got it into my head I was going to join Mother Teresa's Sisters of Mercy in Calcutta…. [Going to meet her at the Indian Embassy] I flung myself past people at her, and she stopped and gently said, "What can I do for you?" And I babbled, "Oh, Mother Teresa, I want to come with you…. I want to pick up dying people in the street, please, please…." And she asked, "You need to do this?" And I said, "Yes, yes, I need to do this!".… She gazed at me and she said, "No, you cannot come…. When you are so filled with love for these people that

you cannot bear to be away from them for another minute, then you can come".... She asked, "What do you do?" and I answered, "I'm in the theater," like confessing this horrible, paltry, putrid occupation. She smiled, nodded, and said, "There are many famines. In my country there is a great famine of the body. In your country there is a great famine of the spirit. That's what you must feed." ... Well, that kept me going for quite awhile and still does.[20]

Ecclesiastes 3 says, *"There is a season for ...every matter under heaven.... [God] has made everything beautiful in its time."* While it is arguable that much of post-Enlightenment history was a season requiring Evangelicalism's special championing of *truth* and *goodness*, now seems to be the season to refocus on the "third leg of the stool"—*beauty*. A key reason to do that is because of culture's shift to postmodernity. As Graham Clay notes,

At modernity's height a naturalistic view of science seemed to swallow up all other forms of knowledge. What could not be proved could not be trusted–and the arts were marginal and treated as an object of suspicion. In postmodernity, aesthetics and literary theory threaten to swallow up everything else. This is creating an intellectual world which has lost any sense of (capital 'T') Truth and replaced it with endless interpretations; games played with the meaning of texts.... [We now] live in a society dominated by images but starved of meaning.[21]

I believe that Schaeffer's strategy for late-twentieth century apologetics needs updating to address twenty-first century realities. Modern man, Schaeffer wrote, had to learn to "bow in the realm of Being... [and] in the realm of morals."[22] Schaeffer thus referenced two of the legs of the stool, "being" (truth) and "morals" (goodness). Let's now add back in the third leg, calling for postmodern people to bow not only metaphysically before the God who is there and ethically before the God who is holy, but also aesthetically before the God who is the measure of all beauty. Seeking to show moderns that faith must be based on knowledge, Schaeffer noted "The Bible teaches in two different ways... in didactic statements... [and] by showing how God works in the world that he himself made."[23] Today we must remind postmodern people that Scripture also teaches in a third way. Beside teaching didactically and historically, Scripture teaches artistically. Consider the three-dimensional meanings found in the God's design of the tabernacle and temple, the hymnody of the Psalms, the dreamscape apocalyptic literature of both Testaments, the nuptial ode Song of

Songs, the prophetic dramas of Ezekiel or Isaiah, and Jesus' (deliberately obscure) parables.

Indeed, according to V. Philips Long, the very nature of biblical history is conspicuously literary in style. He calls it "verbal representational art."[24] Finally, as Schaeffer's strategy stipulated a proper "order for... apologetics in the second half of the twentieth century.... Knowledge precedes faith,"[25] we now need to update that order for the twenty-first century. If knowledge preceded faith for the modern man, perhaps *intuition* of knowledge must precede knowledge for the cynical-about-truth postmodern man.

Long writes:

> [Jean-François Lyotard described] "postmodernism as incredulity toward meta-narratives"...[that is] we can no longer believe in any truth claims that declare themselves to be the key to understanding the whole of life. Whether they are the meta-narratives (grand stories) of Marx or Freud... Christianity, or the Enlightenment, they are no longer credible... In an age when bald statements of capital-T Truth are discounted, society turns to its poets and artists for the most truthful accounts of the human condition. "Grand Stories" may be treated with the utmost suspicion, but people will listen to any number of stories on a human scale, especially those that come from the depths of experience.[26]

I once wrote a poem based on Old Testament imagery. Sometime later, while teaching acting at a state school, I included my poem with the other texts we were performing. The students were rapt. "Where did you get this from?" asked one, a young man who was homosexual and HIV positive. I told them I had written it based on passages in which God speaks to Israel as his adulterous bride, and then we proceeded to work on the text as we would any other.

Some years later another student from that class contacted me specifically to ask for a copy of the poem: "I've lost mine and need it." In conversations with that young man, it seemed to me that the message of the Scriptures had somehow touched his heart.

I do not know whether he might ever have become a Christian. Nevertheless he once said to me, "I have no patience with all those university types who malign Christianity. Do they know what they're talking about? It's such a beautiful religion!" Postmodern man will not easily be evangelized with a propositional tract; we must gain entry by another door. Move his heart with an encounter with real beauty and he may just ask, "Where did you get this from?" After that will be the time to haul out our didactic propositions.[27] And then the truth will set him free.

Wit and Waodani: Attempts at Incarnational Production Practice

One thing Christians need to learn if we wish to work with the professional theater and film world is integrity in our business practices. Many likely would think nothing of editing a play which they found to contain objectionable material. But if a text is not in the public domain, such carving up of the playwright's work not only constitutes not treating my neighbor as I would be treated, it is simply a violation of contractual obligations. Since it's necessary to secure rights to perform a play and rights are generally granted with specific protections stipulated, if I cannot abide by an agreement to present the text "without any changes, additions, alterations or deletions,"[28] I must for love's sake simply forgo producing that particular play.

In 2004, I had occasion to correspond on such a matter with Margaret Edson, author of the 1999 Pulitzer-winning drama *Wit*. *Wit*'s story follows Vivian Bearing, a scholar of John Donne's *Holy Sonnets* who is dying of ovarian cancer. Vivian embodies the reality of *Sonnet 10*, "Death be not proud," as she discovers theoretically, then experientially, how that sonnet is "about overcoming the seemingly insuperable barriers separating life, death, and eternal life."[29] An uncompromising and impersonal scholar, Vivian achieves redemptive self-awareness only through suffering at the hands of her likewise uncompromising and impersonal student doctor Jason Posner. In one particularly gut-wrenching scene, Jason performs an impatient pelvic exam on Vivian, tactlessly recounting all the while how he'd aced her Sonnets class in college. The exam ends abruptly with a loudly uttered expletive as a startled but unapologetic Jason discovers just how huge Vivian's tumor is.

The play's final image, the staging of Vivian's death, reflects an earlier commentary on *Sonnet 10*: "Nothing but a breath, a comma separates life from life everlasting."[30] Thus, almost anticlimactically, following the pandemonium of the Code Team's attempts to shock her back to life, Vivian quietly rises from her bed, removes her ID bracelet, ball cap and gown, and stands naked in a pool of heaven's light, reaching skyward. Lights down; play over. "Very simple, really... death is no longer something to act out on a stage, with exclamation points. It's a comma, a pause."[31]

I was understandably eager to produce *Wit* at our little Christian college. But the play's final nude image, together with some occasional use of blasphemy and foul language, rendered it problematic.

So why not just clothe my actress? Why not edit a few words? Many might have taken that route. But I considered that sticky "love your neighbor as yourself" scripture? What about that bothersome contractual obligation to produce the text as written? How inconvenient that God expects the blameless one will keep his promises, even to his own hurt (Ps. 15:4).

I couldn't do the play. It was that simple.

But I wanted to do the play. I had to do the play.

So what to do? Do unto others as I'd have them do unto me—write to ask the playwright's permission to change her script.

How awful. I assumed she would dismiss me as a fundamentalist crackpot, ball-up my letter, and throw it away.

Still, I wanted to do that play....

So I prayed and prayed about the letter, asking God not only that this Pulitzer-Winning playwright would grant my requested alterations, but that she might even somehow find what I had to write oddly refreshing. When I summoned the courage to actually drop the letter in the mail, I tacked on a last-minute, it-couldn't-happen, yet-nothing-is-impossible-with-God prayer: "While you're at it, Father, would you please bring Ms. Edson to campus to discuss her play?"

Here is the letter I sent in which I tried to think through the issues when selecting a play for production: literary quality, philosophical weight, suitability for a given audience and for the particular cast and crew. The letter also demonstrates, as introduced above, attempts to love—to incarnate Christ for—1) my audience, 2) my actors, and for 3) a theater professional in the wider outside world.

August 10, 2004
Dear Ms. Edson,
Greetings from Lookout Mountain! It is with a measure of fear and trepidation, as well as fan-ish admiration, that I am writing to you.
For several years I have wanted to produce your remarkable play *Wit* here at Covenant College. For so many reasons, it is a play that ought to be produced and seen by the sort of faculty and students we tend to attract. As the college of a small Presbyterian denomination, we work

to achieve an integration of each of our various disciplines with the logical implications of our faith. As such, a play which so wonderfully "enfleshes" the meaning of Donne's Holy Sonnets is a Covenanter's meat and drink. More to the point, given a tendency our Presbyterian culture can sometimes have to produce minds-count-more-than-matter scholars, a play which treats similar characters via Vivian Bearing and Jason Posner might be a dose of much needed medicine. Our folk should hear [character] Professor Ashford's exhortation that, in addition to scholarly rigor, sometimes the pursuit of truth requires that we "Don't go back to the library. Go out. Enjoy yourself with friends. Hmm?"

After struggling for some while with casting difficulties, finally it is my hope to produce *Wit* in February 2005. But before I can do so, I must first ask you an unusual favor. As part of the integration of my discipline and faith, I impress on my student actors the necessity to take seriously the language and actions they employ onstage. It seems to me that the influence enactments have on actors' and audiences' hearts and minds is underestimated in the broader theater education community. What we do onstage really isn't all "just pretend." It isn't reasonable, for example, to expect two actors to walk away from a scene of physical intimacy unchanged. (Indeed, the casting problem I referenced above has to do with this very point. As a teacher, I must guard the tender hearts of my students. How does one ask two teenaged actors to perform a pelvic exam onstage? Enormously dramatically important and compassion-evoking there is no conscionable way to alter the scene. Nevertheless, there is no conscionable way for me to require my young charges to bring it to life in public. Problem solved however, as two of my most capable students were recently married, and when presented with the opportunity to play Vivian and Jason, they jumped at the chance. Hurrah!)[32]

So what, after my lengthy introduction, is the unusual favor I have to ask? It will come as no surprise that in producing plays at a Christian undergraduate institution, we pay close attention to such things as language usage and nudity. I would like to stage the final moment of the play when Vivian passes from death to life with my actress wearing, perhaps, a white satin slip, small enough to have been hidden under her hospital gowns during the show. Also, I am requesting your permission to alter some few instances of language–some few words in the closing Code Team scene, and a few usages of the names "Jesus" and "God" elsewhere in the text. I am aware that it is no minor matter to ask a writer for permission to alter her wording. I feel presumptuous, yet in my situation it is a choice between making such alterations or not producing the play at all. I hope so very much that you will give me your permission, since I want so very much to do your play.

Should you see your way clear to granting permission, I will gladly provide you with a list of specific lines and accept any input about suitable substitutions. Or perhaps you would prefer not to be bothered about such matters any further, in which case I will just go quietly and happily away.

I thank you for your time and consideration and look eagerly for your reply.

With warm regards,
Camille Hallstrom

>Here is Edson's reply:

August 14, 2004
Dear Ms. Hallstrom,
Thank you for writing to me about *Wit*. Of course I am thoroughly opposed to change of one syllable; of course, how would I ever know if you went ahead and did it anyway? You were sweet and honorable to ask, so yes, I give my permission and blessing.

I am interested in you and your work. Got some good grades, did ya? Summa slamma jamma; good for you! (I looked you up.) Theater and religion go so well and so awkwardly together. I'm curious how they're coming together for you and your students.

I have done a lot of speaking in conjunction with the play. I am asking you to invite me to Covenant to speak when you produce *Wit*. To me *Wit* is a hugely Christian play, yet I am rarely asked about that. I'm eager for the chance to talk–and listen–in a hugely Christian context. Inviting me will cause some trouble. (Look me up!) Your superiors will probably say no. In that case, let's meet halfway for a cup of coffee, just us two.

Very truly yours,
Maggie Edson

>She said yes!
>And more than that, she asked *me* if she could come to campus!
>Wow! This prayer stuff works!
>Still she was right. My superiors did have some hesitation about her

coming. For, in "looking her up," I discovered she was gay, living in a long-term relationship with another woman and their two little boys. Some discussion followed with the administration about how best to handle the situation. How might we bring this exceptional literary light to campus for all to benefit by without potentially stirring up a hornet's nest? We did not want a repetition of the infamous Knipper painting vandalism;[33] we did not want catcalls from the audience. Neither did we want impressionable students discombobulated by a currently hot social topic.

For her part Ms. Edson graciously volunteered that, though others might make an issue of her personal life, she had no intention of even mentioning it. She only wanted to talk about, and listen to us talk about, the play. Thus in the months before her visit, I and the cast and crew prayed that God would help us show her genuine hospitality; that he would keep her and us safe from needless, public contention; and that she might even, based on our production of it, see some truth in her own play that she'd never seen before.

What eventually ensued was a witty, erudite, and enthusiastically well-received public presentation by Ms. Edson. That experience has led to an ongoing relationship. Since she lives nearby, I will sometimes travel to Atlanta to see a play and then, perhaps, meet "Maggie" for coffee. Maggie is on the mailing list for prayer letters about my mission work in Uganda and South Sudan and has thanked me for making her aware of realities abroad she might not otherwise have known of. Several years ago she did me the honor of writing a recommendation to attend the Royal Academy of Dramatic Art in London. Perhaps most importantly, when asked whether she'd object to my writing about this history for the current essay, she gave her enthusiastic approval.

A year after getting to know Maggie Edson, I shared the story with a production company I thought might need the encouragement. Every Tribe Entertainment (ETE) had planned to produce a film, *End of the Spear*, in time for the fiftieth anniversary of the death of five missionaries (Jim Elliot, Nate Saint, et.al.) who were murdered in their attempted outreach to the Waodani people in Ecuador. After signing a fine actor, Chad Allen, to play both Nate Saint and his son Steve, ETE discovered Allen was a vocal gay activist. The producers and the families of the martyrs, particularly Steve Saint who served as a go-between for the company, the Waodani, and the families were shocked, but decided after much prayer that God would have them abide by their contract and keep Allen on, even though his lifestyle seemed so at odds with the legacy of the men he played.³⁴ Many Christians condemned, sometimes quite viciously, the film's producer Mart Green and even Saint himself for keeping Allen in the role.³⁵ Allen, for his part, was able to make the following statement concerning his experience with these men:

> I was anxious to meet Steve and when I did, in the most perfect sense, Steve was the realest person I'd met. He cried in our first meeting over dinner, I cried.... I remember writing [in my journal], at the end of the day... if nothing else comes of this movie... that's the kind of man I want to be.³⁶

In an email to ETE, having mentioned my vision to train Christians to become missionaries to the professional stage and film worlds, I thanked ETE for providing my students with such a valuable model.

I praise God for this entire situation! In addition to having a good film to share with my students, I have something even more important —an example of Christian production folk dealing in integrity with a representative of a community who has every reason to view Christians with suspicion and hostility.

Just as the five missionaries and their families had to risk so much to bring the Gospel to the Waodani, Christian dramatists are going to have to risk much to bring Christ to the broken, hurting, needy folk who populate the profession. Who could have foretold that God would use the very men who killed those missionaries to later travel the globe to bring inspiration and God's comfort to countless thousands? Likewise, who knows what God has in mind for the Chad Allen's of the world?

But be sure that your demonstrating Christian love and professional integrity to him when so many were criticizing, even slandering you will bring a great harvest one day. I am eager to see what story God is currently crafting as he intertwines Every Tribe, the Saints', and Chad Allen's lives. Maybe one day another movie will be made about that!

As we seek to share stories and Christ's incarnation with our postmodern neighbors, let's flee the temptation to hide in a comfortable, Evangelical subculture. Taking up his cross and following Christ can have unanticipated results. We may even discover our *"enemies will be those [in our] own household"* (Matt. 10:36). But God, who has made us a theater to the cosmos, is more than equal to the task of also granting us the courage and love we will need to *"endure everything for the sake of the elect, that they also may obtain the salvation that is in Christ Jesus"* (2 Tim. 2:10).

ADDENDUM

Director's Notes from the February 2005 Covenant College Production of Margaret Edson's Wit

Knowledge puffs up, but love builds up.
1 Cor. 8:1 NIV
For this very reason, make every effort to add to your faith... knowledge; and to knowledge... love.
2 Pet. 1:5–7 NIV
Speaking the truth in love, we will in all things grow up into... Christ.
Eph. 4:15 NIV

So what's this play about? Cancer, right? Death and dying, right? The indignities patients suffer at the hands of the almighty doctor, right? Well, no.

"It is a play about love and knowledge," says the playwright in several interviews. But even for one unfamiliar with Margaret Edson quotes, familiarity with the play's characters makes the point clear enough. Plot an axis "K–L"; "K" stands for "knowledge"; "L" stands for "love." Somewhere along this line we can place each of the play's main characters. Vivian and her student doctor Jason are mirror images of each other, both residing in the inhospitable hinterland of knowledge without love; they like facts, not folks. Senior doctor Kelekian moves a bit closer to "L." He is a researcher, but one who works to inject the human touch into his dealings with patients. We admire Kelekian for this attempted compassion; unfortunately though it's often pretty apparent that he is, in fact, *working* at it. At the far "L" side resides nurse Susie who "was never very sharp to begin with," who speaks soothingly to and rubs hand lotion on an unconscious patient, who would rather see Vivian die of cardiac arrest than be kept alive just so Jason and Kelekian can "know more things."

But is there no balance? Must love and knowledge be mutually exclusive? As we can see in the passages above, scripture does warn us of the potential for knowledge to make us arrogant and unloving; nevertheless we are called to increase in both. The trick is to keep the balance referenced in Ephesians. We must seek always to speak *Truth*, while striving ever to do so in *Love*. To overbalance on either side of the equation, to exclude one or the other, is to err. Indeed, to exclude one or the other is actually to exclude its opposite. We've all heard (*smirk*) what "to know in the biblical sense" means. In God's balance book, True Knowledge = Love.

One character in the play seems to embody this balance. Professor E. M. Ashford first strikes us as a ruthless academic, obsessed with the minutiae of semicolons and commas. But we discover that her rigor flows from her concern with "truth," and that for her, "truth" can be discovered both in the library and equally well via genuine human contact. Slowly, slowly, through her sufferings Vivian starts to learn that lesson as well. And here is where another of the play's themes emerges. Edson has said *Wit* is about "redemption," and about "grace." It is about what I've called above "the uses of affliction." Had Vivian never fallen sick, had she never seen her own failings mirrored in her treatment at Jason's hands, she never would have opened her heart.

In her analysis of one of his sonnets, Vivian claims John Donne "finds God's *forgiveness* hard to believe, so he crawls under a rock to *hide*." Whether or not she's right about the poet, this clearly is an accurate assessment of Vivian herself. And so, the God of severe mercies must perform painful surgery in order to save Vivian from her own tendency to "hide behind wit." Modern America doesn't much like believing in such a God. We want "God is love" to always mean "God is nice; God is cozy." But what if coziness turned out to be the enemy of one's eternal soul? *"You say, 'I am rich... and do not need a thing.' But you do not realize that you are wretched, pitiful, poor, blind and naked. I counsel you to buy from Me gold refined in the fire.... Those whom I love I rebuke and discipline"* (Rev 3:17–19). That this is often God's *modus operandi* is plain to Donne. "Batter my heart, three-personed God," he writes, "bend Your force to break, blow, burn, and make me new.... Dearly I love you, and would be loved fain, But I am betrothed unto your enemy.... Except you enthrall me never shall [I] be free, Nor ever chaste, except you ravish me."

Lord, know me. Lord, love me. Lord, have mercy.

1. Author's translation
2. Though this phrase implies I will only discuss the live performance art theater, much that follows also applies to recorded performance, such as in television and film.
3. For a quick history of interactions between church and theater see Camille J. Hallstrom, "Theatre as Incarnation; Toward a Vision for Redemption of Dramatic Art," *Presbyterion* 27/2 (Fall 2001): 132–146. For more detailed treatments see Jonas Barish, *The Antitheatrical Prejudice*, (Berkeley & L.A.: Univ. of California Press, 1981) and Robert Speaight, *Christian Theater*, (London: Burns & Oates, 1960).
4. Max Harris, *Theater and Incarnation* (London: Macmillan, 1990).
5. Todd Johnson and Dale Savidge expand the *incarnational* model to a *trinitarian* one, pointing to theater's "communal" nature which issues forth in sacramental "presence." Todd Johnson and Dale Savidge, *Performing the Sacred: Theology and Theater in Dialogue*, (Grand Rapids, MI: Baker Academic, 2009).
6. Lynn Smith, "Even Those in 'the Biz' Point Fingers at TV Sex and Violence," *Los Angeles Times*, March 15, 1995, http://articles.latimes.com/1995-03-15/news/ls-42955_1_home-improvement-show (accessed April 14, 2012).
7. Cf. the contrast, in Aristotle's study of dramatic art (*Poetics* 3) of *mimesis* (μίμησις "imitation") and *diegesis* (διήγησις "narration"). Mimesis *shows* rather than tells, by means of action that is enacted. Diegesis is the *telling* of the story by a narrator.
8. In recent years theologians are recognizing this similarity between church and theater in a newly developing field , "theatrical theology." Beginning with Catholic Hans Urs von Balthasar's monumental, five volume *Theo-drama*, Protestant writers include Samuel Wells, Kevin Vanhoozer, Shannon Craigo-Snell, et.al.
9. John Peck and Charles Strohmer, *Uncommon Sense; God's Wisdom for Our Complex and Changing World*, (Sevierville, TN: The Wise Press; Knoxville, TN: Master Press, 2000), 246–250.
10. David S. Fetcho, "Art, Action, and Revival," *Christianity and Theater*, 20/1 (Spring 1998): 12–23.
11. Fetcho, "Art, Action, and Revival," 16.
12. "[Sentimentality] denies, evades or trivializes evil… it resists any appropriate, costly action into the world.… Many people young and old maintain a total diet of stories in film and print which have impossibly unrealistic happy endings.… [thus] not facing or dealing with the brokenness that is in myself, my neighbor and in the world.… Christians, who have the right message to confront sentimentality, have instead too often been seduced by it." Dick Keyes, "Sentimentality and Its Costs," *International Newsletter of L'Abri Fellowship*, November 2009: 1–2, http://www.labri.org/inl/pdf/2009/fall-intlabri2009.pdf (accessed April 14, 2012).
13. Oscar Wilde, quoted in Gregory Wolfe, "The Painter of Lite™," *Image*, no. 34 (Spring 2002), http://www.imagejournal.org/back/034/editorial.asp (accessed April 14, 2012).
14. Wolfe, "The Painter of Lite.™"
15. Francis A. Schaeffer, *Art and the Bible*, (Downers Grove, Ill.: InterVarsity Press, 1973), 58.
16. T. Chris Crain, "Turning the Beast into a Beauty: Towards an Evangelical Theological Aesthetics," *Presbyterion*, 29/1 (Spring 2003): 27.
17. Crain, "Turning the Beast into a Beauty," 27.
18. Crain, "Turning the Beast into a Beauty," 28, 32.
19. "[One may suggest a Christian] theme for a play; but if . . . it does not appeal to [the writer, it's] . . . wicked and unwise to undermine his resistance. . . . [lest he] fall into the most disastrous of all errors–that of writing outside the range of his own spiritual experience. Then he will begin to ape the emotions which you have told him he ought to feel, in the effort to communicate to his audience the light which he has not himself received: you will have made his work bogus and himself a hypocrite—all to no

purpose, since bogus plays are without power." Sayers, "Playwrights Are Not Evangelists," 62–63.
20. Susan Jonas, Michael Lupu and Geoffery S. Proehl, eds., *Dramaturgy in American Theater, a Sourcebook*, (Belmont, CA: Wadsworth Cengage Learning, 1997), 409–410.
21. Graham Clay, Foreword to *Art and Soul, Signposts for Christians in the Arts*, 2nd ed. by Hilary Brand and Adrienne Chaplin (Downers Grove, IL: InterVarsity, 2001), xi–xii.
22. Schaeffer, *The God Who Is There*, (Downers Grove, IL: InterVarsity Press, 1968), 134.
23. Schaeffer, *He Is There and He Is Not Silent*, (Wheaton, IL: Tyndale House, 1972), 78.
24. V. Philips Long, *The Art of Biblical History*, (Grand Rapids, MI: Zondervan, 1994), 63.
25. Schaeffer, *God Who Is There*, 129, 142.
26. Brand and Chaplin, *Art and Soul*, 7, 15.
27. I write director's notes for the programs of plays I direct; see an example at chapter's end. Often, we also schedule discussion forums after performances.
28. Wording is taken from Dramatist Play Service's license for nonprofessional performance rights.
29. Margaret Edson, *Wit*, (New York: Dramatists Play Service, 1999), 14.
30. Edson, *Wit*, 14.
31. Edson, *Wit*, 14.
32. Deference to the privacy of the actors and audience was maintained in staging. Vivian lay on the exam table, her head angled slightly toward the audience, her stirruped feet slightly away. Medical drapery provided sufficient "willing suspension of disbelief" that a pelvic exam could be "seen" by the audience without actually being realistically enacted.
33. Edward Knippers' studies of biblical subjects include the use of nudes. Invited to lecture on campus, three of his paintings were slashed by a local Christian activist. "Covenant College Controversy Continues," *Presbyterian and Reformed News* 3/1 (Winter 1997) http://www.presbyteriannews.org/volumes/v3/1/covcol8.htm (accessed April 12, 2012).
34. Mart Green and Steve Saint, "The End of the Spear Controversy: Mart Green and Steve Saint Offer Answers," Eternal Perspective Ministries, posted February 21, 2010, http://www.epm.org/resources/2010/Feb/21/end-spear-controversy-mart-green-and-steve-saint-o (accessed April 14, 2012).
35. Randy Alcorn, "Perspectives on End of the Spear and the Chad Allen Controversy," Eternal Perspective Ministries, posted April 16, 2010, http://www.epm.org/resources/2010/Apr/16/perspectives-end-spear-and-chad-allen-controversy (accessed April 14, 2012).
36. "Excerpt from an Interview with Chad Allen," The DQ Times, http://thedqtimes.com/pages/castpages/other/chadendofthespearinterview.htm (accessed April 14, 2012).

SHARING CHRIST

A MAN WHO TOLD ME EVERYTHING I HAVE EVER DONE!

THE SAMARITAN WOMAN AND THE JOHANNINE THEOLOGY OF CONFESSION

Nicholas Perrin

PhD, Marquette University
President, Trinity International University
Deerfield, IL

It is a privilege and joy to write this essay in honor of my friend and hero Jerram Barrs. I had the opportunity of getting to know Jerram while attending Covenant Seminary in the early 1990s. He has left his mark on my life and thinking in countless ways—I could only wish that the mark could be more visible! As I reflect on Jerram, I am reminded of the Apostle John. There are, I think, several points of comparison. Admittedly, the first point of comparison is not presently so obvious; the second is more so.

First, history tells us that John was actively involved in ministry in Ephesus until the very end of his life. In fact, it is striking that the literary corpus traditionally ascribed to him (the fourth gospel, the apocalypse, and three epistles) are generally dated to his "retirement" years. I am no prophet, but I predict that Jerram, like John, will only grow more effective as he approaches and enters into his own retirement. For all we know, the best is yet to come. Amen!

A second and more presently substantive point of comparison between John and Jerram, and the focus of the following essay, arises as Jerram draws on this Apostle for his theology of mission. This should come as no surprise. Jerram, like many of his colleagues at Covenant Seminary, is a man of the Word. He has been deeply shaped by Scripture, so it is no wonder that we should find his thought overlapping with that of the biblical writers. In fact we would be rather concerned if it did not!

At the same time, most of us in our teaching and writing find ourselves returning to some biblical themes and authors more than others. This is nothing to be ashamed of. Rather this is simply how constructive theology gets done. After all, Martin Luther would not have the legacy he has today were it not for his love affair with Galatians. Likewise Wesley would not be Wesley apart from 1 John, and Yoder would not be who he was apart from the synoptic gospels. Whenever the conversation of theology advances, we can usually scratch the surface and find below that someone has been reading a particular author or portion of the canon in a fresh and interesting way. If Jerram's understanding of mission has a particularly Johannine character, then Amen.

Whether or not Jerram himself would be surprised by this comparison with John, I do not know. What I do know, or at least what I and many others sense intuitively, is that both Jerram's life and his writing have a deeply confessional aspect. That is, he writes and lives without a hint of pretense, as one who is constantly aware of his own sin and redemption, and he speaks of both with equal ease before God and man.

I suspect it is above all this trait that makes Jerram the evangelist he is. If confession is simply truthful talk about God's redemptive activity and oneself as beneficiary of that activity, then I suggest that for John (and Jerram alike), evangelism may be conveniently defined as the intentional act of directing Spirit-prompted confession into the public sphere. Having offered this definition of this way of looking at evangelism, I would like to take the remainder of this essay to explore it further.

Jerram himself speaks toward the necessity for such confession in his treatment of the Samaritan Woman (one of his favorite NT figures, I think). Turning to his book *Through His Eyes: God's Perspective on Women in the Bible*, we find our author quickly homing in on what is clearly an outstanding point of John 4:1–42. Jesus is eager to overcome various barriers. With an eye to the contemporary church, Jerram spells out the implications:

The barriers we raise might come from pride in ourselves and in our own convictions or from hostility to others and their beliefs. They might be barriers of condemnation because of what others think or because of their manner of life. Such barriers may lead to personal separation from other people, both for us and for our children. Believers in Christ can all too readily desire a kind of cultural isolation.[1]

As anyone who is familiar with Jerram's writings and teachings knows, this is a recurring theme. As he sees it, the greatest hindrance to evangelism is not any particular condition within our receptor culture, but rather a condition all too characteristic of the fundamentalist and evangelical sub-cultures, namely, the tendency toward cultural disengagement. The point, I think, can hardly be refuted. Of course the great irony here is that whenever Christian believers engage in this kind of cultural withdrawal, more often than not the nature of the retreat remains superficial. Even as these same Christians inwardly congratulate themselves on their culturally aloof state, or bemoan their beleaguered position, they are all the while unwittingly assimilating the most pernicious assumptions of the very culture which they had been studiously avoiding.

In another book, *Learning Evangelism from Jesus*, in a section also devoted to the Samaritan Woman, Jerram returns to the same basic point. This time he elaborates further on the heart's reasons for such isolation. It is well worth quoting at length:

So often as Christians we think it inappropriate or even ungodly to have friends who are sinners, to have any personal and warm social interaction with unbelievers. Behind this thinking there are several ideas. One is that unbelievers can only influence for the bad, and never for the good. We sometimes behave as if we have everything to give to the non-Christian, and nothing to receive. We imagine that it would be demeaning for us to acknowledge any weakness or need. Christians are supposed to "have it all together," and letting an unbeliever see that I don't have all the answers, and that I need or value what a non-Christian has to give me, or that I value the unbeliever as a person, might discredit both myself and the Gospel.

This is folly, for the truth is that we are always morally flawed, our theology is never perfect, and, like everyone else in this fallen world, we are weak and needy.[2]

At the root of these barriers is an inward pressure toward perfectionism, resulting in an over-estimation of oneself and one's gifts as a Christian and a corresponding devaluation of the unbeliever and the unbeliever's gifts. Perhaps this is due in part to our overselling to others as well as to ourselves the immediate effects of this-worldly salvation (and thus underselling future redemption), all because we have been inwardly convinced by the secular assumption that our fullness ought to be in this life. In any case, in our self-righteousness we as the Church have forgotten our own sin and even our finitude. For Jerram, evangelism cannot even begin to take place apart from the believer's willingness to check these sinful attitudes which stand at the root of the Church's isolationism.

If self-righteous pride is one of the major impediments—if not *the* impediment—to effective evangelism, then one must suppose that humility (the opposite of pride) must be seen as an essential component of the evangelist's demeanor and character. This much should be obvious from several angles. In the first place, imagination and experience would tell us it would be much easier for someone to be won to Christ through gentle appeals than through some kind of finger-to-the-chest remonstrations. In the second place, theologians down through the ages have pointed to humility's fundamental role as a Christian virtue.[3] If evangelism is simply an embodied and verbal extension of Christian being, then the evangelistic effort must depend crucially on humility. Personal experience and tradition concur. When it comes to evangelism, humility matters, and it matters greatly.

And yet despite the fact that most any Christian would agree in theory that pride obstructs effective evangelism, the practical problem remains. The phenomenon Jerram describes is a very real one. On one level, the most important level, this is a spiritual malady which will only finally admit a spiritual solution, a gracious outpouring of the Spirit on our hardened hearts. At the same time, judging from the history of the church, wherever we find spiritual sickness, we know that theological imbalance is usually not far behind. So too, in this case, we may ask ourselves whether, undergirding the condition of Christian self-righteousness and resulting self-isolation, there is a theological construction standing in need of revision.

I believe there is. Exactly what might be wrong with it, I do not claim to know. But in facing the self-righteousness endemic to the church, it does seem relevant that contemporary Evangelicalism, much like western Protestantism as a whole, has historically had an underdeveloped theology of confession.[4]

In part, this has to do with how we are accustomed to think about the Gospel. Inasmuch as "What we win them with, we win them to," it bears reflecting on the nature of the Gospel message as it has been traditionally conveyed in the modern North American context. Here, as one might suspect, there is room for critique. Even if Evangelicalism has rightly laid high priority on the biblical mandate to preach the Gospel to the nations, it has not always—as I have hinted above—formulated that Gospel with the objective and subjective aspects appropriately balanced. As a result, one may discern two lines of evangelistic tradition within Evangelicalism. One line of tradition tends to conceive the Gospel as a set of cognitive-propositional facts, assent to which secures the assurance of eternal life. On this understanding, in its extreme expression, conversion amounts to the successful reception of knowledge and mental agreement with its contents. Another line of evangelistic tradition tends to conceive the Gospel as an account of life which stresses the immanence of the Risen Christ and the pragmatic usefulness of that reality for negotiating day-to-day life. On this understanding, also in its extreme form, conversion amounts to a personal willingness to enter into a subjective experience. Both of these approaches to the Gospel get at important biblical truths, but both are naturally limited in their own way.

One glaring limitation of both of these accounts lies in the fact that they offer a vision of evangelism in which the act of conversion remains essentially private in nature. I remember well sitting through a number of altar calls in a large Baptist church with "every eye closed and every head bowed" where the would-be convert would anonymously slip up her hand for only the preacher to see.

But this common way of thinking about conversion has the unintended effect of radicalizing in our own minds the discontinuity between pre- and post-conversion life. If conversion is a strictly personal decision involving a private transaction between the individual soul and his or her God, then one's public life (including one's gifts, calling, and station) can be seen as having little bearing on that same decision, and vice versa. In this case, for the retrospective Christian, the only abiding significance of the pre-conversion past is its sin, a kind of erasure of the pre-conversion past and its common graces results. While we Evangelicals have been socialized to emphasize the non-redemptive quality of pre-conversion life, we have also been correspondingly reticent to recognize how sin continues to affect the Christian life after conversion.[5] Given these conditions, confession seems to serve most properly as part of a rite of passage into the faith.

Even if there is no objection to confession in principle, it is still far from clear for most western Christians exactly how the discipline of confession finds its place within the on-going Christian life. For most Evangelicals, confession takes place, if you are lucky, during the course of the Sunday morning church service, or as an occasional and *ad hoc practice*, reserved for moments of particularly egregious personal lapse or horizontal reconciliation. For most of us, too, confession is hardly integral to the rhythm of life, and certainly not in any sense intrinsic to our basic identity as Christians. It is simply not on the map in any meaningful sense.

The result of all this in our own formation is predictable. Without confession and without the keeping of short accounts with our personal sin, we will eventually lose our awareness of personal sin. In short order, we come to lose our sense of ourselves as sinners—*simul peccator et justus* (at the same time sinners and justified). "Sinners" become a category for the "other."

This is not to suggest that the cultural isolation Jerram describes can be completely resolved on the church's renewing its commitment to personal confession. The point instead is this: a spirit of self-righteousness plagues the Western church, and, if in the meantime we find ourselves with an inadequate theology and practice of confession, this needs attending to.

To be clear, I am not advocating a self-absorbed worm theology, which is but an inverted pride with alleged scriptural support. Rather, I am asking how we might re-imagine theology, our beliefs, and our practices in such a way as to integrate confession *coram Deo* into the map of our day-to-day existence. Whereas so much theology has focused on what God has done in abstraction from man (and so many evangelists have followed right down this rationalist trail) and so much other theology has focused on human experience so as to occlude the objective work of Christ (and so many evangelists have followed right down this quasi-Gnostic trail), biblical theology and evangelism are best served by their insisting that talk about God and talk about self must be consistently correlated. Such correlation necessarily takes place in the activity of confession, an activity which, again I argue, is assigned a central place in Johannine theology. And thus at this point, I turn to John and his account of the woman at the well.

In reflecting on John's story of the Samaritan woman (John 4:1–42), the evangelist seems to have purposely juxtaposed this woman against an earlier-appearing character, Nicodemus (3:1–15). This in turn gives rise to points of both comparison and contrast. Like the religious leader of John 3, the unreligious woman of John 4 does not immediately comprehend Jesus' layered meaning.

For just as Nicodemus is puzzled over Jesus' statements regarding being born of water and the spirit, the woman too is not entirely sure what to make of Jesus' offer of water welling up unto eternal life. Both conversations are private and semi-confrontational. Both revolve around the image of water and God's redemptive activity. There is a sense in which both characters seem to suspend judgment by the end of their conversations with Jesus, even though in the case of the Samaritan, a much more positive response ensues with the conversion of the townspeople (4:39–42).

So much for the similarities of the two stories, but what about their differences? The Samaritan woman could not be any different from Nicodemus.

He is a male Jew, who belongs to the social and religious elite associated with the temple. She by contrast is a female, a half-Jew (by Jewish standards), a supporter of the wrong temple, and a member—on account of poor moral choices she has made—of the lowest rung of her society. Jerram is quite right in saying that the woman's race, religion, gender, and sin separate her from Jesus. But it is also true that these same identity-markers set her on the opposite end of the spectrum from Nicodemus as well.

Yet it is the Samaritan woman and not Nicodemus who shows a favorable response. This does not mean that Nicodemus has utterly shut the door to Jesus' claims, for the subsequent narrative will show that the night-time visitor eventually comes around to a public faith (cf. 7:50, 19:39). Nor is this to say that the woman has all her doubts completely dispelled on meeting Jesus. Interestingly, as we will see below, the gospel-writer actually takes pains to show that this is not the case. But the very fact that Jesus explicitly reveals himself as the Christ (the Jewish analogue to the Samaritan *Taheb*) (vv. 25–26), together with the fact that she responds by fetching her fellow townspeople (vv. 28–30), demonstrate a level of receptivity that far exceeds anything we find in Nicodemus.

Here, as elsewhere in John, the decisive proof of one's receptivity to Jesus lies in one's willingness to publicly witness about him and even recruit on his behalf. The paired episodes also underscore a standing irony in John's gospel: namely that those whom one might expect to receive their Messiah do not, while those who are not of the Messiah's own ethnicity have embraced him (1:11–13). This is undoubtedly tied in with John's doctrine of election which seeks both to explain Jewish resistance to the Gospel of Jesus and, as part of this agenda, to preserve the absolute freedom of the Spirit to "blow where it will" (3:8) and alight on those who are born of God (1:12–13, 3:3–8).

In considering the contrast between Nicodemus and the Samaritan woman, we have a right to wonder whether the noted timing of the two meetings of John 3 and 4 have an especial significance. The evangelist records that Nicodemus came at night (3:1). By contrast, when Jesus meets the woman at the well, it is "the sixth hour" (4:6), noon in the full light of day. Were we to consider each pericope in isolation, we might be tempted to dismiss the contrast as relatively incidental. The mention of night betrays Nicodemus's shame in publicly meeting with Jesus, while the mention of noon highlights the woman's isolation from other women who would normally draw water in the cool of the day, nothing more.

However, the Gospel of John is not a string of isolated episodes but a masterfully wrought narrative where the various threads and pericopae must be understood in mutual relationship. Thus we should certainly not assume either that the large portion of discourse contained between the two pericopae (3:16–36) was inserted haphazardly or that it stands aloof from the events which precede and follow it. While commentators disagree as to where Jesus' speech to Nicodemus breaks off and where the narrator's editorializing comments break in, there is no need to be detained by the question. Instead, it is enough to point out that 3:16–36 serves not only as a transition between 3:1–15 and 4:1–26, but also as a hinge. As such, the editorial comments help define and fill out the meaning of the two encounters that straddle it. Within that pivotal text, we read as follows:

[19]And this is the judgment, that the light has come into the world, and people loved darkness rather than light because their deeds were evil. [20]For all who do evil hate the light and do not come to the light, so

that their deeds may not be exposed. ²¹But those who do what is true come to the light, so that it may be clearly seen that their deeds have been done in God⁶ (NRSV, 3:19–21).

The sharp contrast between light and darkness suggests a symbolic significance to the nocturnal and diurnal settings which, respectively, precede and follow this digression. John 3:19–21 hints that Nicodemus, at the present moment in narrative time anyway, falls into the category of people who *"loved darkness rather than the light,"* while the Samaritan woman stands among those *"who do what is true"* by coming into the light *"so that it may be clearly seen that their deeds have been done in God."* The added virtue of this reading is that it explains the relevance of Jesus' announcement to the woman that the Father is seeking worshippers who worship in spirit and *in truth* (4:23–24). As we shall find out in the course of the narrative, the Samaritan Woman herself will prove to be a worshipper in truth, which means—in the terms of 3:21—she is one who *"does the truth"* (*poiôn tên alêtheian*).

Tantalizingly, the evangelist gives us little direct explanation as to just what "doing the truth" and "coming into the light" entail. However, if the Samaritan Woman is an example of one who does the truth and comes into the light, we may perhaps find some clues as to the meaning of these phrases within the course of the narrative. Outside of the prologue, the first narrative mention of "truth" or "true" is in connection with Nathanael, who has his curiosity piqued by Philip's claim, *"We have found the Messiah!"* (1:45). Naturally, Nathanael is slightly suspicious and expresses incredulity that anything good could come out of a town like Nazareth (v. 46). At Philip's insistence, Nathanael nevertheless accompanies the early disciple. When Jesus sees Nathanael, he declares him, *"This is a true (alêthôs) Israelite in whom there is no deception"* (v. 47, NRSV). Nathanael in turn is astounded and declares Jesus to be the messiah (v. 49).

There are several interesting connections between Nathanael and the Samaritan Woman.⁷ For our purposes, the most interesting is the fact that both figures are directly or indirectly connected with truth, even as both entertain the possibility of Jesus' messiahship. To be "true" in this sense means ultimately to affirm this messiahship. In this respect, being "true" or "doing the truth" denotes one's membership in the imminently revealed eschatological reality, the community of true Israel.

Judging by Jesus' words to Nathanael (1:47), to be true is also to be free from deceit (*doulos*). We think back (or ahead!) to 3:19–21, where the gospel-writer insists that those who do truth expose the work of God in their own lives by coming into the light (v. 21). Coming into the light here implies not simply choosing a life of obedience but also, and more specifically, choosing to live transparently before God. In fact, obedience and transparency presuppose each other. Interestingly too, in the cases of Nathanael and the Samaritan woman, such self-honesty manifests itself not through immediate acquiescence but through an initial resistance to the claims made on Jesus' behalf.

We should not over-press this point since Nicodemus also asks questions (3:2, 4), as do Jesus' most virulent detractors. Nonetheless, there must be some significance to the fact that when the evangelist leaves us with two models of conversion, he leaves us with two characters who, for a time anyway, intellectually struggle with the claims of Christ's messiahship. This reminds us that conceptual struggle with the claims of Christ is no evidence of moral or spiritual deficiency but, on the contrary, may indicate an underlying—and ultimately God-honoring—commitment to truth. This is a point worth noting for pastors, evangelists, parents, and educators.

In reflecting on the evangelist's characterization of the Samaritan woman in ideal terms, it is helpful to consider not only the woman's reception of Christ's words but also her reaction to them. Picking up the dialogue at 4:16, we find that Jesus asks the woman to call her husband. She responds by claiming to have no husband, a claim which, much to her surprise, Jesus quickly confirms. She is even more taken back when Jesus informs her that she has had five husbands (v. 18). Whatever perceptions the woman may have had of Jesus up to this point in the narrative, clearly now she is giving him her full attention and quickly coming to the conclusion that he is a prophet (v. 19).

While some commentators and preachers have suggested that her turning the discussion to the proper venue of worship (v. 20) is merely an evasive tactic (much like turning a very personal confrontation to an abstract theological debate), this is hardly the case. The proper location of the sacred space was *the* defining issue separating Jews and Samaritans. Any Samaritan who had been convinced that she had met a *bona fide* prophet would naturally want to start with first things first. Who's right and who's wrong when it comes to God's chosen space was no trivial matter. The conversation continues until the climactic moment where Jesus reveals his own messianic identity (v. 26).

At this point, Jesus and his interlocutor are abruptly (*kai epi toutô*) interrupted by the return of the disciples (v. 27). They are undoubtedly surprised, as casual conversation between an unrelated male and female in first-century Palestine verged on the scandalous. The social awkwardness of the moment seems to have prompted the woman's abrupt departure. Headed into the city with the intent of recounting her discussion, the woman, the evangelist carefully notes, leaves behind her water jar (v. 28). Following the narrative thread, the woman's abandoned water jar (*hydria*) would have taken us back to the futile waters jars at Cana (2:6–7), all of which make much the same point. Just as Jesus indicated the imminent redundancy of the cleansing jars and by extension the Mosaic cultus through his miracle at Cana, so too here the woman's leaving behind her water jar implies that she is also poised to exchange the waters of Jacob/Israel (v. 12) for the promised living water (vv. 13–15).[8]

Understood within its own immediate context, the detail of the forgotten water jar also seems to be the woman's way of signaling her imminent return (much like someone at a performance or restaurant who intentionally leaves a coat on the chair while going to the restroom). It is as if the woman were saying, "I will be right back to pick up where we left off." If so, then the woman departs the well scene unsettled and in state of temporary suspense.

This is further borne out by her words to the townspeople: *"Come and see a man who told me everything I have ever done! He cannot be the Messiah, can he?"* (v. 29, NRSV). Initiated by the particle *mēti*, the question expects a negative response (as the NRSV helpfully brings out). Although she is willing to countenance Jesus as the long-awaited Messiah, she nonetheless harbors sufficient doubt to frame the question in negative terms, even to the townspeople she hopes to coax back to the well. Often when this passage is preached, we are led to believe that the Samaritan woman is instantly and entirely smitten with the force of Jesus' messianic claim. But this is simply not the impression the text leaves us with. Rather, it is a story of woman who on a chance encounter with a Jewish messianic claimant, finds herself strangely confronted yet confused. Inward ambivalence notwithstanding, she is willing to speak to this encounter, even to townsmen (*anthrōpois*) who would have likely been generally suspicious of a woman of such reputation.

The message which the woman conveys John labels as "testimony" (*martyrousēs*) (v. 39). Its content was simple: Jesus had told her "All I ever did." There is undoubtedly a hint of hyperbole in the phrase. Even if she and Jesus actually exchanged more information than the gospel-writer preserves, such a short interview would surely not have allowed enough time for Jesus to elaborate on every last detail of the woman's exploits!.Here her report must certainly have entailed some mention of her dubious conjugal history, perhaps along with some attendant details.

The details hardly matter to the evangelist. He simply wishes to draw attention to the fact that her actions ("all I ever did") have been gently brought to light through the incisive gaze of Jesus and that this in turn forms the basis for the woman's public testimony back in the city.

Still, unless we are prepared to dispense with our imagination altogether, it seems as if the evangelist intends for us to fill in the gaps. When we reconstruct the scenario in our own minds, we must surmise not only the woman's willingness to recount publicly the fact of her tainted personal history, but also to relay that this same personal history was a point of interest for the prophetic stranger. This in turn is hardly imaginable. In a society as scrupulous as that of the first-century Samaritans, without our also imagining that in the very act of recounting her story, she was also implying her own repudiation of these same actions. That is, in the very process of rehearsing her conversation with Jesus, she is fulfilling the terms of 3:21: *"But he who does what is true comes to the light, that it may be clearly seen that his works have been wrought in God."* Meanwhile, even as this is taking place, Jesus is explaining to his disciples, *"My food is to do the will of him who sent me, and to accomplish his work"* (4:34). Jesus has indeed been accomplishing the work of God: point in case is the Samaritan woman herself.

In all this, it is easy to forget how little the woman knew about Jesus after all. As I have pointed out, when the woman leaves the jar behind, there is every indication that she is still in process. She can only return to town with her experience of Jesus and a burning question: "This can't be the Messiah, can it?" She has bits and pieces from Jesus. She has much more from her tradition, some of which has already been contradicted by Jesus. There is so much for her to work out.

And yet despite her shortcomings as a theologian, as Jerram himself rightly notes, "[T]his Samaritan woman is a very successful evangelist!" (p. 287). Indeed one would be hard-pressed to find any more effective evangelist anywhere in the pages of the gospels.

The combination of the woman's lack of formation and unsettledness on the one hand and her ability even as a social outcast to rally a sizable portion of the city on the other hand is intriguing. It is meant to be so. For returning to the comparison with Nicodemus, we note the deep irony that whereas the official "teacher of Israel" (3:10) trails off into silence, an unlikely woman of ill-repute becomes the true teacher.

The point here is not that theological training actually impedes the work of the Spirit (unfortunately, such anti-intellectual Romanticism has yet to be fully exorcised from the church). Instead for John's purposes, it speaks to the unpredictable call of God and why Christianity was being resisted by scribal Judaism.

For our purposes, it speaks to the unpredictable call of God and reminds us that "having all the answers" and "perfect theology" (to echo Jerram's words) are not the ideals we have made them to be. If Christians today are made to feel that they need to "have all the answers" and "perfect theology," the question is, Who or what is making them feel that way? We must realize the fact that our most effective witness within the gospels is a woman who actually has very little in the way of answers. She only has a question ("This couldn't be the Messiah, could it?") and a statement ("He told me all that I ever did"). We have every right to surmise that it is not the woman's having the answers that provoked the response among the townspeople, but her willingness to speak publicly to her own struggle prompted by an encounter with Jesus, an encounter that ultimately demanded a new path in life.

The gist of the woman's message ("He told me all that I ever did" [vv. 29, 39]) is simultaneously Christological and self-referential and is thus confessional in the fullest sense. It is Christological inasmuch as it seeks to attribute extraordinary powers to Jesus, powers which one would only associate with a man of God. It is self-referential inasmuch as it involves a recitation of personal actions which violated the norms of the believing community. Her willingness to speak to her past is certainly not under any compulsion from anything Jesus said, but rather is a spontaneous response arising out of repentance. Thus when the Samaritans speak to the effectiveness of the woman's testimony, they seem to be impressed not only by the report surrounding Jesus but also by the response which Jesus had wrought in the life of the town's most wayward woman. In retrospect, palpable signs of repentance evinced by the woman's confession, no less than Jesus' preternatural abilities, seem to have paved the way for Samaria's first recorded mass-conversion to the Jesus' movement.[9]

The woman's forthcomingness in respect to her shame in the midst of an honor/shame culture can hardly be of secondary importance.

Instead, the narrative, together with the crucial interpretive key provided in 3:19–21, leads us to believe that her effectiveness an evangelist is to be substantially tied to her transparency, which in this case involved her own theological dissonance and personal sin.

This is no narrative-critical retrojection of the contemporary infatuation with authenticity. This is simply the evangelist's point. It just happens to be a point which lines up with one of the more promising postmodern concerns. If Enlightenment-style models of evangelism encourages the modern evangelist to assume a posture of mastery, certainty, and control (vis-à-vis both the evidence and our unbelieving interlocutors), the Samaritan woman models a posture of weakness, a good deal of uncertainty, and almost no control (as a social outcast she could hardly bully the townspeople intellectually over her claims). It is of course not only the Samaritan woman's model, but also, implicitly, that of the gospel-writer himself.

That the evangelist has a deep even paradigmatic theological interest in this story becomes clear on review of the broader narrative and its rootedness in the Old Testament. Returning to John 3, we see that John the Baptizer identifies himself as the friend of the bridegroom, even as Jesus is the Bridegroom and Savior (3:27–30). Shockingly, the bride is not, as any first-century Jewish reader might expect, Israel, but the world (3:31–36). When we come to the story of the Samaritan woman in the next chapter, we see the wedding imagery unfolding further as a weary (bridegroom) Jesus sits down by a well. In reciting a story of a tired man of God by a well who is met by an unmarried woman drawing water, the evangelist invokes two patriarchal love stories simultaneously. First is the story of Jacob, who met his future wife, Rachel, also at a well (Gen. 29:1–14, cf. Gen. 24). Second is the story of Moses, who rescued his wife-to-be at the well at Midian (Exod. 2:11–25). The stories and their significance would have been well known. Once both matriarchs take their respective men back home to their families; the rest is, well, salvation history.

It is no accident that the major elements of these patriarchal-courting stories also occur in John's story of Jesus and the woman, including the last-mentioned one when Jesus pays a visit to the kin of his newly acquired female friend (4:40–41; cf. Gen. 24:28–66, 29:9–14; Exod. 2:11–25). The parallels, which John exploits, are hardly arbitrary.

Once we recall that the point of these Genesis narratives is to explain just how the line of Israel would continue, we do well to infer that John is doing exactly the same thing with his "courting scene." If the original story behind the propagation of Israel begins with a man and woman meeting at a well, the story of the propagation of newly-defined Israel likewise begins with the one "greater than Jacob" and the woman at the well. If we wonder how this new Israel would self-perpetuate, the evangelist implicitly invites us to regard the events of John 4:1–42 as an ideal prototype.

Indeed, once the Samaritans conclude that Jesus is truly the "Savior of the world" (v. 42), the astute reader knows that the consummative union between "Savior" and world (3:27–30), promised by the Baptizer, is now underway. In this light, the incident of Jesus and the Samaritan woman is no curious one-off, but a symbolic emblem of the marital union between Jesus Christ and the world.

The Samaritan woman *is* the world. In this case, we must expect that the principles which Jesus uses to reach her (on which Jerram elaborates well in the two above-cited books), as well as the principles which she herself reflects (on which I have sought to elaborate), are paradigmatic for this "work of God," the mission to the world. How are we to carry out the evangelistic mission of God? John seems to say: by following the lead of our own patriarchs, Jesus (=Jacob) and the Samaritan Woman (=Rachel).

On reflection, this makes excellent theological sense. If Jesus serves as the chief exemplar of one who overcomes barriers of various sorts, then, as Jerram insists, Christians too need to be about the business of overcoming barriers as well. However, the mandate to overcome barriers as an integral part of Christian mission does not answer the question as to how, if at all, Christian community can be established so as to prevent the erection of sinful barriers in the first place (including such things as racism, sexism, classism, and regionalism). Herein stands the ecclesial significance of the Samaritan woman. Ironically, it is she as the supreme "other" and not Nicodemus who receives the empowering gift of the Holy Spirit. The outworking of this gift is Spirit-prompted confession, the weakness of which is, paradoxically, the requisite power to level sinful hierarchies and prejudices. As one who speaks to both Christ and her sin, she is not only the ideal convert, but also the ideal believer. It suggests that the tell-tale sign of the Christian is a willing transparency in regard to personal sin and even personal uncertainty. It is precisely these qualities—rather than "having all the answers" or "having it all together"—that mark us off as Christians.

Before leaving this passage, a final word needs to be said about the eschatological character of the woman's confession. As the first-century Jews understood full well, God's eschatological dealings with Samaria coincided with the moment in which God would gather the lost tribes from exile (Jer. 31:4–8; Hos. 8:6–10a). In fact, when John's Jesus speaks to the day when *"sower and reaper are glad together"* (John 4:36), the evangelist likely has in mind Jer 31:5 (*"Again you shall plant vineyards on the mountains of Samaria; the planters shall plant, and shall enjoy the fruit"* [NRSV]),set in the larger context of Jeremiah's well-known prophecy of the New Covenant. Included in this bundle-package is the promise of a new venue of revitalized worship (Ez. 37:26–28), which is obviously alluded to in John 4:24, along with the promise of deep national repentance, all following the pouring out of the Spirit (Ez. 36:29–32). Whether or not the historic Samaritans recognized the woman's repentance as part of the fulfillment of this promise, it is all but certain that the evangelist wants his readers to understand it in just this way.

This means, in the first place, that the source of the Samaritan woman's confession is ultimately not from within, but it is a result of the working of the Spirit, which has broken in through the ministry of Jesus. The Spirit's connection with repentance is touched upon repeatedly in the course of John's gospel (3:5–8, 14:25, 15:26, 16:8–11, etc.); the same Spirit no doubt stands behind the woman's turn in John 4. Thus the woman's request to Jesus, *"Give me this water so that I don't have to keep coming back to this well"* (4:15), is actually fulfilled quite literally through the giving of the Spirit. Moreover it is clear that even in the woman's witness and resulting turnout, *"what has been done has been done through God"* (3:21), that which is done through God is done through the Spirit.

In the second place, this means that confession is not an individualized reality but a corporate one in which all true believers share. As the evangelist seeks to show, the Samaritan woman is a representative example of a larger, redemptive-historical turn where the long-awaited promises of God, involving national-level repentance through the Spirit, were now being realized. Her repentance is not just any repentance. It is part and parcel of *the* repentance, which all believing Israel had been expecting. Confession then is not so much our personal badge we wear as individual Christians, but rather it shows that we are returned-from-exile Israel and the fulfillment of the glorious end-time vision handed down by the prophets.

Lest it be doubted that the thrust of what I have argued so far really stands at the hub of Johannine thought, it should be pointed out that this understanding of confession in John's gospel is consistent with what we find other Johannine writings. In 1 John 1, we read:

> *This is the message we have heard from him and proclaim to you, that God is light and in him there is no darkness at all. [6]If we say that we have fellowship with him while we are walking in darkness, we lie and do not do what is true; [7]but if we walk in the light as he himself is in the light, we have fellowship with one another, and the blood of Jesus his Son cleanses us from all sin. [8]If we say that we have no sin, we deceive ourselves, and the truth is not in us. [9]If we confess our sins, he who is faithful and just will forgive us our sins and cleanse us from all unrighteousness. [10]If we say that we have not sinned, we make him a liar, and his word is not in us.* 1 John 1:5–10

For the author of the epistle (who I, along with many scholars, assume to be co-identical with the author of the gospel), "walking in the light" (v. 7) appears to be a shorthand way of describing a life of confession (v. 8–9), and as such is prerequisite for Christian fellowship. By living this life of confession, Christians may remain confident that their sin has been forgiven (v. 7). Thus, the author very carefully stipulates that the criteria of membership within the community is not utter sinlessness (v. 8), but a demonstrable commitment to admit sin. If this is true, then confession becomes the very trait which sets Christians apart from the world. This coheres with the logic of John 4 because after all, it was the Christians who saw themselves as the recipients of the prophetic promises, including the pouring out of the Spirit.

Whereas we as contemporary Christians identify ourselves in a variety of ways and distinguishing ourselves by certain practices, beliefs, and commitments, very seldom in our thinking does a lifestyle of confession present itself as a compelling badge of Christian self-identification. This is a deficit. And it is a deficit which may have more than a little to do with the long-standing cultural isolation of the Evangelical faithful.

Perhaps the order of the day for our church leaders is a renewed commitment to a life of public, Spirit-engendered confession. Perhaps the order of the day for our evangelists is much the same. Through the narrative of the Samaritan woman, John calls for our willingness to speak not only to Christ's excellence but also to our fallibilities and weaknesses. For John, this is what it means to confess, to come into the light.

In order for many Christians to heed John's message, it would require a radical reversal in how they think about themselves, their unbelieving friends, and the nature of evangelism. For many Christian communities, this would also entail a deep retrenching of the boundaries of socially acceptable self-disclosure. (This also requires wisdom, for confession must be distinguished from such counterfeits as a gloating exhibitionism, a uncruciformed authenticity for authenticity's sake, or a Facebook-style narcissism.) For others, including perhaps Jerram himself, this is added encouragement to continue to come to the light. There is hope. If truthful and transparent talk about God and self are signs of the Spirit's eschatological activity in our midst, the Spirit intends to use the same talk to convince our townspeople that Christ is the Savior of the world.

---

1. *Through His Eyes: God's Perspective on Women in the Bible*(Wheaton, IL: Crossway, 2009), p. 276.
2. *Learning Evangelism from Jesus* (Wheaton, IL: Crossway, 2009), p. 48.
3. The words of Calvin (*Inst.* 2.2.11) are relevant: "I was always exceedingly delighted with that saying of Chrysostom, 'The foundation of our philosophy is humility'; and yet more pleased with that of Augustine: 'As the orator, when asked, What is the first precept in eloquence? answered, Delivery: What is the second? Delivery: What is the third? Delivery: so if you ask me concerning the precepts of the Christian religion, I will answer, first, second, and third, Humility.'"
4. This, however, is not the way it has been from the beginning. Simply to return to Calvin (*Inst.* 3.4.6–24), we see that he has an extensive discussion on the topic. For an overview of the history, including discussion on Bucer and Zwingli, see John T. McNeill, *A History of the Cure of the Soul* (New York: Harper & Brothers, 1951); Annemarie S. Kidder, *Making Confession, Hearing Confession: A History of the Cure of Souls* (Collegeville, MN: Liturgical Press, 2010), pp. 101–62.
5. This surfaces in the genre of the Evangelical testimony where there is some rhetorical pressure to devalue in a wholesale way "life before Christ" and likewise play down the struggle of sin during "life after and in Christ."
6. Where translation is not noted, the translation is my ow
7. Among these is the connection between Jesus' claim to be Jacob's ladder as the Son of Man (1:51; cf. Gen. 28:12) and the woman's reference to Jacob's well (4:6, 12).
8. So too Raymond E. Brown, *The Gospel according to John I–XII* (AB 29; Garden City/New York, NY: Doubleday, 1966), p. 173. Comparisons with the disciples' forsaking their nets (Mark 1:18) seem far-fetched; after all, the woman is presently still undecided on Jesus' messianic claim (v. 29b).
9. To be sure, John is careful to point out, a second wave of belief follows when people meet Jesus for themselves (vv. 39–42), but this hardly negates the importance of the preparatory groundwork laid through the woman's testimony of her own reversal.

LOVE, THE FINAL EPISTEMIC (AND ONTOLOGY TOO)

Esther L. Meek

PhD, Temple University
Professor of Philosophy, Geneva College
Beaver Falls, PA

People who have the privilege of knowing Jerram Barrs cannot help but hear him and his heart as they read his book *The Heart of Evangelism*. And that is a wonderful thing. He artfully models gentleness and respect and insists explicitly and emphatically that gentleness and respect are critically to any effort to invite others to Christ.

It is impossible to improve on Jerram's example or his counsel. But I would like to try to put them in a philosophical context, and thereby, show them all the more as the things one ought to be and do. I want to show that Barrs' approach to evangelism is of a piece with a healthy epistemology and ontology.

Epistemology is the philosophical study of how people know what they know. We all tend to picture knowledge as statements and proofs, as I will show. Our picture informs the way we understand Christianity and the Gospel, and also how we envision evangelism: it's all about statements and proofs. Where the emphasis is on statements and proofs, such things as gentleness, respect, and love are rendered incidental to knowledge. They are marginalized as "technique."

But if gentleness and respect are techniques, they are not gentleness and respect. If love is marginalized with respect to knowledge of the Gospel, the Gospel is not the Gospel. I submit that we've been pretty bad at evangelism at least partly because of a defective epistemology, one which can be judged to be a noetic effect of sin. Fixing our epistemology will contribute strategically to our efforts to witness to others regarding the good news of Jesus Christ. And it won't just make us better at the technique; it will change the entire dynamic to one that accords with our humanness, creation, and the Word of the Lord.

I appreciate this opportunity to acquaint you with the proposals of covenant epistemology, and to do that in honor of Jerram Barrs. In effect, I want to show that love is the final apologetic—a famous and true aphorism of Francis Schaeffer's and Jerram Barrs'—because it is first the final epistemology, and ontology, too. Simply put, love is the core of knowing and being.

First I'll talk about what I call our defective epistemological default. I will suggest how this defective default has adversely impacted all our knowing, our Christian discipleship, and specifically in this context, our evangelism. Then I will my propose how knowing works, for which I have appropriated the term covenant epistemology. Covenant epistemology is the thesis we take as our paradigm for all acts of knowing the covenantally constituted interpersonal relationship. Covenant epistemology places love at the core of knowing, thus rendering love the final epistemology. I will draw out its implications for knowing and bearing witness. Finally I will briefly suggest how love is arguably the core of being, rendering covenant ontology the final ontology, too.

Our Defective Epistemic Default

Epistemology is the branch of philosophy that studies how we know whatever it is we know. Education guru Parker Palmer writes that this six-syllable word doesn't exactly leap to people's lips. But:

The patterns of epistemology can help us decipher the patterns of our lives. Its images of the knower, the known, and their relationship are formative in the way an educated person not only thinks but acts. The shape of our knowledge becomes the shape of our living; the relation of the knower to the known becomes the relation of the living self to the larger world.[1]

According to Palmer, epistemology is unavoidable and critically important to consider. The shape of our epistemology is the shape of our lives. It shapes how we engage reality and how we apprehend God.

In thinking about how we know, a key preliminary matter is the question: what is knowledge? I argue that all of us children of the Western thought-tradition share a preconceived idea about what sort of thing knowledge is. We all are inclined to think that knowledge is information: facts rendered in statements.[2] The tacit assumption is that these facts stand by themselves and are disconnected from each other and from us. We tend to think of knowledge as static and timeless. We think our acquisition of it is linear and passive: we open our eyes and read timelessly true information off of the world. We tend to think that getting an education involves collecting information and that doing science is collecting data. I call this our epistemic default—our built-in, preset assumptions regarding what knowledge is.

Our Western epistemic default fosters pairs of opposites. It tends to privilege one member of the pair, knowledge, as over against the other, not knowledge. We privilege knowledge over belief. For example: fact over value, science over art or religion, reason over emotion or faith, objective over subjective, mind over body, theory over application, and so on. I picture this as "Esther's Daisy of Dichotomies." Put all the privileged members in the shared center of the daisy and that puts all the delegitimated members of each pair on this and that petal.

I do not need to argue to make the point that we do have an operative epistemic default. We all have preconceived notions about knowledge that inevitably shape how we go about knowing. Further, we may surmise that a problem with the default—a defective default—might adversely affect our efforts to know. And since knowing permeates every corner of our lives, that bad effect could be widespread. Since in our knowing we engage the world, other people, and our cultural projects, and since knowing is the fabric of our relationship with God, our Christian discipleship, and witness, all these could be damaged as a result.

We have our Christian version of this default. Many Christians, especially Evangelical Protestants, tend to think Christianity is about comprehensive Christian information. Christian information is what we listen to the sermon for, go to Bible studies for, and go to symposia for. It's what we die for—in the sense of, "When we get to heaven, we will know everything."

The dichotomies are widely operative, also. We regularly distinguish theory from application and truth from obedience. We distinguish the Gospel's informational content and presentation from our technique. Our technique is seen to include acts of kindness and mercy along with gentleness and respect; and these are deemed secondary.

I don't mean to pan information, facts, and theory, *except as an epistemic paradigm,* a model of knowledge and knowing that, as such, skews knowing throughout. This paradigm excises from our picture of knowledge and knowing several critically important aspects.

One central aspect is the very active dynamism of transformativly coming to know and be known. It excludes dimensions of knowing without which information cannot even occur or count as knowledge. Its dichotomies are false dichotomies. It cuts knowledge off from both knower and known (reality) and cuts the knower off from the known. It depersonalizes both and dishonors both. It foments disengagement, irresponsibility, indifference, boredom, cluelessness, hopelessness, skepticism, cynicism, atheism, secularism, and societal and environmental damage of all sorts. It excludes adventure, confidence, risk, wonder, and wisdom. I believe that it excludes Jesus, the Truth. It has actually thwarted our efforts to know and skewed our attempts to educate: we do not know or teach how to listen deeply to the real and therein to invite its gracious self-disclosure.

And the defective epistemic default, we may reasonably surmise, is contorting our well-intentioned efforts to reach our neighbors for Christ. Information, facts, and theory are problematic as an epistemic paradigm; the theoretical paradigm has also shaped our posture as persons. That there could be such an integral connection between epistemology and posture is something that the defective default gives no framework to understand—a sure sign of its inadequacy. But this has not stopped its shaping knowers' orientation to the world into one that is dismissive, disengaged, and thus damaging.[3] It has bred epistemological arrogance along with its privileging of analysis and critique.

In theology and evangelism this has fostered a snobbish exactitude, an adversarial and argumentative approach. In the best works of apologetics, many verbs reflect war: defense, offense, challenge, argue, combat, destroy.[4] In these activities, of course, the mismatch of approach to agenda (advocating the preeminence of *Christ*) is glaring, and damagingly offensive. It engenders an interpersonal approach that unbelievers rightly sense fails to accord with the Gospel. I believe this situation persists because Christians have not considered epistemology; or where they have, they have not imagined there being an alternative to the defective default. As Palmer says, the shape of our epistemology is the shape of our lives.

What I have somewhat playfully caricatured here as a defective epistemic default is widely acknowledged to be a modernist epistemology: an understanding of knowledge to which the entire Western tradition of thought and ideas has been inclined since its inception with Plato, but has been exacerbated—put on steroids, so to speak—in connection with modern philosophy beginning with Rene Descartes in the 1600s through the eighteenth century Enlightenment ascendancy of reason and to the present day.

Several Christian scholars have made the point that Evangelical Protestants have proved to have absorbed modernist epistemology deeply. One obvious irony here is that modernist epistemology delegitimates religion, faith, Christianity, and God. No wonder prospective Christians have epistemic issues! Missiologist Lesslie Newbigin argues that people in the West cannot even hear the Gospel due to the epistemological crud in their ears (my term, not his!).[5]

Other scholars confirm what I am saying here about Protestant Christianity and modernist epistemology. David Kettle, of the Gospel and Our Culture Network, designates modernist epistemology, the "theoretical paradigm." He writes: "In 'modern' society a theory of knowledge has established itself that turns theoretical knowledge into a paradigm for all knowing, including—in an act of 'logical inversion'—knowledge of God."[6] He says, "according to modern thinking, 'value' can be separated from 'fact' and is subjective and private." Kettle argues that the theoretical paradigm "has subverted the exploration of reality at the level of our deepest and most lively personal engagement with the real."[7] Working in the tradition of Newbigin, Kettle passionately argues that revising our understanding of knowing is critical to the reality of the Gospel and the church's effective mission in the world.

Recently, Old Testament scholar Walter Brueggemann has written, "A substantive decision is required of us, for modernity has eroded even our readiness to hold to the miraculous scandal [of the Resurrection]."[8] He also comments that "matters of life and faith cannot be expressed in the tongues of modernity, for [its technical epistemology, incapable of doxology], has consigned us to death and despair." Brueggemann has devoted decades to calling the church of contemporary Western society to re-appropriate a prophetic imagination that will subvert the royal consciousness of consumerist satiation.[9]

Our epistemology should shape our orientation or posture to something parallel to the Lord's. I argue that the epistemic paradigm, rather than being theoretical, should be the gracious, redemptive, transformative in-breaking of the reality of Christ that is the Gospel. I believe that the defective default actually hampers the Gospel: it prevents us from unleashing its rich resources for epistemology and knowing. We love Jesus, but we don't go to the bank on that epistemically because we don't do epistemology (and mistakenly think we are getting by without doing it), or we do epistemology in the tradition of the defective default, the theoretical paradigm.

There are successful knowings in everyone's lives which put the lie on this defective default—places where we get knowing right, and where a deeper, proper default of humanness in knowing appears. It's just that the defective default has blinded us to the epistemic significance of the places we get it right, maybe even discredited them as knowings, and induced them to atrophy. I maintain that being known redemptively by Christ is one such knowing, in fact, the paradigmatic knowing.[10] Redemptive encounter is the paradigm of good knowing.

So, Christians' defective epistemic default damages both our apprehension of the Gospel and our evangelistic effort. In the evangelistic situation, this is all the more damaged by the fact that people considering Christianity fall into the defective epistemic default too. Considering Christianity raises all kinds of epistemic reversions to a defective default because unbelievers in the West also persist in the defective default. This can come to the fore with a vengeance when they are asked to consider Christianity.

Unbelievers hear believers to be asking them to surrender their minds and rationality. Being faced with the risk of a life-altering commitment to a being who claims to claim you brings forth a stubborn demand for certainty and proof that one would have thought outmoded. One of the things that can help in this situation is for the epistemologically savvy believer to keep the epistemic playing field oriented to the Gospel. But this crucial epistemic move is just what is happening when believers exercise gentleness and respect (whether believers can explicitly articulate the epistemic value of what they are doing or not!). Love is the final apologetic.[11] A look at covenant epistemology will show how this is the case.

Additionally, the discipline of philosophy hasn't helped matters. Much current philosophizing, known as the analytic tradition and also used by Christian philosophers, tacitly presumes the defective epistemic default.[12] It is not that these efforts are of no value. But I believe there is a fundamental epistemic reorientation that has been overlooked and must be implemented if we are to salvage just about anything. Covenant epistemology provides this reorientation.

Coming to Know as Subsidiary-Focal Integration

Covenant epistemology is the thesis that we take as our paradigm of all acts of knowing the covenantally constituted interpersonal relationship. Covenant epistemology intertwines three strands of ideas. The first is Michael Polanyi's account of knowing as subsidiary focal integration, augmented to a more profound "personal" than he articulated in his *Personal Knowledge*. The second is a theological vision of biblical covenant as relationship. The third is a cluster of theses that I refer to as "interpersonhood." Briefly describing these three strands will give a sense of covenant epistemology.[13]

Twentieth century Hungarian scientist Michael Polanyi turned philosopher because he saw the need to reform modernist epistemology. In order to save science, he wanted an epistemology to reflect what scientists do.[14] He developed an alternative epistemology to offer what he felt Western philosophy had never furnished: an account of knowing that makes sense of scientific discovery—of first acts of coming to know. Polanyi's refreshingly innovative alternative model of knowing makes good sense of all our knowing, resonating healingly with our humanness and bringing knowing back into accord with what Scripture indicates about it. When I found Polanyi's work,[15] for me it was the missing piece I needed personally to justify my own Christian belief and to feel confidence in engaging reality.

Here's how Polanyi describes knowing: First the knowing experience we should be trying to make sense of is not explanation—information, after-the-fact statements, and proofs. The real question is about discovery—how do you come to know in the first place? This is a dilemma Plato posed which has never been resolved in Western epistemology and culture. How can we come to know anything at all? For either you know it or you don't. If you know it, you don't need to come to know it; if you don't know it, you can't come to know it. Coming to know—discovery—has been discredited by the defective default, just like faith and emotion have. Yet knowing is the act in which humans are most glorious and most engaged. Polanyi argued that the dilemma only stands as long as knowledge is restricted to what can be explicitly articulated—that is, stated in words. But people on the way to knowing, like a sleuth endeavoring to solve a mystery or a scientist on the track of a discovery, rely on clues that they half understand and on hunches they would be hard pressed to verbalize. And they must do so. Therefore we must accredit this tacit knowledge to these tacit powers. "We know more than we can tell," was Polanyi's famous aphorism.[16]

The act of coming to know, according to Polanyi, involves a risky, responsible trajectory of scrabbling to rely in the right way on clues to elicit a coherent pattern. This struggling feat he calls integration. We are aware of the clues, on which we rely and indwell them "subsidiarily." The pattern is "focal"—we focus on it. The integrative trajectory of a discovery can span minutes to years to a lifetime. When we achieve the pattern or make the discovery, we can experience an *aha!* moment. It is a moment when the clues we have been struggling to make sense of are transformed and we shift from looking at disconnected particulars to indwelling them subsidiarily—looking *from* them—to see the new focal pattern . The pattern transforms the appearance of the clues, and it transforms their meaning. We can experience surprise and a kind of recognition simultaneously. The achievement of this pattern, along with an exciting, unspecifiable sense of future prospects, inclines us to submit to it as a token of reality. Subsidiary-focal integration characterizes not only the first act of coming to know, but the responsible, sustained, developing, grasp of it. Thus, no knowledge can ever be exhaustively focal or explicit; the focal is always outrun by the inarticulate, subsidiary roots which ground it.

You are, this minute, performing subsidiary-focal integration, integrating from subsidiaries to a focal pattern. You are trying to get inside the clues of my comments to understand my message. You are reading, too: in this you are subsidiarily attending to marks on a page and hand and eye movements to focus on epistemology, of all things! If we were together talking, you would also be indwelling my facial expression, my gesticulating hands, and my tone of voice, to attend to my guidance and strive to make sense of the pattern. Subsidiary-focal integration is easily exemplified in reading, in athletics, in the creative artistic experience, in any learning endeavor. It helps to have in mind any one of these common activities as you process what I am saying about subsidiary-focal integration.

I learned from theologian John Frame that all acts of human knowing always have three interpenetrating aspects.[17] These aspects reflect the three ways God is Lord. God's Lordship, for Frame, is the single definitive feature that shapes our knowing as human creatures, "servant thinkers." God's Lordship, which is the capacity in which he covenants with us and all reality, manifests itself in his authority, control, and presence (or solidarity). This suggests a triad of the normative, the situational, and the existential. A single epistemic act—anything from calculus to cooking, from knowing God to knowing how to bodysurf—evidences these three interpenetrating aspects.

The normative is whatever authoritative word, theoretical framework, coach or teacher contributes direction or guidance and teaches us to see what is there. The situational is what is there—whatever setting surrounds us and the issue that draws us. The existential is whatever we the knowers, creationally and culturally embodied, bring to it—the place from which we move outward to engage the real, the situation, under the guidance of the normative. There is no human knowing which does not include all three inseparably. Dr. Frame insists that each is ultimate in its own way.

Frame's account is a responsible identification of biblical parameters of human knowing. But I believe that Polanyian epistemology reveals the mechanism of how knowing works. It helps us see that presuppositions or fundamental belief commitments, as well as theoretical frameworks in any field, are subsidiarily indwelt as we rely on them to move from them to a farther pattern. Also, Frame's three dimensions identify three sectors of subsidiary clues on which we rely in any act of coming to know. We subsidiarily indwell authoritative words and guides (the normative), the place of our puzzlement (the situational), and our own lived, felt, body (the existential), in scrabbling toward an integrative focal pattern.

In subsidiary-focal integration, the relationship of the focal to the subsidiary is transformative. Because of this asymmetrical, transformative relationship, coming to know cannot be a linear summation of information. It neither begins with nor results in exhaustive clarity. It vectors from formerly unspecifiable subsidiaries toward unspecifiable future prospects. Mysteriously, these unspecifiable clues and possibilities bind us more deeply and concretely in the world and beckon us further. Guided by a coach, you come to master snowboarding. You have a felt body skill that connects you with snow and slopes, and that opens future prospects to you; and the world comes to you in ever bigger mountains.

Coming to know is thus something more like my groping overture and reality's surprisingly gracious response. What's more, that overture involves my finding my way to living on the terms (including, anticipatively, its deeper rationality) of the as-yet undiscovered reality that beckons me. When reality self-discloses, the knower herself undergoes transformative change: we find ourselves changed in the knowing event. Often a discovery doesn't answer our questions so much as explode them, interrogating us.[18]

Knowing involves propositions, but not propositions as exclusively focally asserted. It involves them as professed[19] and embodied subsidiarily, as bearing indeterminately on a wondrous, mysterious, three-dimensional reality, a reality that breaks in and breaks open and transforms and ought thereby to reduce us to silence! And do not think that this dishonors words. Rather, it honors them more profoundly as we indwell them and let them guide us through doorways of allusiveness that evoke the real.[20]

Polanyi's innovative subsidiary-focal integration effectively redraws the playing field in therapeutic opposition to all the dichotomies of Western thought. It also challenges what is perhaps its most unexamined presumption—that knowledge is wholly focal and explicit.[21] Philosopher Marjorie Grene has pronounced that Polanyi's central epistemic proposal is "grounds for a revolution in philosophy."[22] I believe that it holds the prospect of healing culture and Christendom. Colin Gunton, Lesslie Newbigin, and David Kettle are others who have striven to appropriate Polanyi's insights to this end as well.[23]

Covenantal Dimensions of Knowing

The curious dimensions of the act of coming to know, as I have described them here, came to strike me as person-like. It suggested that not only the knower but also the yet-to-be-known, in some way, is personal. This led me to develop the idea that knowing, the relationship between knower and known, might be more fruitfully understood as an unfolding personal relationship. If so, then what knowers do is "invite" the real.

What is more, it appeared to me that good knowing practices involve a kind of covenantal self-binding. In particular, I found that Annie Dillard's chapter on stalking muskrats in *Pilgrim At Tinker Creek* furnished a telling example of how we bind ourselves covenantally in order to "invite" the as-yet-undiscovered reality.[24] Longing to know is like saying, "I do"—a promise to love, honor, and obey—in advance of and in invitation to a responding, gracious, self-disclosure.

My thought developed in the context of an intellectual friendship with theologian Mike Williams as we team-taught at Covenant Seminary what we together came to call covenant epistemology. Williams' important theological claim is that biblical covenant is first of all a historically unfolding relationship (in contrast to a mere contract).[25] The beginning of such a relationship is the gracious initiative of God; Williams emphasizes that the motion of the biblical story is never ascent, but rather descent—the descent of God. The end of such a relationship is not exhaustive information but rather the intimacy of interpersonal communion in friendship. This is not to eliminate pledge-like dimensions, but rather always to place them in the context of relationship and view them as constitutive of relationship.

The central covenantal relationship of Scripture and of history is an unfolding relationship that is a knowing of God. The definitive features of covenant thus describe an act of coming to know. It is reasonable to infer that, for human knowers in the biblical world that is itself the covenanting word of God, the definitive features of knowing him are also helpfully suited to all other acts of coming to know. We may acknowledge a fundamental accord between Polanyian epistemology and Williams' understanding of biblical covenant as relationship.

Interpersonhood

Even once we reconfigure the idea of covenant like this, we, in the substantially abstract Western tradition, hear the word "covenant" and automatically "noun-ize" it, depersonalize it, as Friedrich Nietzsche and Martin Heidegger rightly object.[26] We need an extra dose of attention to what I call interpersonhood. John Macmurray argues that an account of personhood, and a sense of one's own personhood, involves being-in-communion.[27] To be a person is to be in communion. It takes at least two to be one. This powerful argument effectively challenges the substance ontology endemic in the Western tradition, which has simultaneously depersonalized and divorced us from one another. The primordial, prototypic, instantiation of persons-in-communion, without which you would not be you, is the mother and child. The original constituting and the culminating and transforming instantiation of it, also without which you would not be you, is God and the human. From one to the other is a span of interpersonal communion that makes us persons. The fundamental dynamic of being, then, has more to do with love, pledge (covenant), and trust than with substance and attributes.

Grounded as it is in this all-enveloping dynamic, from mother and child to God and the human, human knowing itself has the dynamism of interpersonal, covenantally shaped, unfolding relational communion. What is more, this dynamic has a centering core: the face-to-face, transformative encounter. Here I have in mind Martin Buber's well-known I-You encounter. And James Loder offers a moving account of insight as transformation, in which the knower is re-centered through the gracious in-breaking deliverance of the face of the Holy.[28] Knowing —insight—requires something graciously breaking in from outside you. Knowing is Gospel-like, because knowing is Gospel at the core.

You should be able to guess that this account of knowledge resonates profoundly with Calvin's treating knowing self and knowing God as reciprocally coterminous.[29] It helps us appreciate that the reciprocity at the beginning of the *Institutes* is no mere logical technicality or even epistemic innovation (though it is that), but rather the palpable interpersonal relationship which is the core and context of human knowing. I believe that there is a back and forth of overture and response, a kind of dance of knower and known, that unfolds their relationship, toward the end of communion.

Having connected knowing and covenant, the yet-to-be-known can be seen as a person, personated, or person-like, and knowing as an interpersonal relationship. It's as if persons are in the vicinity. It is wonderful to have an epistemology that makes interpersonal— rather than impersonal—knowing the basic form of knowing. It is especially valuable, both for our spirituality and for our epistemology, to "accommodate" knowing God with such a model. But what may we say about non-human creation? I am convinced that treating the yet-to-be-known as one would treat a person yet-to-be-known is effective. The knower who comports her- or himself in person-welcoming ways invites the real's self-disclosure.

A motif that gets at all of this is that of reality as gift.[30] Where there is gift, persons are in the vicinity. Only persons give gifts; gift-giving is distinctively personal. It is always embedded in interpersonal relationship. As the Lord's instant-by-instant worded creation, reality is his gracious gift. So it is entirely fitting that we take for the epistemic paradigm a cultivating of relationships between persons, even if the yet-to-be-known isn't a person.

Love, the Final Epistemology and Ontology Too

To know is to invite the real. What we do in good knowing is not passively demand bits of information to the end of power and control. Rather, we may invite it the way we invite a person to self-disclose. We must therefore practice "epistemological etiquette."[31] If you want to know something, you need to comport yourself in a covenantally self-binding way. Think of any effort to come to know that you have undertaken; I wager that you can identify covenantal features in your behavior with respect to the yet-to-be-known!

To invite, to welcome, is active and passive simultaneously. It is to create a hospitable space of noticing regard in which the yet-to-be-known is welcomed to freely self-disclose.[32] It means conferring dignity, in delighted notice, on the yet-to-be-known, being committed to attending patiently to it. Delight, says David Bentley Hart, is the premise of any sound Christian epistemology.[33]

The fundamental dynamic of coming to know is a responsible, risky, passionate commitment, where commitment is this disposing ourselves toward the yet-to-be-known. This fundamental dynamic is, thus, longing and love. This means caring in hope of knowing. I argue that we do not know in order to love; we love in order to know. This involves what Catholic mystic Simone Weil calls, creative attention. It actually brings reality to be more itself in a new way. "Love sees what is invisible," she says; she is talking about the Good Samaritan's attention to the inert lump of flesh in the gutter, which thereby creates him as a human person.[34] You can see how this would be healing: knowing for shalom.

We love in order to know. In addition to love, the effort calls for faithfulness, patience, respect, and humility. It involves putting yourself in the way of the yet-to-be-known—in the place it is likely to reveal itself. It involves learning to live life on the terms of the yet-to-be-known.

It means listening long and beyond our preconceived categories. As Martin Buber says of his famous I-You mode of being, it involves "Saying 'You' and listening."[35] It requires exercising a humility and vulnerable, risky openness to being known in the process. As Abraham Joshua Heschel indicates, in contrasting the Greeks and the Jews, we must learn not in order to comprehend so much as in order to be apprehended.[36]

The act of coming to know is an event that unfolds through time, from nothing to notice to imaginative striving guided by an unspecifiable sense of proximity to the solution (Polanyi's phrase), to an *aha!* moment that reconfigures everything we thought we were endeavoring to rely on and more besides. It takes us up in an adventure, a quest, a pilgrimage from need toward shalom. This unfolds dynamically as a relationship of mutuality between knower and known, a dance of overture and response.

The integrative moment of insight, when it comes, also gives us a sense that reality didn't answer our questions so much as change the questions and transform us in the process. You also have the sense that reality has disclosed itself in an act of unmerited grace and that in this you have been blessed by the descent of God.

Your heart that loves Jesus may now be resonating with this picture of knowing. All this suggests that in even the simplest effort to know there is a gracious coming of God, and that the paradigm of knowing, the proper epistemic default, is none other than our being encountered redemptively by Christ. Indeed, the Supper at Emmaus, in which the disciples' eyes were opened in the breaking of the bread, and our regular enactment of it in the Eucharist, gives us the model for all knowing. Yes, this pertains to knowing muskrats and neurology as well as to knowing your neighbor and your community. But what else would you expect in a creation that is God's gracious self-revelation?

That leads me to say: we may affirm that love is the core of all things, as Colin Gunton says.[37] Reality is gift, God's moment-by-moment gift. He says, "let there be"—he consents to being—and that is utterly gracious. Each atom with its mysteries, and the whole taken together, is his word, his presence, the exuberant overflow of the Trinity's dance of delight and love. Thus, love is the final epistemology because it is first the final ontology. Relationality is the core of reality, rendering reality, even the ordinary, wonder-full through and through.[38]

Covenant Epistemology and Evangelism

Covenant epistemology redraws knowing in such a way that love is its core dynamism. This may come as a surprise to you, but I think you might find it a welcome one. It accords with our heart's cry, our humanness. It accords with that wherein we image God: love.

Yes, sin warps all of us and sets us in rebellion against God. But do we not have to acknowledge that love outruns rebellion, and good, evil?

And when we consider the noetic effects of sin, as I have already noted, does that not include disinterested information gathering and proof in a world yet charged with the grandeur of God? To affirm these claims is not to minimize the ravages of rebellion, but rather to maximize the greater reality of God. In fact, understanding the core relationality and intimacy of knowing and being makes better sense of how sin is so tragic and catastrophic. For truth is troth, as Parker Palmer argues.[39] Knowing is shot through with the dynamic of trust, as is all of being.

I submit that covenant epistemology shows that the dynamics of healthy evangelism are the dynamics of healthy knowing. Understanding that we love in order to know orients us in a posture of care, disposed to engage the real. The not-yet-believer is deeply real and displays the glory of God in good measure. Their rebellion against God, Calvin indicates, is as intimate as our submission; and they are not far from the kingdom.

To know them is to invite the real. In the evangelistic relationship, it is to invite the real in unbelievers—to invite them in a way that draws them more fully to being truly themselves. It may be an act of creative attention. Also, it is to invite God himself—to look for and welcome what God is already at work doing in unbelievers' lives. It is to welcome humbly the incursion of the real in our own lives, for which unbelievers may serve as God's instrument of choice. It is to invite the real in relationship between us and them. All this should describe our relationship not only with individuals but with our communities in their need of healing and wholeness.[40]

Gentleness and respect, Jerram Barrs' signature qualities and stipulations, are practices of epistemological etiquette that invite the real. These create the welcoming space of noticing regard. With the orientation of covenant epistemology to the adventure of knowing for shalom, what he recommends as the heart of evangelism ceases to be an awkward technique and begins to be the heart of healthy knowing, being, and doing.

Covenant epistemology accords deeply with evangelism not only because love is the final apologetic, but because the unbeliever's conversion is itself the paradigm of all knowing; for conversion is the gracious, redemptive, transformative, descent of God. Understanding that this is what we invite in an especially meaningful way orients us to live life on its terms. Anticipating this—and nothing short of it—accords the event its true *gravitas*. For while assent—or better, profession—is conversion's critical component, if it is bare assent it is liable to be untrue. When Thomas understood that he perceived Jesus raised from the dead, he did not say, "That's correct." He said, no doubt from the floor where he suddenly lay on his face, *"My Lord and my God!"* (John 20:28).

Also, covenant epistemology makes it clear that conversion is embedded in an ongoing transformation that develops us to be more fully human, more fully who we are. We become more fully ourselves in the delighted gaze of the face of the Other.[41] We grow in love and in imaging the one who is love—these are Barrsian themes as well.[42] And this personal growth in love, to come full circle, will make us better knowers. We believe—and trust and love—in order to understand. And that is the heart of evangelism.

---

1. Parker Palmer, *To Know As We Are Known: Education as a Spiritual Journey* (San Francisco: Harper Collins SanFrancisco, 1966), 21.
2. Esther Lightcap Meek, *Loving to Know: Introducing Covenant Epistemology* (Eugene, OR: Cascade, 2011), 3–30. The following several paragraphs partially reflect this chapter, titled, "The Need for Epistemological Therapy."
3. These assessments are from Colin Gunton, *The One, the Three, and the Many* (Cambridge: Cambridge University Press, 1993). I engage this book in ch. 11 of *Loving to Know*.
4. I will refrain from naming the particular book from which I cull this list. I understand the deep love of the Lord that regularly prompts such zeal. Comparing this book and Barrs' *Heart of Evangelism* reveals that both endeavor to make sense of 1 Peter 3:15. That the two books contrast glaringly with regard to posture makes my case convincingly. I understand that there is biblical warrant and the example of Jesus to support confrontation. Speaking the truth in love—what that looks like and how to embody it —is a matter for deep wisdom. What I am arguing here is that a defective epistemic default common to the Western tradition fosters—and blinds us to—this discordant posture. Additionally, in the reformational tradition an adversarial posture has resulted from undue emphasis on antithesis over common grace. But this too, I would argue, can be rectified with an epistemological reorientation and an epistemology that accounts for their coexistence. I believe that covenant epistemology achieves both. See Meek, "Anticipative Knowing and Common Grace," *Loving to Know*, Texture 4, 184–192.
5. See Lesslie Newbigin, *The Gospel in a Pluralist Society* (Grand Rapids, MI: Eerdmans, 1989); Lesslie Newbigin, *Proper Confidence: Faith, Doubt and Certainty in Christian Discipleship* (Grand Rapids, MI: Eerdmans, 1995).
6. David J. Kettle, *Western Culture in Gospel Context: Towards the Conversion of the West; Theological Bearings for Mission and Spirituality* (Eugene, OR: Cascade Books, 2011), 30.
7. Kettle, *Western Culture*, 32.
8. Walter Brueggemann, *Truth-telling as Subversive Obedience* (Eugene, OR: Cascade Books, 2011), 50–51.
9. Walter Brueggemann, *The Prophetic Imagination*, 2nd ed. (Minneapolis: Fortress, 2001).
10. I suggest that many Christians also have a defective apprehension of the Gospel, one that thwarts their apprehension of it in the most personal way. Their experience often is not characterized by the delighted anticipation of the continual coming of Christ in intimate encounter and transformation. This malady has its epistemic dimension. But

of course, defacing the Gospel is the thing that sin would target preeminently. That's why the Apostle Paul gets crass in his anger against legalism (Galatians 5).
11. Francis Schaeffer, *The Mark of a Christian* (Downers Grove, IL: IVP Books, 1971), 29. This exact phrase does not appear there, but has become a common way in which Jerram Barrs and many others speak of the way the Lord calls Christians to interact with unbelievers.
12. Esther L. Meek, "Michael Polanyi and Alvin Plantinga: Help From Beyond the Walls" *Philosophia Christi* 14: 1 (2012), 57–77. There is also much philosophical work, especially in the twentieth century Heideggerian tradition, which effectively challenges the defective Western default. See Martin Heidegger, *Basic Writings*, rev. and expanded ed., David Krell, ed., (New York: HarperCollins, 1993).
13. These three are the topics of Parts 2, 3 and 4 of *Loving to Know*.
14. The definitive biography of Polanyi is William Taussig Scott and Martin X. Moleski, S.J. *Michael Polanyi: Scientist and Philosopher* (New York: Oxford University Press, 2005).
15. I first learned of Polanyi's work from a young man who had visited Francis Schaeffer at L'Abri in the 1970s, and who had lent me his copy of *Personal Knowledge*. Michael Polanyi, *Personal Knowledge: Towards a Post-Critical Philosophy* (Chicago: University of Chicago Press, 1962).
16. Michael Polanyi, *The Tacit Dimension* (Chicago: University of Chicago Press, 2009), ch. 1. This lecture, called "Tacit Knowing," provides a short entrée into his work. The synopsis I provide can be found there, as well as in several other essays.
17. John Frame, *The Doctrine of the Knowledge of God* (Phillipsburg, NJ: P&R, 1987).
18. Esther Lightcap Meek, *Longing to Know: The Philosophy of Knowledge for Ordinary People* (Grand Rapids: Brazos, 2003), 192–198.
19. In *Loving to Know*, I follow Polanyi's account of truth as responsible personal commitment with universal intent. I use the word "profession" to represent this. Meek, *Loving to Know*, 63 et passim.
20. I make this point because I know of Jerram's scholarship in and appreciation for literature. From Calvin Seerveld I draw the wonderful word "allusive." See Calvin Seerveld, *Rainbows for a Fallen World: Aesthetic Life and Artistic Task* (Toronto: Tuppence, 1980). See also Graham Dunstan Martin, "The Tacit Dimension of Poetic Imagery," *British Journal of Aesthetics* 19 (Spring 1979), 99–111.
21. See further Meek, "Polanyi and Plantinga."
22. Marjorie Grene, "Tacit Knowing: Grounds for a Revolution in Philosophy," *Journal of the British Society for Phenomenology* 8 (October 1977), 164–71.
23. Gunton, *The One, the Three, and the Many*; Newbigin, *Proper Confidence*; Kettle, *Western Culture*.
24. Annie Dillard, *Pilgrim at Tinker Creek*, (New York: HarperCollins, 1974), ch. 11; Meek, *Loving to Know*, ch. 2.
25. Michael D. Williams, *Far As The Curse Is Found: The Biblical Drama of Redemption* (Phillipsburg, NJ: P&R, 2005). Meek, *Loving to Know*, ch. 7.
26. Nietzsche speaks mirthfully of the "Egypticism" of philosophers, who turn concepts into concept mummies by sucking the life out of them. Friedrich Nietzsche, *Twilight of the Idols*, in *The Portable Nietzsche*, trans. and ed. by Walter Kauffman (New York: Penguin, 1954), 479. Martin Heidegger's *Being and Time* employs the phenomenological method to expose our penchant for substantival ontology which easily eclipses the continual question of fundamental ontology along with our *Dasein*. Martin Heidegger, "Introduction," *Being and Time* (San Francisco: HarperSanFrancisco, 1962), 21–66.
27. John Macmurray, *Persons in Relation* (Atlantic Highlands, NJ: Humanities, 1991). Meek, *Loving to Know*, ch. 8
28. Martin Buber, *I and Thou*, trans. Walter Kaufmann (New York: Charles Scribner's Sons, 1970); James E. Loder, *The Transforming Moment*, 2nd ed. (Colorado Springs: Helmers and Howard, 1989); Meek, *Loving to Know*, chs. 9 and 10.

29. John Calvin, *Institutes of the Christian Religion*, Ford Lewis Battles, trans., John T. McNeill, ed. Library of Christian Classics, 2 vols. (Philadelphia: Westminster, 1960), I,1.1. It also accords with Herman Dooyeweerd's location of the human as before God in the intimacy of the first verses of Psalm 139: *"Oh LORD, you have searched me and you know me." In the Twilight of Western Thought,* (Nutley, NJ: Craig, 1980), 189. The same depersonalizing tendency must be combated with respect to the word "heart".
30. I interact with this concept in the work of Phillip Rolnick in *Person, Grace, and God* (Grand Rapids, MI: Eerdmans, 2007) in *Loving to Know*, 365–82
31. The following and several other practices of epistemological etiquette I describe in *Loving to Know*, 425–68.
32. The notion of welcome I draw from George Steiner, *Real Presences* (Chicago: University of Chicago Press, 1989), 146–9.
33. David Bentley Hart, *The Beauty of the Infinite* (Grand Rapids, MI: Eerdmans, 2003), 253.
34. Simone Weil, *Waiting for God*, trans. Emma Craufurd (New York: HarperCollins, 2001), 92.
35. Martin Buber, *I and Thou;* trans. Walter Kaufmann (New York: Charles Scribner's Sons, 1970), 62.
36. This is my colleague Robert Frazier's paraphrase of Heschel's outlook. Personal conversation.
37. Gunton, *The One, the Three and the Many*, 179.
38. Esther L. Meek, "It's a Wonder-full Life." 2012 Commencement Speech, Providence Christian College, Pasadena, CA, May 5, 2012.
39. Palmer, *To Know as We are Known*, 31–32.
40. Esther L. Meek, "Knowing for Shalom in Aliquippa," Conway Alliance Church Symposium on Biblical Justice, Feb 25, 2012.
41. Meek, *Loving to Know*, Texture 6: "A Sense of Personal Beauty," 298–309.
42. Ranald Macaulay and Jerram Barrs, *Being Human: The Nature of Spiritual Experience* (Downers Grove, IL: InterVarsity, 1978), ch. 1.

TURNING MY EASTERN WORLDVIEW UPSIDE DOWN

InKyung Sung

Director, L'Abri Fellowship Korea
Lecturer, School of Christian Worldview
Yangyang, Korea

The Story of My Name

Everyone's name comes with significant meanings and memories. Behind my name is an interesting history of three Eastern worldviews. Let me first tell you the story of my name before I explain what has happened to my worldview.

My family name, "Sung," goes back to AD 1144 when In Bo Sung started a new clan in the southeast of the Corea Dynasty—the kingdom from which modern Korea derives its name. Indirectly, In Bo's lineage can be further traced to the ancient Zhou Dynasty in China, but records of this era are scarce. In Bo was a scholar and public official who did not leave much of a legacy except as the officially recognized founder of the Sung family. I belong to the twenty-fifth generation of Sungs since In Bo and am the first of my parents' four children.

The second character of my given name, "Kyung," means "feast." It is a generation character assigned by convention to virtually all male Sungs in my generation. My parents used to call me "Kyung-A" as an affectionate nickname.

But by far the most interesting part of my name is the first character, "In." I wasn't called by that name when I was young; I had two other names before I received my current name.

When I was born, I was called "Pat Kyung," meaning "farm feast," because I was born under an apple tree on a farm. Despite the generation character, it wasn't a particularly festive birth. My parents' landlords had a six-month-old son, and they had a Shamanist/Taoist superstition that if two babies are born under the same roof in the same year, one of them would catch a disease and die. So, my mother was asked to leave at the last moment of her labor. Having nowhere to go in the midsummer heat, she sought the shade of an apple tree.

A few years later, my father was diagnosed with stomach cancer and I caught a mild case of polio. In accordance with the Buddhist belief that any illness could be healed if one made an offering of a golden Buddha, my parents made the very expensive gift to a local temple. A monk at the temple unexpectedly gave me a new name, "Pan Kyung," meaning "sold feast." Some of my parents' friends still call me by that name, remembering me as the child who was sold to Buddha in exchange for health.

But the golden idol, of course, could not give us anything regardless of how expensive a gift we gave him. My father soon discovered that his cancer would kill him, and that his only hope would be the one and truly powerful God. After my family became Presbyterian Christians through a miraculous healing of my father's cancer, my father decided to change my name again, this time to "In Kyung." Little did he know that he had merely switched the symbol of one non-Christian worldview with that of another. "In," meaning "sincerity," "benevolence," and "love of heavens and neighbors," is the central idea of Confucianism according to the Korean philosopher, Yak Yong Jung (1762–1836).

These three worldviews, Taoism, Buddhism, and Confucianism, as Alfred North Whitehead pointed out, are religions as well as philosophies, and their histories together define the history of the East.[1] Since I was so deeply immersed in them as to have had names corresponding to each of them, it comes as no surprise that my life was profoundly influenced by a mixture of the three, not only religiously but also intellectually.

It was Jerram Barrs, along with my other tutors Ranald Macaulay,

Barry Seagren, and Richard Winter, who helped me to overcome the false religions of the East during my stay at English L'Abri in 1984–87. I had to turn two fundamental assumptions upside down in the process: the concept of truth and the way of knowing it. In this essay, I would like to introduce you to the reality of three major Eastern religions and philosophies—Taoism, Buddhism and Confucianism—and how much I struggled under their deleterious influences until, one day, Jerram asked me to write an essay to find out the Truth.

Taoism

The function of Tao is well expressed in three concepts: production without possession, action without self-assertion, and development without dominion. The three categories called possession, self-assertion, and dominion are the virtues that Western and Eastern people have been seeking for a long time.

The word "Tao" is literally equivalent to the Greek *he hyedos*, which means "the way." But it is not easy to translate the exact concept of Tao into English, because it is an extremely complicated idea. For example, Tao can be understood as "the Way," "the Rationality," "the Supreme Reason," "the Divine Being," "a Way of the Sages," "How Things Happen," etc. Today Tao is often interpreted as "the Ultimate Reality."[2]

Not True to the Way Things Are but Anything Goes

Lao Tzu, in his book *Tao Teh Chin*, wrote, "There is nothing better than *moderation*. The student of Tao is free from his own ideas. Tao is as accepting as the sky, as consistent as the sunrise, as solid as a mountain, as flexible as a bamboo in a breeze."[3] The images of sky/accepting, sunrise/consistent, mountain/solid, and bamboo/flexible hardly seem to fit together, but one very clear image fits together, which is that the truth is moderation. The idea of moderation or anything goes in Taoism was designed for the middle way just like Aristotle's Golden Mean in the West was designed to avoid taking excessive positions. *Anything goes* is not about making easygoing compromises with everything. Rather it is about the best wisdom the old sages found, not only for survival in the political jungle, but also, for proper understanding of universal reality and daily cunning in the world.

When Lao Tzu taught, "Tao is Tao, Tao is Tao no more," he meant that the moment you think you succeed in defining Tao you find that

Tao is not the Tao as you defined it just before, because the reality of Tao is ever changing. While Westerners looked for the unchangeable and everlasting truth, Easterners looked for the changeable yet permanent truth. Tao is not the unchangeable and everlasting truth; it changes moment by moment. The only permanent truth is the continuity of change.

Politically, Tao is a form of anarchism. Cosmologically, Tao is the ultimate source of all existence. Ethically, Tao is the ground for morality. Epistemologically, Tao is the moderate and skeptical truth. The nature of Tao in itself is indescribable, imperceptible, and unknowable. It is, as a phenomenon, a mode of being. Taoism in Korea was deeply baptized by Shamanism and became a primitive religion as well as daily wisdom of life.

When I was a child, my mother often admonished me with a Korean proverb: "Angled people always get hit. Live like the wind blows in the sky." It means inflexible people always topple down, so that it's better to live like flexible wind. It is a good application of the moderation of Taoism because I might be criticized or attacked by my opponents if I take sides or extremes in society. Taoism provided me a highly political neutrality and skeptical concept of truth until I found the absolute and objective truth that is true to the way things are.

Not for Understanding but for Embodying

Can you understand what Tao is? Maybe you cannot at all. "If you have trouble understanding Tao it may be because Tao is not to be understood, but embodied." Understanding may be a way of knowing truth, but not of knowing Tao. Taoists teach at least three ways to embody the truth.

Let intuition guide you. Taoists do not trust their logic, but only their intuition. They believe reason and logic are artificial and manipulative. Lao Tzu once said, "When what is happening in learning isn't clear, do not work too hard to figure things out. Instead, relax and let your mind's eye see what is happening. Let your perceptions and intuition be your guides."[4] The very best way of learning is intuition, not reason.

Empty the heart. Students of Taoism say that emptying the heart is crucial in embodying Tao. Emptying in Taoism is not "vacancy of space," but "making potential room for truth." Emptying the heart, then, is not "self-denial of sinful natures" as in the Christian life, or "anti-intellectualism" as in Western philosophy. Rather it is a purity of heart unpoisoned with unnecessary and artificial knowledge. Taoists emphasize simplicity of life and a calm, indifferent attitude toward all situations. Purity, simplicity, and calmness constitute the nature of emptying the heart.

Take no action. If anything shows off or creates any competition, it is regarded as an artificial and manipulative action. Korean Taoist Young Oak Kim judges such actions as "hypocritical, self-righteous and partial."[5] So taking no action does not mean idleness or doing nothing. Rather, it means doing no artificial or manipulative action. Because taking no action prevents artificial and human activity, it is one of the best ways of knowing the Taoist truth.

Taoism provided a highway for my intellectual suicide and dehumanized life. It gave me a justification for doing nothing not only in thinking but in living as well. One of the consequences of Taoism was that I was quite reluctant to make strenuous effort to study, make money, think hard, or any other kind of human activity.

Buddhism

It is true that one of the epochal affairs of the twentieth century was the meeting of Christianity and Buddhism. So many western Christians are amazed by the Four Noble Truths of Buddhism because of their simplicity. Humans' existence is full of conflict, sorrow, and suffering; all difficulties and pain are caused by the selfish desires of humans; freedom can be found, and it is the *Nirvana*. The Noble Eight-Fold Right Path is the way to this liberation.

I myself had been brainwashed by the political phrase, "follow the right path," which literally means "practice justice." The real meaning of "the right path" is "the middle way" which is far from justice or the absolute right. Even though it appears as righteousness or justice in Chinese characters, it is not the absolute concept of righteousness or justice as in Christianity.

Not Unchangeable but Moderate Right

Buddha described the Eight-Fold Right Path as follows:

A man should seek a way of moderation between self-indulgence and self-mortification. This moderation consists of right view, right thought, right speech, right action, right mode of living, right endeavor, right mindfulness, and right concentration.[6]

As Buddha clearly states, the word "right" here does not stand for the absolute or antithetical right. "Right" stands for the middle way, which is no other than moderation and synthesis.

When Buddha went out and met a harp player, the harp player asked him a question: "Sir, what does it mean to live a moderate life in this world?" Buddha answered, "A moderate life is something like a harp that creates a beautiful melody when the strings are tuned properly."[7] "Properly" simply means not too tight, not too loose, but just right. That is the middle way, not the absolute right.

Again in Buddha's book called *The Avatamsaka Sutra*, Buddha said, "Do not be consumed with lust and unenlightened behavior. Also, do not practice asceticism or too much suffering, which is not holy or righteous. If you could turn away from the two extremes, it is the moderation or the middle way." Buddha himself saw that only the middle way could bring peace and harmony in the world by putting an end to conflicts and wars between the two extremes. Therefore, the middle way is an existential and psychological solution for everything.

The Dalai Lama once explained this moderate concept of truth in this way: "We believe that nothing is unchangeable." Buddha himself once said, "The things which are made will always change. But there is one and only one unchangeable thing. That is *Sunya*." So in Buddhism, everything can be changed except *Sunya*, which literally means nothingness. *Sunya* cannot be changed because it is neither being nor non-being, but being and non-being at the same time.

If I understand *Sunya* correctly, it has no actual reality, no absolute, no unchangeable truth, and no clear concept of good and evil. This unfortunately justified me in getting into, not only spiritual nothingness with God, but also into total nothingness of my life. The nothingness led my life to debauchery without doing something meaningful.

Not Self-denial but Self-dismissal

There are a few liberating or enlightening ways in Buddhism. The most well-known Buddhist Indian ways of knowing the truth are *Nirvana*, *Anatman*, and the *"Don't-know" mind*.

Nirvana. In Sanskrit *"nirvana"* means "put out the fire" or "cast away the fire." The best way of attaining liberation and enlightenment and to understand the truth is to put out the fire of all your human desires. It's not the self-denial of sinful natures as in the Christian teaching, but the self-destruction or self-discipline of all kinds of normal desires such as eating, sleeping, resting, etc. There are Buddhists who have not spoken a word for ten years, never lain down or slept on a bed for eight years, and spent all of their time isolated in mountains.

Anatman. The Sanskrit word *"anatman"* literally means "self-abandonment" or "self-dismissal," a spiritual state of nothingness and a causational reality of meditation. Again, *anatman* is not the self-denial of sinful natures as in the Christian life, but the dismissal of human nature. It is eccentric, pessimistic, and ascetic, like the Gnostic way of life in the early church.

The "Don't-Know" Mind. The minds that cut off all thinking become "Don't-know" minds. When all thinking has been cut off your mind becomes empty. This is before thinking. Unless you throw away all your opinions, all your likes and dislikes, and only keep the mentality that you don't know anything, you cannot know truth. A student at Harvard Divinity School, Paul, met the Great Master Seung Sahn, the Korean Zen Buddhist, and they enjoyed a Zen dialogue as follows:

Paul: "Sir, what is life?"
Master: "Do not think about your life too seriously. Go drink a cup of coffee."
Paul: "Drinking coffee doesn't make me see the truth. Could you tell me what the truth is, sir?"
Master: "Do not think about truth. Truth is everywhere. Only be enlightened by the 'don't-know' mind."
Paul: "What is the 'don't-know' mind, sir?"
Master: The 'don't-know' mind is the empty mind or the mind-before-the-mind."

Paul took his advice seriously and escaped from his reason and practiced "don't-know" mind. Soon Paul was saying, "I love both Jesus and Buddha." The "don't-know" mind led him to commit intellectual suicide and become a religious pluralist.

Confucianism

I have been brought up in a strong tradition that "the men of virtue shall be quick to adapt themselves to circumstances." Confucius encouraged this kind of behavior in his book *Moderation*: "A man of virtue conforms to *moderation,* while a little man opposes *moderation.*

Moderation for a man of virtue is to behave appropriately for the time, and *moderation* for a little man is to feel no shame in being a little man."

Mencius, one of Confucius's best students, interpreted *a man of virtue* as "a person who takes a serious view of the times." Here "the times" means *circumstances* that vary at times and places. "Moderation" refers to "the middle way" without settling down somewhere. Is that a wise wisdom or another expression of Aristotle's Golden Mean?

Not Absolutes but Situational Middle

Why is it that a man of virtue shall be quick to adapt himself to circumstances? Because, Confucius believed, a man of virtue takes *the situational middle* seriously while a little man takes the extremes or absolutes. Therefore, in Confucianism, *a man of virtue* is a person who is impartial and conforms to whatever situation he might be in.

Chu Hsi, an important Chinese scholar of Neo-Confucianism, interpreted *moderation* as ". . . never inclined to anything. For any affair, *moderation* is neither excessive nor deficient. It is an ordinary practice, which can be a norm anytime and anywhere."

Hak Ju Kim, a Korean scholar, interpreted *moderation* more clearly: "There can never be an absolute good or evil in the practice of *moderation*. The principle of the distinction between good and evil is relative rather than absolute. Therefore, even the act of *moderation* itself is neither absolutely good nor absolutely evil. Even in evil there are good intentions, and even in good there is a seed of evil."[8]

Tetsuji Morohashi, a Japanese scholar, correctly interpreted *moderation* like this: "The *moderation* of Confucius is not only *moderation* between matters, but between being and nothing, pleasure and suffering."[9] As you see, *moderation, or the middle way*, is the only truth in Taoism, Buddhism. and Confucianism. If you are against it, you are considered not only as a foolish person but also a little man or a narrow-minded man in Asia.

I was always afraid of being regarded as a little man or narrow-minded man because of the influence of the story my grandmother told me when I was young. There was a prime minister called Hwang Hee in the Chosun Dynasty of Korea. He served four kings for about forty years. There are good reasons he survived such a long period in a jungle of politics. One day, as Hwang Hee came home from work, he saw two of his servants quarreling in the garden. He went to his room directly, without interrupting them, because of the custom that a noble man should keep away from any danger or conflict.

A few minutes later, one of the servants who were quarreling came into Hwang Hee's room and explained the situation to him. After listening to the servant's story, Hwang Hee said, "Yes, what you say is true." Then the other servant came in, and also defended his position. After listening to another story, Hwang Hee said, "Yes, what you say is also true." Hwang Hee's nephew had been watching everything that was going on. He asked Hwang Hee, "Why did you do that? It cannot be that both of them are true." Do you know what Hwang Hee replied? "Yes, after all, what you say is also true." Maybe, we can name Hwang Hee's philosophy "This is true, and that is also true." There are at least three ideas suggested by this story:

1) "This is true, and that is also true" is the worldview without standards. It is tremendously flexible and adaptable, as you see it allows people to lack consistent perception and a clear standard of values upon which to make judgments. 2) "This is true, and that is also true" is the philosophy of *moderation*. It avoids all conflicts, helps the holder be free of enemies, always searching for the middle way. 3) "This is true, and that is also true" is the methodology of non-logic. As for this way of thinking, the Eastern mind emphasizes sensitivity rather than reason and intuition rather than logical procedure.

The art of Hwang Hee's living has profoundly influenced my grandmother. Her nickname was "Madam Hwang Hee." She respected him very much not only because he was politically adaptable but morally above corruption. She was pleased most when she was told, "You are just like Hwang Hee," or, "You live without laws." This influence meant that everyone in our family should be as smoothly mannered as a well-rounded rock.

Not Logic on Fire, but Logic on Sentiments

Historically, the theory of *moderation* was developed side by side with the concept of the *Theory of Li and Ki*. It is a form of Asian dualism which divides and categorizes all existence into two inseparable components, *Li* and *Ki*. *Li* is the formative element (the basic principle and normative logos), while *Ki* is the energizing element (the material force and energetic power). Chu Hsi, the Chinese scholar of Neo-Confucianism, believed that *Li* and *Ki* were independent of each other and yet inseparable, since *Li* cannot exist concretely without *Ki*, and *Ki* would be formless and directionless energy without *Li*. He made an ethical and psychological code called *The Theory of the Four Truths and the Seven Sentiments* based on the theory of *Li* and *Ki*. *The Four Truths* are benevolence, righteousness, propriety, and wisdom. *The Seven Sentiments* are joy, anger, sorrow, fear, love, hate, and lust.

Chu Hsi believed *The Four Truths,* which originate from *Li*, are always good, while *The Seven Sentiments,* which originate from *Ki*, can be good or bad. He believed that *Ki* is prior to *Li*. He thought that empirical sense comes before ideological reason, because in conceiving the truth and achieving moral establishment, reason is not the best way. Rather, pure emotion is the best way because, while reason is always influenced by human greed, pure emotion or intuition always leads to the purest and highest truth. That's why he insisted on the fasting of the mind as the best way of understanding truth.

Two distinct schools of Neo-Confucian epistemology developed in Korea three centuries later. Toe Gye Lee stressed the primacy of *Li*, the logos or normative, and Yul Gok Lee gave emphasis to *Ki,* the energy or power. Especially, Toe Gye Lee slightly changed Chu Hsi's ideas in two senses. First, he believed that *Li* is prior to *Ki* ("*Li-first-Ki-after*") and secondly *Li and Ki* are interrelated and reciprocal in perceiving the truth.

The theory of *Li* and *Ki* was a highly sophisticated idea and was something like the idealism and empiricism or the subject-object discussion today. Even though I need more supplementary lessons on this area, I was mixed up enough, not with the "the logic on fire" or "balance of intellect and emotion" like many good Christians were, but with the logic on sentiments.

Conclusion

As you have read the short history of my name and three religious and philosophical influences, you may have recognized that I was heavily conformed to the worldviews of Asia in two areas: the concept of the truth and the way of knowing the truth. I felt that truth was relative and the way of knowing the truth was simply through intuition. I summarize the beliefs of *"moderate intuition," "creative feeling,"* as Yong Oak Kim described it for his Harvard thesis, or *"relative sentiments"* of the three religions and philosophies as follows:

. . .

Taoism
The concept of the truth—*Not true to the way things are but anything goes*
The way of knowing the truth—*Not for understanding but for embodying*

Buddhism
The concept of the truth—*Not unchangeable but moderate right*
The way of knowing the truth—*Not self-denial, but self-dismissal*

Confucianism
The concept of the truth—*Not absolutes but situational middle*
The way of knowing the truth—*Not logic on fire but logic on sentiments*

The terminologies in the concepts of truth such as "anything goes," "the middle way," and "the situational middle" are slightly different from one another. The "anything goes" of Taoism is a cosmological and phenomenal moderation; "the middle way" of Buddhism is existential and psychological moderation; and "the situational middle" of Confucianism is social and moral moderation. But the key idea is *moderation*. The *moderation* has developed to solve not only philosophical and universal conflicts, but also historical and human conflicts people face day-to-day.

The terminology about the way of knowing such as "embodying," "self-dismissal," and "logic on sentiments" is also slightly different from each other. "Embodying" is experiential and phenomenal intuition; "self-dismissal" is psychological and ascetical intuition; and "logic on sentiments" is emotional and pure intuition. But the main idea is *intuition*. The *intuition* has developed to solve not only the problems of ideological and theoretical ways of approaching reality, but also to provide a more purified way of understanding the truth. The concept of *intuition* is not without utility. It is one of the most popular ways of understanding truth in the East, similar to the empiricism of the West. It was more than useful, but created a society centered on experience.

After I became a born-again Christian when I was about twenty-one years old, I was somewhat aware of my *moderate intuition* without fully realizing "its endless logical dichotomy between the epistemological methodologies of reason and experience," as Dong Hwan Park well described the inner dilemma of the Eastern people.[10] I was surprised how much I was seriously *"tossed to and fro by the waves and carried along by every wind of doctrine, by human cunning, by craftiness in deceitful schemes"* as the Apostle Paul describes in Ephesians 4:14. The conclusions of my Eastern mindset had been waiting to be reformed for many years:

- No absolute but moderate truth.
- No confrontation but compromise.
- No discernment but accepting anything.
- No paradigm but harmonization.
- No practice but idealizations.

The consequences of these conclusions are enormously painful: no objective criteria exist for the truth, no clear moral standard, no grounds for social justice, and no religious absolutes. A culture of shame developed rather than a sense of guilt, a harmony of dual forces rather than 'checks and balances', and a reverence for reputation rather than a solid basis for good and evil. I realized that my belief system may not be totally wrong, but it may not be big enough to solve my experiential conflicts in daily life as well as my philosophical conflicts.

Turning my Eastern worldview upside down began with the Word of God, in the same passage the Apostle Paul says, *"Until we all attain to the unity of the faith and of the knowledge of the Son of God...we will no longer be children...."* (Eph. 4:13–14). Am I still an infant or an immature child? I came to the conclusion that if I don't try to reach unity in faith and knowledge, I'm simply an infant spiritually and intellectually even though I was physically an adult. The message struck me and opened my eyes to a new dimension of my life. I realized I should *"not be conformed to this world, but be transformed by the renewal* [my] *mind"* (Rom. 12:2). Later, I found there was a clear paradigm for the "integrative union" of spiritual and intellectual experience (2 Cor. 10:4–6).

---

1. Alfred North Whitehead, *Religion in the Making* (London: Macmillan, 1926), 49.
2. Lao Tzu, *The Texts of Taoism*, trans. James Legge (Mineola, NY: Dover, 1962), 14–15.
3. See http://classics.mit.edu/Lao/taote.2.ii.html
4. Pamela K. Metz, *The Tao of Learning* (Atlanta: Humanics New Age, 1994), chap 14.
5. Young Oak Kim, *Dohol Talks with the Dalai Lama* (Tongnamu), 664–6.

6. Charles Van Doren, *A History of Knowledge* (New York: Ballantine Books, 1992), 22.
7. *Hankyoreh Daily Newspaper*, September 23, 2000.
8. Hak Ju Kim, *Moderation*, (Seoul National University Press), 203–9.
9. Tetsuji Morohashi, *Confucius, LaoTzu, Buddha, East Asia*, 192–5.
10. Dong Hwan Park, *Heart of East and Mind of West*, 3–5.

FREEDOMS AND LIMITATIONS

C. S. LEWIS AND FRANCIS SCHAEFFER AS A TAG TEAM

C. John Collins

PhD, University of Liverpool
Professor, Old Testament
Covenant Theological Seminary
St. Louis, MO

I count it a great delight to contribute this essay in honor (or should I say, in hono*u*r?) of Professor Jerram Barrs, especially since he (together with his associate Ranald Macaulay), Francis Schaeffer, and C. S. Lewis have done so much to shape my own thinking and living as a Christian. To have Professor Barrs as a colleague, and a friend, is a privilege beyond my wildest imagining. And if I focus on Genesis 1–11 in this essay, consider that a tribute to my sharing the 2010 Francis A. Schaeffer lectureship with Professor Barrs on that topic.

Francis Schaeffer Introduces "Freedoms and Limitations"

Francis Schaeffer (1912–84) had a major influence on Jerram Barrs. Schaeffer served as a Bible Presbyterian pastor in St. Louis and then as a missionary in Europe; he founded and operated L'Abri, with its orientation toward young people. As a pastor and apologist within the great Christian tradition, Schaeffer was convinced that there was not a final conflict between the sciences and the Bible when both are properly understood.

But many do interpret the sciences and the Bible as being in conflict; and these alleged conflicts can be most acute when it comes to the story of origins: the origin of the universe, of life, of the varieties of life forms, and especially of humankind. Christians have tried various ways to address these conflicts; Schaeffer, being both an evangelist eager to remove barriers to coming to the Christian faith and a theologian knowing that we must preserve the true Christian faith without diluting it, aimed to give some guidance on just how to address those potential barriers. Schaeffer was also a churchman, considering unnecessary conflict within the church to be destructive of Christian well-being and witness.

For these reasons Schaeffer articulated an approach to origins that he called "freedoms and limitations": there is a range of reasonable scenarios by which we may address the apparent conflicts between the Bible and the sciences, and yet there are limits to this range, limits set both by basic biblical concepts and by good human judgment.[1]

Schaeffer was willing to consider, among other freedoms, the possibility that Genesis 1 describes God creating a grown-up universe (nowadays called the appearance of age hypothesis); or that God was reforming a creation that had been partially deformed by Satan's fall; or that the "days" refer to long ages. He concluded, sensibly and generously:

> I urge you again to remember that I am not saying that any of these positions are my own or that they will prove to be the case. I am simply stating theoretical possibilities as we consider the correlations between what the Bible sets forth about cosmogony and what we can study from general revelation.[2]

At the same time he wanted to insist on God's special creative activity at certain places; in particular, at the original creation, at the creation of conscious life, and again at the creation of man, the result was discontinuous in some way from what had preceded. He also thought it essential to say that Adam was the first man and that Eve was made from him. This left him with a careful view of what is called theistic evolution: he saw no support for the molecule-to-man sort of naturalistic evolution, and he imagined that anyone who held to his limitations would not be an evolutionist in the fullest sense of the word.

When it comes to assessing Schaeffer's version of specific freedoms and limitations, the first thing to do is to recognize that he has covered the main options that Evangelicals in his day had explored. And surely his instincts are right: these explorations come from obviously good people who are competent scholars; why should we get worked up over their differences? At the same time, a great deal of water has gushed on by under the exegetical bridge since his booklet first saw publication in 1975, and thus I would take his list of freedoms as enumerative and suggestive, rather than exhaustive. The limitations strike me as eminently reasonable, and indeed generous—and, as we will see, they fit well with the arguments of C. S. Lewis.

Further, Schaeffer's approach allows what we might call a glass half-full style of ministry, whose main goal is to help people adequately face the facts about their humanness—we are distinct from the other animals, and we all need God—without quibbling over every detail. This approach allows us to affirm people and leave them to develop their own perspectives further—traits that I have seen vividly embodied in Jerram Barrs!

So all these factors certainly make me admire Schaeffer. In addition, I think another factor, unstated, comes into play as well: namely, a sane Christian has a hierarchy of commitments, and thus, for example, should insist more strongly on the tenets of mere or basic Christianity —say the Trinity or the resurrection of Jesus—than on some other matters that are important, but not quite so vital—say the number of sacraments and their exact effects. Since I am, like Schaeffer and Barrs, a Presbyterian, I appreciate as well the ideal of "generic Calvinism,"[3] which allows a range of possible views on a number of matters, within the circle of the Reformed ministry.

My admiration for Schaeffer's approach grows even greater when I add into the mix some insights from C. S. Lewis, the literary scholar. In my judgment, Lewis' insights show that the very nature of the material we have in Genesis leads to some sort of freedoms and limitations rubric, since the material both resists a purely literalistic reading and invites a recognition of its historical impulse.

In this essay I want to develop these insights from Lewis, and in places to refine them (since they touch on my own area of specialization, namely Genesis). I will also draw on Lewis to defend this approach against some of its critiques, which are still current. And if at times I think I can improve on some particulars in their outlooks, I still think that a "broadly Lewisian"[4] and "broadly Schaefferian" tack when it comes to Genesis will provide us with the intellectually and morally robust tools we need for bringing the message of Genesis to each culture.

What Kind of Introduction Does C. S. Lewis Need?

C. S. Lewis (1898–1963), famous both as a defender of Christian faith and as the writer of imaginative fiction, actually had a day job: he was a professional scholar of medieval and Renaissance European literature. From 1925 until 1954, he was a Fellow and Tutor in English Literature at Magdalen College, Oxford; and from 1954 until he retired in 1963 (shortly before he died that same year), he was Professor of Medieval and Renaissance Literature at Cambridge University. In the course of his academic work he produced books and papers on topics in ideological history, English philology, and literary interpretation, many of which still show considerable value.

Nowadays the general public knows Lewis primarily for the theological, apologetic, and imaginative works; nevertheless, his total work hangs together, and the same personal traits come through in all of his writings.

Lewis the apologist wrote when the standard narrative in the Western world was that the advances of the sciences were relegating the archaic beliefs of traditional religions such as Christianity to the museum. As he put it:

> It is a common reproach against Christianity that its dogmas are unchanging, while human knowledge is in continual growth. Hence, to unbelievers, we seem to be always engaged in the hopeless task of trying to force the new knowledge into moulds which it has outgrown. I think this feeling alienates the outsider much more than any particular discrepancies between this or that doctrine and this or that scientific theory.[5]

For Lewis it seems clear that if our ancestors had known what we know about the universe Christianity would never have existed at all.

As Christians sought to adapt to the new knowledge, many skeptics held these efforts in contempt; as Lewis put it:

> My friend Corineus has advanced the charge that none of us are in fact Christians at all. According to him historic Christianity is something so barbarous that no modern man can really believe it: the moderns who claim to do so are in fact believing a modern system of thought which retains the vocabulary of Christianity and exploits the emotions inherited from it while quietly dropping its essential doctrines. [6]

Lewis took it to be his job to defend the essentials of Christian belief, and to show that these essentials wear well as they encounter modern trends of thought.

Lewis portrayed himself as a purveyor of traditional Christianity; but he made his own contributions as well. For example, it has been common in Christian thinking to treat the Bible as a virtually disjointed collection of stories, poems, doctrinal treatises, ethical discourses, and so forth. Since about 1990, Christian students of biblical theology have become more explicitly aware of the overarching story of the Bible and of the powerful role that story plays in forming the worldview of a community. As Albert Wolters and Michael Goheen put it:

> To miss the grand narrative of Scripture is a serious matter; it is not simply a matter of misinterpreting parts of Scripture. It is a matter of being oblivious to *which story is shaping our lives*. Some story will shape our lives. When the Bible is broken up into little bits and chunks—theological, devotional, spiritual, moral, or worldview bits and chunks—then these bits can be nicely fitted into the reigning story of our own culture with all its idols! One can be theologically orthodox, devotionally pious, morally upright, or maybe even have one's worldview categories straight, and yet be shaped by the idolatrous Western story. The Bible loses its forceful and formative power by being absorbed into a more encompassing secular story. [7]

One way of marking key episodes in this unfolding story is the rubric, "Creation, Fall, Redemption, and Consummation."[8]

Lewis was, at least with respect to mainstream biblical theology, ahead of the game in his attention to the narrative unity of the Christian message.[9] As early as 1947, in his book *Miracles*, he was describing world history (with its redemptive component) as "this great story… a very *long* story, with a complicated plot."[10] In his 1950 essay, "Historicism," he was even more explicit: "For Christianity… history is a story with a well-defined plot, pivoted on Creation, Fall, Redemption, and Judgement."[11]

And again, in his Cambridge lectures introducing the medieval picture of the world, published posthumously in 1964 as *The Discarded Image*, he wrote:

> History, in a word, was not for them [the Greeks] a story with a plot. The Hebrews, on the other hand, saw their whole past as a revelation of the purposes of Yahweh. Christianity, going on from there, makes world-history in its entirety a single, transcendentally significant story with a well-defined plot pivoted on Creation, Fall, Redemption, and Judgement. [12]

Many theologians are coming to recognize that their doctrinal formulations must do justice to this narrative structure, and I will return to this theme. For now, I simply want to notice that a literary scholar, with no special training in biblical studies or theology, had seen something that is now acknowledged as old hat. Perhaps his further observations, as I will discuss below, will be likewise fruitful.[13]

Lewis Discusses Textual Features of Genesis

In his *Reflections on the Psalms*, Lewis made it clear that he was not what he called a Fundamentalist; he did not define the term, but it appears from the context that he meant someone with "a prior belief that every sentence of the Old Testament has historical or scientific truth." And Lewis added, "But this [prior belief] I do not hold, any more than St. Jerome did when he said that Moses described Creation "after the manner of a popular poet" (as we should say, mythically) or than Calvin did when he doubted whether the story of Job were history or fiction."[14] (By the way, this version of fundamentalism is often assumed to be entailed by another principle that Schaeffer held to, namely the inerrancy of the Bible. No doubt this frequent assumption is due to the fact that plenty of inerrantists exist who do indeed fall into that kind of fundamentalism. But the overall principle does not require it. Interestingly enough, Lewis himself touches on some of the linguistic, literary, and philosophical matters that, combined with disciplines such as speech act theory and rhetoric, can provide the tools for articulating a sound notion of biblical truthfulness — but I shall have to develop that elsewhere.)

Lewis here refers to Jerome, but no one has located the exact spot in which Jerome makes this claim. The closest source is a passage in the English proto-Reformer John Colet (1467–1519), who wrote in a letter to one Radulphus:

> Thus Moses arranges his details in such a way as to give the people a clearer notion, and he does this *after the manner of a popular poet*, in order that he may the more adapt himself to the spirit of simple rusticity, picturing a succession of things, works, and times, of such a kind as there certainly could not be in the work of *so great a Workman*.[15]

With this principle in mind, Lewis addresses the possibility that the creation story in Genesis is in some way "derived from earlier Semitic stories which were Pagan and mythical"—a view that had become widely spread by his time, and which was held to discredit Genesis. But Lewis shows his good literary and philosophical sense by first insisting, "We must of course be quite clear what 'derived from' means. Stories do not reproduce their species like mice."[16] He observed that it is *persons* who do the retelling, and revising of stories, for various ends:

> Thus at every step in what is called—a little misleadingly—the "evolution" of a story, a man, all he is and all his attitudes, are involved. And no good work is done anywhere without aid from the Father of Lights. When a series of such re-tellings turns a creation story which at first had almost no religious or metaphysical significance into a story which achieves the idea of true Creation and of a transcendent Creator (as *Genesis* does), then nothing will make me believe that some of the re-tellers, or some one of them, has not been guided by God.[17]

Hence, although Lewis found much that he deemed poetical, or even mythical, in the Genesis creation story, he was nevertheless willing to attach to it some kind of referent. For example:

We read in *Genesis* that God formed man of the dust and breathed life into him. For all the first writer knew of it, this passage might merely illustrate the survival, even in a truly creational story, of the Pagan inability to conceive true Creation, the savage, pictorial tendency to imagine God making things "out of" something as the potter or the carpenter does. Nevertheless, whether by lucky accident or (as I think) by God's guidance, it embodies a profound principle. For in any view man is in one sense made "out of" something else. He is an animal; but an animal called to be, or raised to be, or (if you like) doomed to be, something more than an animal. On the ordinary biological view (what difficulties I have about evolution are not religious) one of the primates is changed so that he becomes man; but he remains still a primate and an animal.[18]

Now, Lewis elsewhere makes it clear that he thought this "changing" of one of the primates to become man was both historical and supernatural.[19] Thus the poetical or pictorial style of the Genesis story does not prevent it from referring to a real event in the history of the world.

Several ways of qualifying and refining Lewis' observations here immediately come to mind; and as I consider them, I hope that we do not lose sight of the broadly Lewisian character of the revision that results.

The first refinement addresses Lewis' interpretation of the phrase in Jerome or Colet, "after the manner of a popular poet" as "mythically," or as "in the form of a folktale" (in the parallel passage in *Miracles*).[20] A chief difficulty in appreciating what Lewis meant here comes from the multiple definitions of the English word "myth," together with the fact that Lewis himself did not consider that word a derogatory categorization. From Lewis' own discussion it appears that he does *not* intend to suggest that the tale has no historical referentiality; but he is clear that we do not discern whatever referentiality it has by way of a literalistic reading.

For the reader not attuned to all of Lewis' intended nuances, it would be better to turn to the context of the passage in Colet, the only known source for Lewis' description. Colet's phrases "give the people a clearer notion" and "simple rusticity" point the way; and earlier in the same place, Colet indicates that Moses' object "was not to give to the learned of future generations a scientific statement of the manner and order of the creation of the universe, but to teach a *moral* lesson to the people whom he was leading out of the bondage and idolatry of Egypt."[21] That is, Colet is not contrasting the literary type of myth or folktale with a literary type of history, but rather the popular account with the scientific. The popular account does not even pretend to give the kind of details that learned scholars seek about the exact order of events or the inner workings of the things described. It is content with vivid, pictorial description which entrusts to the reader or hearer the responsibility of using the account properly, namely by allowing the story to capture the imagination and loyalty of the community that owns it.

A further refinement speaks to Lewis' acknowledgement that other ancient Near Eastern origin stories are relevant to the meaning of Genesis. Much has happened in the study of the ancient Near East since Lewis' time. While it was once common to suppose that the Babylonian poem *Enuma Elish* was the relevant ancestor of the Genesis creation story,[22] and though some biblical scholars still think this way, Assyriologists now find in Genesis 1–11 a set of parallels to some much older Mesopotamian sources.[23] To call them parallels highlights the problems connected with derivation; it allows that Genesis is a response to, a comment upon, or even a refutation of the Mesopotamian stories, without saying what the exact literary relationship is (or even whether specific texts were in mind).

And what do these parallels tell us about the function of Genesis 1–11? The Mesopotamian sources provide what Assyriologist William Hallo calls "prehistory"—the story of the period of human existence before there are any secure written records—and "protohistory"—tales of the earliest stages for which there are records.[24] Another way to put this is to recognize that these materials provide what we can call the front end of the official Mesopotamian worldview story. Further, it appears that the Mesopotamians aimed to accomplish their purpose by founding their stories on what they thought were actual events, albeit told with a great deal of imagery and symbolism. Thus it is reasonable to take Genesis 1–11 as having a similar purpose in Israel, expecting similar attention to history without undue literalism: these stories explain to ancient Israel where they came from, how things got to be the way they are, and why God has called Israel to exist in the first place (to restore the whole of God's world to a condition of blessing".[25]

Lewis rightly, therefore, recognized the hermeneutical caution that good readers should exercise when approaching Genesis 1–11. His own scholarly studies had made him vividly aware of the problem. In discussing a medieval writer who takes older poetical works too literalistically he says,

> The poet is ranked with the scientist as authority for a purely scientific proposition. This astonishing failure or refusal to distinguish—in practice, though not always in theory—between books of different sorts must be borne in mind whenever we are trying to gauge the total effect of an ancient text on its medieval readers. [26]

Lewis speaks further of "the medieval failure to distinguish between writers of wholly different kinds," and gives as an example, "A highly lyrical passage from Job (xxxix. 19–25) is here being turned into a proposition in natural history."[27]

A further example of a failure along the lines that Lewis exposes is the effort to describe the biblical picture of the world, as a flat place, possibly disc-shaped, with mountains at the extremities supporting the sky, which is a solid dome with an actual body of water above it; below the land we find an ocean and the subterranean pillars of the earth. Unlike the medievals that Lewis was writing about, scholars' purpose for this description is not to adopt it, but to warrant rejecting the biblical picture for its primitivity. Such a description appears in, for example, the United Bible Societies' (USB) *Handbook on Genesis*, which makes its appeal to passages such as Psalm 104:2–3, 5–9; 148:4; Job 26:11; 37:18; 38:4–11; Proverbs 8:28–29; and Amos 9:6.[28] In view of the general sensitivity to linguistic, literary, and rhetorical matters in the UBS series, it is surprising to realize that the list of texts is entirely of poetical passages, with no assessment of the different kinds of texts and what one might have to do to ascertain their presupposed picture of the world.[29] I wonder what Lewis would say about this way of reading!

Further, Lewis the historian of literature helps us to appreciate that one of the literary techniques at work in Genesis may well be what we call anachronism, portraying past events in light of the author's and audience's present world. This was certainly a feature of medieval European literature; as Lewis noted, the medievals "pictured the whole past in terms of their own age. So did the Elizabethans.... It is doubtful whether the sense of period is much older than the Waverley novels."[30] This need not detract from the historicity of the text, since the text can still refer to actual events without making any kind of strong claim about the details of the characters' circumstances. An example in Genesis would be the term "city" for the very early kind of settlement in Genesis 4:17.

Some may prefer a higher level of literalism in their reading of Genesis than Lewis did, and that preference is legitimately open to discussion. Nevertheless the broadly Lewisian points still stand: first, the possible effect of pagan stories on the origin of Genesis need not detract from its inspiration; and second, the possibility (in my mind, the near assurance) of shared motifs and literary conventions with other ancient Near Eastern stories need not detract from the referentiality, nor even from the historicity, of the Genesis material—so long as we do not identify historicity with literalism in interpretation.[31]

An Example: The Origin and Fall of Human Beings

The flow of this essay is headed toward the conclusion that the presence of pictorial material and literary conventions in Genesis 1–11 shows that an approach like Schaeffer's is surely the best way for believers to hold and commend their faith in the larger world.

C. S. Lewis fits into this pattern. For example, he was happy to entertain a variety of scientific-historical scenarios for the origin of humankind, but none of them would be valid if they were to deny the mystery of reason, or any implications that follow from that mystery. Likewise, these scenarios must not deny the objectivity of ethical judgments.

Consider, for example, his treatment of human origins in the context of his chapter on "The Fall of Man" in *The Problem of Pain*.[32] In discussing the biblical story of Adam and his sin, and the degree to which that event may have affected the rest of us (traditionally the descendants of Adam and Eve), he acknowledges this about the Fathers (the leading theologians in the first few Christian centuries), "Wisely, or foolishly, they believed that we were *really*—and not simply by legal fiction—involved in Adam's action."[33]

Now Lewis wanted to do justice to this belief, at the same time as he recognized that twentieth century scientific beliefs ran contrary to a literalistic reading. So he set about addressing, with his characteristic clarity, how these two sets of beliefs might relate to one another. "Many people think that this proposition"—that God created man good, but then man fell by disobedience—"has been proved false by modern science," with its view that "men have arisen from brutality and savagery."

There seems to me to be a complete confusion here. *Brute* and *savage* both belong to that unfortunate class of words which are sometimes used rhetorically, as terms of reproach, and sometimes scientifically, as terms of description; and the pseudo-scientific argument against the Fall depends on a confusion between the usages. If by saying that man rose from brutality you mean simply that man is physically descended from animals, I have no objection. But it does not follow that the further back you go the more *brutal*—in the sense of wicked or wretched—you will find man to be.[34]

Lewis insisted, "Science, then, has nothing to say either for or against the doctrine of the Fall," and proceeded to offer a scenario that he thought might be "a not unlikely tale"

For long centuries, God perfected the animal form which was to become the vehicle of humanity and the image of Himself. He gave it hands whose thumb could be applied to each of the fingers, and jaws and teeth and throat capable of articulation, and a brain sufficiently complex to execute all of the material motions whereby rational thought is incarnated.... Then, in the fullness of time, God caused to descend upon this organism, both on its psychology and physiology, a new kind of consciousness which could say "I" and "me", which could look upon itself as an object, which knew God, which could make judgments of truth, beauty and goodness, and which was so far above time that it could perceive time flowing past.... We do not know how many of these creatures God made, nor how long they continued in the Paradisal state. But sooner or later they fell. Someone or something whispered that they could become as gods.... They wanted some corner in the universe of which they could say to God, "This is our business, not yours." But there is no such corner. They wanted to be nouns, but they were, and eternally must be, mere adjectives. We have no idea in what particular act, or series of acts, the self-contradictory, impossible wish found expression. For all I can see, it might have concerned the literal eating of a fruit, but the question is of no consequence.[35]

It is clear from the context, and from Lewis' other writing, that by "God caused to descend upon this organism, both on its psychology and physiology, a new kind of consciousness," he meant something that was *super*natural; as he said in *Miracles*, "To believe that Nature produced God, or even the human mind, is, as we have seen, absurd."[36] And notice that this "new kind of consciousness" enables the creature to reason about transcendent moral realities, which again cannot be a simple outgrowth of its material capacities.

We might want to revise this scenario in some of its particulars; I have offered my own revisions for it elsewhere, and my result is still broadly Lewisian.[37] The point here is that, according to Lewis, whatever the details of the story we tell about human origins, there are limits to what we may suggest and still be within the bounds of good critical thinking—which, as Lewis would insist, is necessary if we want to be practicing good science.

What applies to the origin of humankind applies to evolutionary theory in general. Lewis mentioned evolution frequently in his writings, generally to distinguish the scientific theory from the ideological extrapolations some made of it (which he ranked as a "Myth"). But he said a few things about the theory itself. A fair sample would be this:

Again, for the scientist Evolution is a purely biological theorem. It takes over organic life on this planet as a going concern and tries to explain certain changes within that field. It makes no cosmic statements, no metaphysical statements, no eschatological statements.... It does not in itself explain the origin of organic life, nor of the variations, nor does it discuss the origin and validity of reason. It may well tell you how the brain, through which reason now operates, arose, but that is a different matter. Still less does it even attempt to tell you how the universe as a whole arose, or what it is, or whither it is tending. But the Myth knows none of these reticences.... "Evolution" (as the Myth understands it) is the formula of *all* existence. [38]

The kind of evolutionary theory that did not bother Lewis theologically "does not in itself explain the origin of organic life, nor of the variations, nor... of reason;" that is, it does not insist beforehand that we may only allow a purely naturalistic scenario for the whole development of life (though he has not ruled that out).[39]

Nominally, at least, some leading evolutionary biologists support Lewis on this. For example, D. M. S. Watson (1886–1973), Professor of Zoology and Comparative Anatomy at University College, London (1921–1951), acknowledged: "But whilst the fact of evolution is accepted by every biologist the mode in which it has occurred and the mechanism by which it has been brought about are still disputable."[40] The National Science Teachers Association (NSTA) says something very similar: "There is no longer a debate among scientists about whether evolution has taken place. There is considerable debate about how evolution has taken place: What are the processes and mechanisms producing change, and what has happened specifically during the history of the universe?"

Even though these statements sensibly refuse to decide ahead of time what kinds of factors can be involved, other statements are emphatic in ruling some things out. The National Association of Biology Teachers (NABT) insists:

Evolutionary biology rests on the same scientific methodologies the rest of science uses, appealing only to natural events and processes to describe and explain phenomena in the natural world. Science teachers must reject calls to account for the diversity of life or describe the mechanisms of evolution by invoking non-naturalistic or supernatural notions. [41]

(I do not suggest here that Lewis thought that "non-naturalistic" notions *must* be involved in any extensive fashion, nor whether any of these would be readily perceptible to human students, nor even whether it was appropriate for him to have much of an opinion— except, of course, in the origin of humankind.)

It is therefore reasonable, in light of what kind of text Genesis 1–11 is, first, to refuse to dictate to the paleontologist what he or she may find in the fossils or a geneticist in the genome. At the same time, when that geneticist or paleontologist wants to try to put those findings together into larger theories that tell the human story, then that person is reasoning as a human being, and his or her reasoning must comply with good reasoning. As Lewis wrote in another context,

Now I dread specialists in power because they are specialists speaking outside their special subjects. Let scientists tell us about sciences. But government involves questions about the good for man and justice, and what things are worth having at what price; and on these a scientific training gives a man's opinion no added value. [42]

A white lab coat does not confer a privileged status to one's dicta in every subject!

Consider some more of the features that Lewis touches on, which distinguish humans from the rest of the animals. The motivation for science itself is distinctively human: "One of the things that distinguishes man from the other animals is that he wants to know things, wants to find out what reality is like, simply for the sake of knowing."[43] Human friendship is another feature that resists explanation purely in terms of natural development of animal capacities:

Friendship is—in a sense not at all derogatory to it—the least *natural* of loves; the least instinctive, organic, biological, gregarious and necessary.... We can live and breed without Friendship. The species, biologically considered, has no need of it.... [Friendship] has no survival value; rather it is one of those things which give value to survival.[44]

Some researchers have indeed tried to argue that human friendship is continuous with some aspects of animal behavior, but they must rest their argument on defining friendship down. A 2003 survey article in *Science News*, entitled "Beast buddies," concludes: "Harder to understand though, according to Silk, are the bonds so close and widespread in *Homo sapiens*. She says, 'None of our models of reciprocity [among nonhuman animals] can accommodate the psychology of human friendship.'"[45]

Humans even carry out their romantic loves in a way that shows both their animality and their distinctiveness:

For I can hardly help regarding it as one of God's jokes that a passion so soaring, so apparently transcendent, as Eros, should thus be linked in incongruous symbiosis with a bodily appetite which, like any other appetite, tactlessly reveals its connections with such mundane factors as weather, health, diet, circulation, and digestion.... It is a continual demonstration of the truth that we are composite creatures, rational animals, akin on one side to the angels, on the other to tomcats. It is a bad thing not to be able to take a joke.[46]

The other animals are uniformly serious!

Lewis would have us believe that there is something fundamentally unreasonable in the insistence (such as the NABT has apparently made) that even humankind arose by a purely natural process; and since it is unreasonable, it is bad scientific history. And Lewis had undoubtedly met people who made just such an insistence, even in the name of "science." Of them he said:

> They ask me at the same moment to accept a conclusion and to discredit the only testimony on which the conclusion can be based. The difficulty is to me a fatal one; and the fact that when you put it to many scientists, far from having an answer, they seem not even to understand what the difficulty is, assures me that I have not found a mare's nest but detected a radical disease in their whole mode of thought from the very beginning.[47]

To see how Lewis' approach helps us to face contemporary challenges, consider this example. Anthony Cashmore is a professor of biology at the University of Pennsylvania, specializing in "the mechanism by which plants respond to light."[48] He was elected to the National Academy of Sciences in 2003, and the *Proceedings of the National Academy of Sciences* published his inaugural article, "The Lucretian Swerve: The Biological Basis of Human Behavior and the Criminal Justice System," in 2010. Cashmore aims to show that, since human behavior is the product of genes, environment, and "stochastic" factors (that is, they are probabilistic), therefore there is no such thing as free will. This in turn means that "individuals cannot logically be held responsible for their behavior"; which then leads to Cashmore's purpose for writing, namely a proposal to reform the American criminal justice system.

In making the argument about how the biological factors determine behavior, Cashmore does cite a few studies in cognitive science, regarding the relationship between measurable brain activity and human choices. He does not claim that anyone actually understands the brain processes, or what consciousness is; he rather expects that at some point we will have a full explanation for how it arises from the chemical properties of the nervous system. He nevertheless insists, "as living systems we are nothing more than a bag of chemicals... not only do we have no more free will than a fly or a bacterium, in actuality we have no more free will than a bowl of sugar. The laws of nature are uniform throughout, and these laws do not accommodate the concept of free will."[49]

Because "progress in understanding the chemical basis of behavior will make it increasingly untenable to retain a belief in the concept of free will," therefore "it is time for the legal system to confront this reality." All of the reforms he proposes stem from "the elimination of the illogical concept that individuals are in control of their behavior in a manner that is something other than a reflection of their genetic makeup and their environmental history," and this will "hopefully minimize the retributive aspect of criminal law." Persons convicted of crimes will then be given the appropriate psychiatric help (as specified by a "court-appointed panel of experts").[50]

There is much to say about the overall logic of Cashmore's argument and many of the details as well. For now, I will content myself with observing that Lewis would surely point out that Cashmore, in declaring our thoughts to be merely a biological phenomenon, has undercut anyone's right to believe such a claim. Cashmore seems to have taken it as fundamental to science that we must seek purely material and, apparently, reductionistic, explanations for everything.

Lewis, who wrote, "A man's rational thinking is *just so much* of his share in eternal Reason as the state of his brain allows to become operative,"[51] would not be surprised at the close connection between brain activity and decisions, although he would likely also point out how little these findings actually do explain. He would surely also note what problems we make for ourselves if we suppose that it is even reasonable to posit that chemical events in the brain, strictly speaking, *cause* thoughts or choices.

Further, we recognize that free will and moral responsibility are parts of a larger realm of discourse, in which there is some transcendent norm that we are obligated to comply with. And Cashmore has not evaded such transcendence. Why does he not suggest that we simply eliminate those who commit crimes—whether from the population, or at least from the gene pool (say, by sterilization)? Surely it is because he sees as clearly as anyone else that we *should not* do such horrors to our fellow humans. Why does he think we ought to restructure our criminal justice system? Is it not because he considers it *unjust* to punish people for things for which they are not responsible? And who gets to choose these panels of experts, what kind of decision-making does he expect from them, and to whom will they be accountable? Will they be wrong if they accept bribes or other favors? I must believe that Cashmore expects everyone to behave with the utmost honesty and fairness, and that they are blameworthy if they do not. And even to make the case for something, to try to persuade us that it is *true*, is in effect to insist that the readers *ought to* believe it, and are culpable if they do not.[52]

It is to Cashmore's credit that he commits these inconsistencies: they are his humanity breaking through. As Lewis put it, "Holding a philosophy which excludes humanity, they yet remain human.... They know far better than they think they know."[53]

We might suspect that Lewis would add, along with his Professor Digory Kirke, "Logic! Why don't they teach logic at these schools?"[54]

Objection: These "Adjustments" Take Leave of the Biblical Presentation

I have already cited a passage from Lewis where he imagined his friend Corineus objecting to a project such as I have discussed here, namely that we are no longer talking about the *biblical* world.

Indeed, in words that oddly echo Corineus, the biblical scholar Peter Enns has made exactly this objection to my own study on Adam and Eve:

> Collins's synthesis requires an ad hoc hybrid "Adam" who was "first man" in the sense of being either a specially chosen hominid or a larger tribe of early hominids (Collins is careful not to commit himself to either option).... Further, this type of hybrid "Adam," clearly driven by the need to account for an evolutionary model, is not the Adam of the biblical authors.[55]

For now I leave aside the question of whether Enns has presented and analyzed my argument carefully (I think he clearly did not), because I am not aiming to defend the specifics of my own work here, except insofar as I am "broadly Lewisian."⁵⁶ I will instead focus our attention on his words, "not the Adam of the biblical authors," with its echo of Corineus.

How does Lewis help us think through such an objection? First, Lewis has reminded us that the material in Genesis 1–11 contains a good deal of pictorial description: and this means, *both* that we must be careful of undue literalism, *and* that the material can still have a referent. Enns seems to be suggesting that only a literalistic reading of the Genesis material is true to the Bible writers on their own terms, and that any effort to relate that to science departs from the Bible writers altogether (a departure he advocates).⁵⁷

The British New Testament scholar N. T. Wright seems to understand things better than Enns when he discusses the Apostle Paul's use of Adam in Romans 5:

> Paul clearly believed that there had been a single first pair, whose male, Adam, had been given a commandment and had broken it. Paul was, we may be sure, aware of what we would call mythical or metaphorical dimensions to the story, but he would not have regarded these as throwing doubt on the existence, and primal sin, of the first historical pair. Our knowledge of early anthropology is sketchy, to put it mildly. Each time another very early skull is dug up the newspapers exclaim over the discovery of the first human beings; we have consigned Adam and Eve entirely to the world of mythology, but we are still looking for their replacements. What "sin" would have looked like in the early dawn of the human race it is impossible to say; but the turning away from open and obedient relationship with the loving creator, and the turning toward that which, though beautiful and enticing, is not God, is such a many-sided phenomenon that it is not hard to envisage it at any stage of anthropoid development. The general popular belief that the early stories of Genesis were straightforwardly disproved by Charles Darwin is of course nonsense, however many times it is reinforced in contemporary myth-making. Things are just not that simple, in biblical theology or science.⁵⁸

Lewis deals with the ideas at the base of this objection:

> Remembering, as I do, from within, the attitude of the impatient sceptic, I realize very well how he is fore-armed against anything I might say for

the rest of this chapter. "I know exactly what this man is going to do," he murmurs. "He is going to start explaining all these mythological statements away".... I freely admit that "modernist" Christianity has constantly played just the game of which the impatient sceptic accuses it. But I also think there is a kind of explaining which is not explaining away.... I am going to distinguish what I regard as the "core" or "real meaning" of the doctrines from that in their expression which I regard as inessential and possibly even changed without damage. [59]

Lewis draws a distinction between the "core" of a Christian doctrine and the particular form by which some people might picture the relevant events, and he reminds us, "Christianity is not to be judged from the fancies of children any more than medicine from the ideas of the little girl who believed in horrid red things."[60]

He then asks us to imagine a scenario:

We can suppose a Galilean peasant who thought that Christ had literally and physically "sat down at the right hand of the Father." If such a man had then gone to Alexandria and had a philosophical education he would have discovered that the Father had no right hand and did not sit on a throne.... Even if it could be shown, then, that the early Christians accepted their imagery literally, this would not mean that we are justified in relegating their doctrines as a whole to the lumber room. Whether they actually did, is another matter. The difficulty here is that they were not writing as philosophers to satisfy speculative curiosity about the nature of God and of the universe.... Hence the sort of question we are now considering is never raised by the New Testament writers. When once it is raised, Christianity decides quite clearly that the naïf images are false.... We do not find similar statements in the New Testament, because the issue has not yet been made explicit: but we do find statements which make it certain how that issue will be decided when once it becomes explicit. [61]

Or, as he puts it in another place:

The answer is that the alternative we are offering [the early Christians] was probably never present to their minds at all. As soon as it was present, we know quite well which side of the fence they came down on.... The earliest Christians were not so much like a man who mistakes the shell for the kernel as like a man carrying a nut which he hasn't yet cracked. The moment it is cracked, he knows which part to throw away. Till then he holds on to the nut, not because he is a fool but because he isn't. [62]

Besides Alexandrian analysis, what sorts of principles do we have that can guide us, ensuring that we are keeping the kernel? One overlooked factor in Lewis that I have alluded to is the notion of the overarching storyline of the Bible. The story begins with a transcendent God who made a good world, with its human inhabitants morally innocent. By some sort of disobedience they pulled themselves and their offspring astray from God's good plan, and God's activity is thereafter redemptive—that is, he is constantly aiming to provide "forgiveness for having broken, and supernatural help towards keeping, that law," that universal law embedded in the good creation.[63] The freedoms leave some room for discussion over just what kinds of scenarios we will be intellectually satisfied with. But the shape of the story puts a limit on our speculations. We want to be sure that we are still telling the same story. This, by the way, is why we should not take Lewis' image of the kernel and shell too strictly: that is, the biblical way of describing things retains its value as the proper way to envision the events and scenery, because that imagery shapes our attitudes. Hence, we are not free to "throw it away" in every sense, and Lewis himself did not.

Corineus' objection, then—as exemplified by Peter Enns—stems from a drastic oversimplification, and thus from actual misunderstanding.

Conclusions

C. S. Lewis, Francis Schaeffer, and Jerram Barrs have shown us how the biblical story, sometimes summarized as Creation, Fall, Redemption, and Consummation, rings true: it actually accounts for what we find in ourselves and in the world. That story is, in fact, the true Big Story that makes sense of our lives. I admire the passion with which these men have sought to bring the truth of this Big Story to bear on a wide range of human activities—indeed, on all of life.

Such an endeavor will meet difficulties, and our faith obligates us to make our best effort to address these difficulties with full intellectual rigor and honesty. By combining the profound insights of Lewis and Schaeffer into a sensible program of "freedoms and limitations" we have the tools we need for responsible and faithful discussions of our origins.

1. Francis A. Schaeffer, "No Final Conflict." In *The Complete Works of Francis A. Schaeffer* (Westchester, IL: Crossway, 1982), 131.
2. Schaeffer, "No Final Conflict," 136.
3. Robert Letham, *The Westminster Assembly: Reading Its Theology in Historical Context* (Phillipsburg, NJ: P & R, 2009), 3, 176, 182.
4. Steven Jon James Lovell, *Philosophical Themes from C. S. Lewis* (University of Sheffield PhD, 2003), 10.
5. C. S. Lewis, *God in the Dock: Essays on theology and ethics* (Walter Hooper, ed.; Grand Rapids: Eerdmans, 1970), 38 ("Dogma and the universe," 1943). Since many of Lewis' works appear in several editions, with different page numbers (and some of these are online), and since the collections of essays gather things written at different times, my convention for citing Lewis is the following: the books I will cite from the edition I own, but also with the chapter or section number; the essays I will cite from the collection, but also with the title and (probable) date.
6. Lewis, *God in the Dock*, 63 ("Myth Became Fact," 1944).
7. Albert M. Wolters and Michael W. Goheen, *Creation Regained: Biblical Basics for a Reformational Worldview* 2nd ed. (Grand Rapids, IL: Eerdmans, 2005), 125.
8. Wolters and Goheen offer the idea of a play in six acts, Creation, then Fall, then Israel, then Jesus in the gospels, then the post-Easter Church, and then the consummation—thus splitting Redemption up into three parts.
9. One can find various titles such as Abraham Oakes, *A Short Essay on the Creation, Fall, and Redemption of Man* (London, 1750), and T. R. Birks, *The Difficulties of Belief In Connexion With the Creation and the Fall, Redemption and Judgment* (London, 1876). One might further find this narrative structure to underlie the famous "fourfold state of man" of authors such as Thomas Boston; but the influence of this structure on biblical studies and theology seems (to me at least) small. Readers of the Greek Christian theologian Athanasius (296–373) will recognize that he has structured his two major apologetic works, *Against the Heathen* and *On the Incarnation of the Word of God*, around just this storyline.
10. C. S. Lewis, *Miracles: A preliminary study* (1st edition; London: Geoffrey Bles, 1947), 119–20 (ch. 12); (2nd edition; New York: Macmillan, 1960), 98–99.
11. C. S. Lewis, "Historicism," in *Christian Reflections* (Walter Hooper, ed.; Grand Rapids, MI: Eerdmans, 1967), 103.
12. C. S. Lewis, *The Discarded Image: An introduction to Medieval and Renaissance literature* (Cambridge: Cambridge University Press, 1964), 174.
13. For more general reflections on aspects of Lewis' thought, see my essay, "A Peculiar Clarity: How C. S. Lewis Can Help Us Think About Faith and Science," in John G. West, ed., *The Magician's Twin: C. S. Lewis on Science, Scientism, and Society* (Seattle: Discovery Institute Press, 2012), 69–106.
14. C. S. Lewis, *Reflections on the Psalms* (London: Geoffrey Bles, 1958), 109 (ch. 11).
15. From his second letter to Radulphus (1497); English translation from Frederick Seebohm, *The Oxford Reformers* (London: Longmans, Green, & Co., 1869), 51 (italics original). Another translation, with the Latin original, appears in J. H. Lupton, ed., *Letters to Radulphus on the Mosaic Account of the Creation, Together with Other Treatises, by John Colet, m.a.* (London: George Bell, 1876), 9–10. The wording quoted suggests that Lewis had read the Seebohm edition of the letters (Lupton's rendering is "after the manner of *some* popular poet," which is also close). It is possible that Lewis mistakenly attributed this to Jerome, since he is well-known to have quoted often from memory — see Walter Hooper's "Preface" to Lewis, *Selected Literary Essays* (Walter Hooper, ed.; Cambridge: Cambridge University Press, 1969), xvii. But it is also possible that Colet did actually derive this view from Jerome, as he did so many other views. In the first

letter to Radulphus, Colet had mentioned Jerome as a careful scholar familiar with the original Hebrew. Credit for tracking down this reference goes to the blog post and comments at alltheblognamesarealreadytaken.wordpress.com/2008/05/29/cs-lewis-and-st-jerome/.
16. Lewis, *Reflections on the Psalms*, 110.
17. Lewis, *Reflections on the Psalms*, 110–111.
18. Lyle W. Dorsett, ed., *The Essential C. S. Lewis* (New York: Scribner, 1988), 404–405.
19. This point follows from Lewis' argument in his *Miracles*, regarding the special status of mind, which cannot be explained as merely the material operations of the brain. See also his *The Problem of Pain* (London: Geoffrey Bles, 1940), ch. 5.
20. Lewis, *Miracles*, 33 (ch. 4); *God in the Dock*, 42 ("Dogma and the Universe," 1943).
21. Frederic Seebohm, The Oxford Reformers (London: Longmans, Green, & Co., 1869), 29.
22. See the discussion in Alexander Heidel, *The Babylonian Genesis* (Chicago: University of Chicago Press, 1951)—a book that addresses issues that were current in Lewis' time.
23. For discussion and documentation, see my *Did Adam and Eve Really Exist? Who They Were and Why You Should Care* (Wheaton, IL: Crossway, 2011), Appendix 1.
24. William W. Hallo, "Part 1: Mesopotamia and the Asiatic Near East," in William W. Hallo and William K. Simpson, eds., *The Ancient Near East: A History* (Fort Worth, TX: Harcourt Brace College Publishers, 1998), 3–181, at 25.
25. I make these points more fully in chapter 2 and Appendix 1 of *Did Adam and Eve Really Exist?* An example of missing this point comes from Daniel Harlow, "After Adam: Reading Genesis in an age of evolutionary science," *Perspectives on Science and Christian Faith* 62.3 (2010): 179–95; at 185–87, Harlow notices symbolic and pictorial elements in both Genesis and the Mesopotamian sources, and pronounces them both unhistorical. He is confusing historicity with a literalistic scheme of interpretation, without argument.
26. Lewis, *Discarded Image*, 31.
27. Lewis, *Discarded Image*, 147–48.
28. William D. Reyburn and Euan McG. Fry, *Handbook on Genesis* (New York: United Bible Societies, 1997), 27.
29. Likewise, in what is actually a good book (which I have commended), Davis Young and Ralph Stearley, *The Bible, Rocks and Time* (Downers Grove, IL: InterVarsity, 2008), dismiss appeal to phenomenal language as an "attempt to avoid the force of the [Genesis] statement" (207), apparently unaware of all the linguistic, literary, and rhetorical issues they have swept under the rug.
30. Lewis, *Discarded Image*, 183. "The Waverley novels" refers to a class of historical fiction that began in the early nineteenth century (as in Sir Walter Scott's *Waverley*, 1814).
31. For more detail, see my *Did Adam and Eve Really Exist*, §2b. I also employ a number of Lewisian and Schaefferian ideas in my contributions to Matthew Barrett and Ardel Canaday, eds., *Four Views on the Historical Adam* (Grand Rapids: Zondervan, 2013)—not only in my chapter, but also in my comments on the other contributions.
32. Lewis, *The Problem of Pain*, ch. 5.
33. C. S. Lewis, *The Joyful Christian* (New York: Simon & Schuster, 1977), 49.
34. Lewis, *The Problem of Pain*, 75 (ch. 5).
35. Lewis, *The Problem of Pain*, 75 (ch. 5).
36. Lewis, *Miracles*, 32 (ch. 5).
37. See my discussion in *Did Adam and Eve Really Exist*, §5d; I propose my own "freedoms and limitations" in §5c. In my discussion of Lewis, I draw attention to his bafflement over the solidarity concept that underlies the biblical picture. Hence it fascinated me to discover after my book's publication that Lewis continued to wish for greater light on this topic: in a letter written in 1951, more than 10 years after *The Problem of Pain*, he wishes he had known more about how the notion of "members of one another" works; letter, 12 September 1951, cited in Richard Purtill, *C. S. Lewis' Case for the*

Christian Faith (San Francisco: Ignatius, 2004), 56. This idea is part of what New Testament scholars now call "interchange," and it is part of the larger question of corporate solidarity among the people of God.

38. Lewis, *Christian Reflections*, 86 ("The Funeral of a Great Myth," ca. 1945). Lewis may very well be reflecting a comment by G. K. Chesterton, whom he admired: "No philosopher denies that a mystery still attaches to the two great transitions: the origin of the universe itself and the origin of the principle of life itself. Most philosophers have the enlightenment to add that a third mystery attaches to the origin of man himself. In other words, a third bridge was built across a third abyss of the unthinkable when there came into the world what we call reason and what we call will," in *The Everlasting Man* (Garden City: Doubleday, 1955 [1925]), 27. A work that Lewis praised, Arthur James Balfour, *Theism and Humanism* (New York: Hodder & Stoughton, 1915), makes this point as well. And, interestingly enough in view of Schaeffer's connection to "Old Princeton" Seminary, David Livingstone has shown that Benjamin Warfield wound up with a very similar approach to evolution; see Livingstone, *Darwin's Forgotten Defenders* (Grand Rapids: Eerdmans, 1987). Hence Lewis' reservations about what natural "evolution" can accomplish resonate with Schaeffer's freedoms and limitations cited at the head of this essay.
39. J. B. S. Haldane, whom Lewis mentioned often, certainly did want to claim that evolutionary biology ruled out any possibility of conventional theistic religion being true. He states this plainly in his essays "Darwinism today," "When I am dead," and "Science and theology as art forms" in *Possible Worlds and Other Essays* (New Brunswick, NJ: Transaction Publishers, 2002 [1927]); see further Gordon McOuat and Mary P. Winsor, "J. B. S. Haldane's Darwinism in its religious context," *British Journal for the History of Science* 28.2 (1995): 227–31.
40. Watson, "Adaptation," *Report of the Ninety-Seventh Meeting British Association for the Advancement of Science* (London: Office of the British Association, 1929), 88–99, at 88.
41. These two statements were accessed in January of 2016: "NSTA Position Statement: The Teaching of Evolution," 2003, http://www.nsta.org/about/positions/evolution.aspx. "NABT Position Statement on Teaching Evolution," adopted in 1995 and modified in 1997, 2000, 2004, 2008, and 2011, http://www.nabt.org/websites/institution/?p=92. (Earlier versions held that "natural selection…has no specific direction or goal," but this has been removed—so at least a teleological reading of the whole process is allowed for.)
42. Lewis, *God in the Dock*, 315 ("Is progress possible? Willing slaves of the welfare state," 1958).
43. Lewis, *God in the Dock*, 108 ("Man or rabbit?," 1946).
44. C. S. Lewis, *The Four Loves* (London: Geoffrey Bles, 1960), 70, 84 (ch. 4). In the same chapter Lewis observes, "To those—and they are now the majority—who see human life merely as a development and complication of animal life all forms of behaviour which cannot produce certificates of an animal origin and of survival value are suspect" (71).
45. Susan Milius, "Beast Buddies," *Science News* (November 1, 2003): 282–84.
46. Lewis, *The Four Loves*, 116 (ch. 5).
47. C. S. Lewis, *The Weight of Glory and Other Addresses* (Walter Hooper, ed.; New York: Simon & Schuster, 1996 [1980]), 103 ("Is Theology Poetry," 1944); cf. *Christian Reflections*, 89 ("Funeral of a Great Myth," ca. 1945). See also *God in the Dock*, 135 ("Religion Without Dogma?," 1946), where Lewis notes that there are different levels of openness to religion in the different scientific disciplines: "It is as their subject matter comes nearer to man himself that their anti-religious bias hardens."
48. Information from the university's web page on Professor Cashmore, http://www.bio.upenn.edu/faculty/cashmore/index.html.
49. Anthony Cashmore, "The Lucretian Swerve: The Biological Basis of Human Behavior

and the Criminal Justice System," *Proceedings of the National Academy of Sciences*, January 12, 2010, www.pnas.org/cgi/doi/10.1073/pnas.0915161107.
50. Cashmore, "The Lucretian Swerve."
51. Lewis, *Miracles*, 37 (ch. 6).
52. This last point comes from Stephen R. L. Clark, *From Athens to Jerusalem: The Love of Wisdom and the Love of God* (Oxford: Clarendon Press, 1984), 96–97; see further at 28–30 for a position similar to Lewis'. Along the same lines as Cashmore is Tamler Sommers and Alex Rosenberg, "Darwin's nihilistic idea: Evolution and the meaninglessness of life," *Biology and Philosophy* 18 (2003), 653-68. They claim that Darwin's naturalism and materialism undermine any notion of teleology for human life, and thus any notion of ethical normativity. Again, these authors are nevertheless assuming an ethics of belief, in the sense that they aim to persuade. Indeed, they get explicitly moralistic when they speak of "every naturalist's *obligation* to be a Darwinian about how ethical beliefs arose in the first place" (667), and later conclude, "If it is the right conclusion then we *must* respond to Dennett's final question… with a simple 'no'" (668). I should recommend a dose of Lewis's essays in *Christian Reflections* as a helpful antidote.
53. Lewis, *Miracles*, 37 (ch. 5).
54. C. S. Lewis, *The Lion, the Witch and the Wardrobe* (New York: HarperCollins, 1950), 48 (ch. 5).
55. Peter Enns, "Still in the Weeds on Human Origins," review of *Did Adam and Eve Really Exist?*, by C. John Collins, *Perspectives*, December 16, 2011, 19–22, at 19 (italics added). Enns has similar points in his book, *The Evolution of Adam: What the Bible Does and Doesn't Say About Human Origins* (Grand Rapids: Baker, 2012), but the remarks in his review allow us to focus.
56. I am inclined to excuse his misreadings in light of Lewis' concession to Dr. Pittenger, who had likewise misread and mischaracterized Lewis: "we all know too well how difficult it is to grasp or retain the substance of a book one finds antipathetic," in *God in the Dock*, 179 ("Rejoinder to Dr Pittenger," 1958). Nevertheless, I must comment on an obvious mistake in the quoted words from Enns: In my book I said nothing about a "synthesis" that "requires an ad hoc hybrid"; rather, I set out my freedoms and limitations, and then considered several scenarios in light of those. I thought I made it clear that I did not endorse any of them. Perhaps my strategy only makes sense if one accepts a freedoms and limitations model to begin with?
57. Enns makes it clear in his *Evolution of Adam* that this is indeed what he means; e.g., "The biblical writers assumed that the earth is flat, was made by God in relatively recent history (about 4,000 years before Jesus) just as it looks now, and that it is the fixed point in the cosmos over which the sun actually rises and sets" (xiii); he also refers to a "strictly literal/historical reading of Genesis" (xv), apparently equating literalism in reading with historicity. Ironically, he does actually mention the essay by Lewis that has the Corineus quotation, but only to use its title, "Myth became fact" (Enns, 76), with no engagement with its content.
58. N. T. Wright, "Romans," in Leander Keck et al., eds., *New Interpreter's Bible, Volume X* (Nashville: Abingdon, 2002), 393–770, at 524ab (italics added). (I am not implying that Wright would agree with my own position; that will be another discussion!)
59. Lewis, *Miracles*, 69–70 (ch. 10). A very similar discussion appears in Lewis, *The Weight of Glory*, 100–101 ("Is theology poetry," 1944); see also *God in the Dock*, 45–46 ("Dogma and the Universe," 1943).
60. *Miracles*, 74 (ch. 10). Compare what he said about the medieval world picture: the learned were well aware that the world is round, but "There were ditchers and alewives who… did not know that the earth was spherical; not because they thought it was flat but because they did not think about it at all" (Lewis, *The Discarded Image*, 20).
61. Lewis, *Miracles*, 75–76 (ch. 10).
62. Lewis, *The Weight of Glory*, 100–101.

63. C. S. Lewis, "On Ethics" in *Christian Reflections* (Walter Hooper, ed.; Grand Rapids, IL: Eerdmans, 1967), 46–47.

EVANGELISM AND THE CULTURAL MANDATE

William Edgar

DThéol, Université de Genève
Professor of Apologetics, Westminster Theological Seminary,
Philadelphia, PA
Professeur Associé at Faculté Jean Calvin
Aix-en-Provence, France

A significant portion of this content appears in another from in *Created and Creating: A Biblical Theology of Culture* (IVP Academic). © 2016 by William Edgar. Used by permission of InterVarsity Press, www.ivpress.com.

Is the unity of evangelism and the Cultural Mandate a perennial discussion? It flares up regularly, especially over the past few centuries. The latest form is a debate over the two kingdoms view. Many Evangelicals are heated about the issue of evangelism and cultural activity in general or the gospel of social justice in particular. Corwin, Moreau, and McGee describe missiologists as often being divided between those who fear an emphasis on social justice will undermine evangelism and those who believe the church should be engaged in social justice far more than it is.[1] New York pastor Timothy Keller puts the divide this way:

> On the one hand there are Christians who want to work for social reforms, citing only Biblical reasons, and speaking aggressively against those who do not share their religious beliefs. On the other hand there are those who counsel Christians not to seek social justice at all, predicting that such efforts only make Christians more like the world. Instead, they say, Christians should concentrate on only bringing individuals to faith in Christ and building up the church.[2]

His own view is that the first group is too triumphalist, while the second group is too pessimistic about real cultural change and social reform.

John Gladwin bluntly states that this dichotomy stems from a rabid individualism produced by the Enlightenment and not Scripture. He writes, "Scripture does not appreciate our modern distinctions between the different works of evangelism and social action. Certain things flow from the Gospel as a matter of course...." One of them is "the apostolic *public* testimony to Christ."[3] John R. W. Stott, principal architect of the Lausanne Covenant (1974), a statement of faith which attempted to redress an imbalance between so-called spiritual and so-called physical needs, states that evangelism is appealing to people to come to Christ for conversion, whereas mission is "Christian service in the world comprising both evangelism and social action."[4]

Perhaps what got us off to a bad start in more recent times is H. Richard Niebuhr's *Christ and Culture*.[5] The book is brilliant, lucid, compelling, and it represents several of the major ways the church has viewed culture over the years.

The book begins by stating that there is an enduring problem of relating Christ, who is filled with the love of God, and culture, which he defines, following Bronislaw Malinowski, as "the 'artificial, secondary environment' which man superimposes on the natural." As such, culture includes "language, habits, ideas, beliefs, customs, social organization, inherited artifacts, technical processes, and values."[6] Niebuhr then outlines five possible positions in response to the enduring problem:

- Christ Against Culture
- The Christ of Culture

- Christ Above Culture
- Christ and Culture in Paradox
- Christ the Transformer of Culture

Niebuhr finds strengths and weaknesses in all these views, although he appears to lean most towards Christ the Transformer of Culture, which he attributes to Augustine and also to F. D. Maurice (1805–1872), the controversial Anglican Christian socialist.

Niebuhr unintentionally sets up a contrast which stems from a category mistake. Instead of relating the Triune God to the creation (once perfect, now fallen, and being redeemed), by means of omnipresence and accommodation, he contrasts a rather abstract "Christ" to the "artificial, secondary environment" human beings have developed. That is quite different. The result is that the Gospel of Jesus Christ must somehow always be in tension with something called culture. The root problem is that Niebuhr's scheme does not sufficiently begin with a creation that is *tov me'od* (Hebrew for "formless and void"). Nor does he consider that the Second Person of the Trinity was from the beginning the mediator of Creation, who holds everything together (Col. 1:16–17). Thus Jesus was no foreigner needing to define his relation to the world, whether against it, of it, above it, etc.

Even after the Fall, God having decided to save the world and not abandon it, Christ is still the mediator, but of the new creation (Col. 2:18–20; 1 Tim. 2:5). To be sure, because of the introduction of evil, his role is now corrective as well as contemplative. The tragedy of sin is that it blinds people from seeing him as he is: The Apostle John writes, *"All things were made through him... He was in the world, and the world was made through him, yet the world did not know him"* (John 1:3, 10). Still, Christ is not an entity that must somehow be placed in tension with the world. The Gospel is the power of God unto salvation, approving and developing what is good, correcting and overcoming what is awry in every realm of life (Rom. 1:17–18). The disjunction caused by sin does not introduce a Christ who is radically different from the mediator of creation, but reintroduces him as the conciliating mediator between God and his people (1 Tim. 2:5).

Perhaps a better way to approach the question (largely unexplored it seems to me) is to conduct a biblical-theological study of the relation between the Lord's call of Genesis 1:28–30 to subdue the earth and his commission in Matthew 28:18–20 to make disciples of the nations. Among the many suggestive claims set forth in Harvie M. Conn's landmark study, *Evangelism: Doing Justice and Preaching Grace*, is that there is an essential unity between what Reformed theologians call the "Cultural Mandate" and the "great commission." That is, when Jesus tells his disciples to *"Go therefore and make disciples of all nations..."* (Matt. 28:19), he is in continuity with the much earlier commandment to *"be fruitful and multiply and fill the earth and subdue it..."* (Gen. 1:28). Conn argues that, "It is not an either/or, not a both/and, not even simply a primary/secondary." These two mandates are not two different commands, but rather two stages in God's covenant relationship with mankind. He adds an eschatological note: "The so-called 'missionary mandate' is the covenant mandate's anticipated fulfillment in redemptive grace."[7]

Similarly Bruce Waltke faults pietism and counters, "The great commission to baptize all nations in the name of the Father, Son, and Holy Spirit and the Cultural Mandate complement, not compete against, each other. God's erupting kingdom in a world that needs taming entails a people who purpose to develop a culture that pleases him."[8] In this brief article, lovingly dedicated to my dear friend Jerram Barrs, a man who is thoroughly convinced of its conclusions, I will attempt to suggest some of the ways a proper biblical theology of the two mandates can be explored, and then I will make some reflections on the question of evangelism and cultural activity.

The Image

At the dawn of the world, after he had created the light, the expanse, the dry land, the vegetation, the luminaries, the birds and the fish, and then all the living creatures, God paused to make the crown of his creation. The narrative slows down. Something crucial is about to take place: *"Then God said, 'Let us make man in our image, after our likeness'"* (Gen. 1:26). A good deal of ink has been spilled over the use of the first person plural. Some see this as an early reference to Jesus Christ, or to the Holy Spirit, or even to the entire Trinity.[9] No doubt, "The new is in the old concealed, the old is in the new revealed," and yet one should be very cautious not to read the mature doctrine of the Trinity back into the ancient text in any kind of forced manner.

It could be as Meredith Kline suggests, following a good many Jewish commentators, that God is addressing his heavenly court.[10] There is biblical evidence for the reality of this kind of council. Isaiah 6:1–8 pictures the Lord sitting upon a throne with the seraphim in his court. When he asks *"Whom shall I send, and who will go for us,"* it is possible that the "us" includes these angels (see Job 38:4, 7). When God responds to the people of Shinar's boast, *"Come let us make bricks,"* with his own *"Come, let us go down..."* it is possible that an angelic court is in view (Gen. 11:1–9).

Still another set of commentators see this as a plural of majesty, or even a plural of self-deliberation. Cassuto makes a strong case for a "plural of exhortation." That is, when we determine to do something, we will often say, "Let us go!," or "Let us rise up!" and the like. For example in 2 Samuel 24:14, David, having sinfully taken a census of the people, is asked to choose his punishment. One of them comes with high risk, and yet the certainty that it will be utterly fair: committing to God's will. *"I am in great distress,"* he said to Gad, *"Let us fall into the hand of the Lord,"* rather than into the hands of man.[11] Paul Joüon believes the expression is a plural of self-deliberation on grammatical grounds.[12]

Each of these positions has merit. Perhaps, as David Clines puts it, the view that it refers to self-deliberation has fewer disadvantages than the others.[13] At the same time, as Gordon J. Wenham points out, there may not be all that many disadvantages to the view that God speaks in his heavenly court.[14] And if we accept the Bible as a united text, then it would not be wrong either to include an early reference to the Trinity here. Likely it is impossible to be dogmatic. I am drawn to the self-deliberation or "plural of exhortation" view.

What matters for our purposes is that this is a special moment. Cassuto writes, "Only in the case of man, because of his special importance, does Scripture allude to the Divine thought preceding the act of creation."[15] This special moment is the creation of mankind after God's own image. "Whereas the other creatures are created 'according to their kinds' (Gen. 1:21, 24, 25), humanity is made 'in the image of God.'"[16] This concept is unique in any religion or any philosophy. What then does this mean? Again, a great deal has been said about the subject. Rightly so, for it is one of the most significant teachings in the biblical worldview.

The terms *tselem* and *demût* help us a little. The first is often used to denote figurines or even relief carvings (Ezek. 23:14). The second is a general term for "likeness," which can mean a resemblance, as in Daniel 10:16, which describes an angel, one "in the *likeness* of the children of man," touching Daniel's lips. The angel looks like a man. A very close parallel to the use of these two words has been found at Tell Fakhariyah (northeastern Syria) in a bilingual Assyrian inscription of an Aramaic paraphrase: the statue is a likeness and an image.[17] This means that there is an essential resemblance and yet also a distinction. As C. John Collins puts it, "Thus, we can paraphrase Genesis 1:26: 'Let us make man to be our concrete resemblance, to be like us.'"[18]

Context should be our primary guide for understanding exactly what the image is, and what it leads to. A number of possibilities present themselves. One is that the image refers to the mental and spiritual attributes. This is the view of Jerram's and my mentor, Francis A. Schaeffer. For him, the image represents at least four faculties: man is moral and can make moral choices; man is rational, able to think; man is creative, able to make works of art; and man can love.[19] This view is quite plausible, although we lack clear connections in the specific texts which refer to the image of God (Gen. 5:1; 9:6; 1 Cor. 11:7; Eph. 4:24; Col. 3:10; Jas. 3:9).

Certainly man shares certain attributes with God. What is certain is that there is a tacit connection between the image and the honor due the human being. A considerable number of ethical issues come to the fore. Put positively, as J. Douma says, "Confessing man as the image of God should make us think highly of (the life of) our neighbor and, in comparison, think modestly of ourselves and our own life." Put negatively, Douma writes, "We may say that whoever assaults human life assaults the image of God."[20]

Another crucial consequence is the equality of the sexes. Both male and female are in God's own image (Gen. 1:27). They have equal dignity. They jointly share the task of subduing the earth. Indeed, they cannot be fruitful and multiply into successive generations unless both are image-bearers. Genesis 5:1–4 makes it clear that both male and female are generically named "man" (*adam*), and so Adam the person was able to father a son in his own image (see also Gen. 9:6).

The most comprehensive view is that the image makes mankind a true likeness, and God's true representative on earth. Immediately following the declaration of man's special creation as God's image-bearer we find the unique mandate, *"And let them have dominion..."* (Gen. 1:26). In good Hebrew fashion, after the "intent" comes the "accounting" of how it happened: *"So God created man in his own image... And God blessed them, and God said to them, 'Be fruitful and multiply and fill the earth and subdue it...'"* (1:27ff.).

This ruling and subduing is a royal task. One can find many examples in scripture, and some outside of it, of the kingly calling to have dominion. An outstanding example is Solomon. When his kingdom was finally settled, he could then exercise proper dominion (1 Kgs. 4:24).

Psalm 8 specifically connects man's identity with royal rule, when it speaks of his being *crowned* with glory and honor, giving him dominion (vv. 5–6). Waltke connects the image with our being set apart for God: "We are to be distinguished by our godlike compassion in connection with our ruling. Like God, we are to be merciful kings."[21]

Waltke makes further points about the nature of the image.[22] First, there is a psychosomatic unity to the human being. That is, there is no dualism of body and soul, and certainly no superiority of the soul or the mind. The term *selem* refers to a "formed body."[23]

Second, the image is a faithful, or adequate representation. Mankind is "theomorphic" in relation to the original. Even though, unlike us, God is pure Spirit, yet he is able to see (Ps. 94:9) and hear (Ps. 34:17), so that our human structure is a faithful representation, much like a mirror image is faithful to the original.

Third, and this is most important, the image of God means life. Just as God is alive, so mankind is a living being. Waltke notes how well Michelangelo captured this in his masterpiece on the ceiling of the Sistine Chapel: a lifeless Adam, a mere candidate for humanity, awaits the touch of God to give him life.

And fourth, Waltke reflects on the function of the image, particularly the capacity to rule. We have "representative authority," he argues. And he points out as others have, that unlike the Assyrian tradition, where only kings were thought to be in the image of God, and therefore authorized to rule, in the Old Testament, all mankind is endowed with this status. "God has called humanity to be his vice-regents and high priests on earth." Had the Fall not occurred nothing would threaten human dignity, and no class barriers would exist.

The Mandate

The image of God is both constitutive and functional. God not only made mankind in a certain way, but calls him to certain tasks. In the first iteration of that function, connected with the Lord's "intent" (Gen. 1:26), dominion over the creation is underscored: *"And let them have dominion over the fish of the sea and over the birds of the heavens and over the livestock and over all the earth and over every creeping thing that creeps on the earth."* In the second, the "accounting" (Gen. 1:27–30, 31), there is a blessing, then the command to procreate and fill the earth, and then dominion over the earth, underscoring that what is ruled is God's gift.

The point not to be missed is that God is at the center of everything in mankind's calling. After the statement about God's blessing the human beings, what might be taken as a passing comment, *"And God blessed them,"* becomes actually foundational for what follows. Whereas God had blessed the fish and birds and animals and told them to *"be fruitful and multiply"* (Gen. 1:22), when it comes to human beings, verse 28 qualifies that, *"God said to them,"* stressing the personal presence of the God who commands in a special way. God's blessing then is really at the heart of this Cultural Mandate and of all the successive iterations of it. Put differently, God enters into a covenant relationship with his people. Everything else stems from that central arrangement.

In the first version of the mandate, before the Fall, the Lord says, *"Let them have dominion (radah)"* over the entire animal world (Gen. 1:26). In the second (Gen. 1:28), the command is repeated in the context of the others to fill the earth and subdue it (*kabash*). Many have written about these two terms, to have dominion and to subdue. Critics of biblical religion have assumed that they give license to exploit or even violate the creation. Some have blamed these verses for pollution.[24] It is true that *radah* can signify harsh or punitive dominion (Num. 24:19; Neh. 9:28). But it also can mean a just and peaceable rule (1 Kgs. 4:24; Ps. 145:13) or simply honestly gotten wealth (2 Kgs. 20:13). The norm for a good Near Eastern king was that he devote himself to the welfare of his subjects and to favor the vulnerable (Ps. 72:12–14). The term *kabash* is rare, but it connotes the idea of getting under control or even taming (Mic. 7:19; Zech. 9:15). A parallel word, *mashal*, is often used as a parallel to both *radah* and *kabash*. Surely, the context of Genesis 1–2 makes it clear that the rule of the world by humanity is the rule of a benevolent king.

Although the finished creation was "good" and "very good," ruling and subduing were still a necessary part of directing the history of the world. At the most elementary level, tilling the earth and accepting God's gifts of plants, trees, and animals requires labor and wisdom (Gen. 1:29–30). At the broader level, humanity was called to spread the blessings of Eden to all the earth. Collins writes, "This would mean managing all of its creatures and resources for *good* purposes: to allow their beauty to flourish, to use them wisely and kindly, and to promote well-being for all."[25] This management is in imitation of God's greater stewardship over his creation. The so-called "nature psalms" attest to the overarching sovereignty of God over his creation, and yet to his delegating analogous power to mankind. Psalm 104:14–15 tells us, *"You cause the grass to grow for the livestock and plants for man to cultivate, that he may bring forth food from the earth and wine to gladden the heart of man, oil to make his face shine and bread to strengthen man's heart...."* Psalm 8, to which we will return, points out that man's significance is not from his size, for he is minuscule, but from his task: *"You have given him dominion (mashal) over the works of your hands..."* (v. 6).

The balance is delicate. As Richard Bauckham puts it, "The close relationship between the image of God and the dominion means that the latter is an exercise of rule *on behalf of* God, not *instead of* God."[26] He points out that Psalm 145, which is a celebration of God's glory and a commentary on his rule over all creation, alludes to his grace and mercy. Paralleling the words of Exodus 34:6, the Psalm tells us, *"The Lord is gracious and merciful, slow to anger and abounding in steadfast love,"* and then adds, *"The Lord is good to all, and his mercy is over all that he has made"* (vv. 8–9). Thus it is that God rules in a way that models our rule. Human dominion is meant to be a form of caring responsibility for God's creatures.[27]

The stipulation for accomplishing such dominion is that mankind must *"be fruitful and multiply and fill the earth"* (Gen. 1:28). Crucial for the Cultural Mandate is the increase of the human race through reproduction, and then spreading throughout the earth. If it were not clear enough that mankind was to spread over the face of the earth from these verses, the second version of the creation, after the *toleh doth* ("generations of," the first of ten such markers in the book of Genesis) makes it abundantly clear that Adam and his wife, Eve, were to continue the human line. The man from now on would leave his father and mother and establish a new family. Childbearing was to be the normal calling of families even in a fallen world (Gen. 4:1–2, 5:3). Much later, reflecting on the Genesis account, Paul tells us that God *"made from one man every nation of mankind to live on the face of the earth..."* (Acts 17:26; see Mal. 2:10).

Paul adds, *"... having determined allotted periods and the boundaries of their dwelling place, that they should seek God, in the hope that they might feel their way toward him and find him"* (Acts 17:26–27). This is an important statement. With good and necessary consequence, we may infer that the original purpose of the creation of humankind was that we should have progressed to a state of glory and happiness, beyond even the perfection of Eden. This is the meaning of the probation, wherein the Lord prohibits taking of the fruit of the tree of the knowledge of good and evil. Had Adam, our first representative, succeeded in obeying God, he would have led his posterity into an eternal state of consummate bliss, represented by the tree of life. As we know, he failed, and our first parents, instead of moving toward this joy, were found guilty, naked, and ashamed, and they were ultimately banned from the Garden. Access to the tree of life was denied (Gen. 3:23–24). Yet, by the unspeakable mercy of God, a way was left open to regain eternal life, through Jesus Christ. In the end after centuries of the history of redemption culminating in the death and resurrection of the Savior, God's people could finally have access to the tree of life, whose leaves are for the healing of the nations (Rev. 22:2).[28]

Blessing is God's gift, procreation, populating the earth, and dominion—all of these constitute what is sometimes known as the Cultural Mandate. While this nomenclature is acceptable, we would want to unpack the term "culture" carefully if we were going to be sure it aptly describes what is going on in these Genesis passages.

Space prohibits such a full treatment. Many people associate culture with the arts or with leisure activities. This is the assumption made in our newspapers which often relegate "culture and the arts" to the last section, as though politics, economics, science, etc. were not cultural activities. The term can also be used of symbols and values we assign to knowledge and experience of the world. In that way almost everything we think and do as human beings is cultural.[29]

John Murray's nomenclature of "the creation ordinances" aptly describes the intent here. Marriage and procreation, labor in all its contours, and worship, the true worship of the Lord God, while they have an ethical tone to them, are at the same time meant to be comprehensive.

The sense that emerges from Genesis is somewhat more developmental than our modern idea of culture. Perhaps the term "civilization" would be closer to the biblical data. Admittedly civilization has a checkered history. In the eighteenth century it often meant something rather elitist. To be civilized was to rise up from barbarism. The etymology is less discriminatory. Civilization derives from the Latin "civilis," which we translate as "civil." In turn this relates to "civis," meaning citizen, and "civitas," meaning the city. To be civilized, then, means to be an honorable citizen. For Mirabeau, human flourishing is the goal of "populations," and religion is the foundation for human growth.[30] Generally civilization refers to the material or instrumental side of human culture, particularly when these lead to the development of science, agriculture, sophisticated trade, and the better aspects of urban culture. Civilization further refers to such developments as standardized writing, measurements, methods of communication and the like. The arts hold a special place in the development of civilization. Art ennobles nature and also gives a well-crafted account of human existence.[31] Whether we settle for the term culture or civilization, the point is that Genesis underscores the human calling to develop and extend God's purposes in the world.

At this point we encounter the notion of progress. Here is a delicate matter.

First because, so popular in the eighteenth and nineteenth centuries, the idea of progress has been challenged by more recent events. It is difficult to believe in human progress when we have seen so much destruction around us. In the wake of two world wars, terrorism, market upheavals, and all kinds of abuses, it is tempting to believe that human history is simply in decline.

Second, because many of the formulations of the idea of progress have come from humanist and rationalist sources which do not square with realism. The Renaissance, with all of its marvels, was at least in part a statement of man's grandeur. It claimed to bypass the Middle Ages (a pejorative term) and go back to the source (*ad fontes*) with the rediscovery of Greek philosophy. At the Enlightenment, the notion of progress became identified with optimism. Philosophers such as Leibniz and Voltaire proclaimed progress in indisputably confident and sanguine terms. The nineteenth century built on the idea of progress. It is safe to say that many (not all) significant philosophers and even theologians during this time connected onto Immanuel Kant's idea that although progress is not automatic, nevertheless we can expect a sometimes painful passage from barbarism (or primitivism) through civilization toward a truly enlightened culture, which includes the abolition of war. Much of this should take place through education.[32] But now it is not so easy to believe in progress.[33]

Christians got into the act. Usually they saw progress as divinely guided. Consider Abraham Kuyper, who is in many ways the father of Christian worldview thinking. He also revived the doctrine of common grace in a way that set the tone for his successors, whether or not they agreed with him in every detail. Indeed, Kuyper was not inclined to use the term culture a great deal. And it was not he, but most likely Klaas Schilder who coined the term "Cultural Mandate."[34] But Kuyper's views are flavored with the idea of progress. Some of them border on what C. S. Lewis called "chronological snobbery," at times with a tinge of racism, in fact. In his chapter on science in *Wisdom and Wonder*, Kuyper compares the "dark-skinned tribes of Africa" with contemporary Europeans, where human society "bears a far nobler and elevated character," not only among Christians, but among unbelievers as well because of common grace. Without God's common grace, science would have been in decline. He qualifies this kind of statement somewhat by reminding the reader of the essential equality of all human beings as well as their equal propensity to sin.[35]

Notwithstanding the problems associated with the idea of progress, it can be fairly stated that there is a progressive unfolding in the history of redemption which results from both special grace and common grace. This is what is meant, in part, by the opening statement in the book of Hebrews: *"Long ago, at many times and in many ways, God spoke to our fathers by the prophets, but in these days he has spoken to us by his Son..."* (Heb. 1:1–2).

A proper notion of progress can also be surmised from statements about building the Church (Matt. 16:18; Eph. 2:20–22). Building is by definition progressive. But does this progress in revelation, culminating in Jesus Christ, followed by the preaching of the Gospel to all the nations, have anything to do with common grace? While the two must never be confused, the one cannot exist without the other. Common grace serves the purpose of saving grace in a number of ways. First and foremost, God's redemptive purposes are served in the wider context of history. Here is how John Murray puts it, in his magnificent article on the subject:

Without common grace special grace would not be possible because special grace would have no material out of which to erect its structure. It is common grace that provides not only the sphere in which, but also the material out of which, the building fitly framed together may grow up into a holy temple in the Lord. It is the human race preserved by God, endowed with various gifts by God, in a world upheld and enriched by God, subsisting through the means of various pursuits and fields of labor, that provides the subjects for redemptive and regenerative grace.[36]

Culture and the development of history cannot be separated from God's purposes of redemption. Neither the church nor the individual believer can be abstracted from the context of the wider history of the world. Indeed the Gospel would make no sense to an unbelieving person who comes to faith without the workings of culture and civilization.

If the essence of the Cultural Mandate could be distilled into three headings, it would be these:

1. The blessing of God on the human race. The heart of humanity's calling is to know the covenant presence of the Lord God, who is our God just as we are his people. As he has done everything to shower his love on us, he has given us all the gifts we need to flourish and return his love.

2. To be fruitful and multiply and fill the earth with our productive presence. The human race was to populate the entire earth, always with the purpose of discovering God's life-giving purposes for us, in all our diversity and talents.

3. To rule over the creation with gentle lordship. Always under the greater lordship of God, we are vicegerents in this marvelous place, taming what is untamed so that it redounds to God's greater glory.

After the Fall

The question naturally arises: What happened to the Cultural Mandate after the Fall? On the surface, it would seem that everything about it was put into question. To cite Murray's creation ordinances, marriage and childbearing were seriously damaged (Gen. 3:16); labor has now become drudgery, with death as the reward for living in a fallen world (3:17–19); and worship has become idolatry (4:5). If we look for any reiteration of the Cultural Mandate, we will find Genesis 4:17–24, where indeed cultural pursuits are undertaken but by the line of Cain, which lived outside of God's presence, east of Eden (4:14–16). By contrast, Cain's failed vocation as the first born was replaced by Seth, whose son Enosh initiated the practice of calling upon the Lord, that is, of true worship. Things go from bad to worse, so that by the time of Noah, the Lord became sorry he had made mankind to dwell upon the earth. So he eradicated the human race through a great flood, with the exception of Noah's own family. And then, after a few more generations, the people build a city and a hideous tower, meant to draw God down to earth on their own terms. Again, the Lord scattered them and confused their language (11:1–9).

At this point the so-called "two kingdoms" approach becomes plausible. This theology is age-old. Martin Luther set forth one version of it. For him life was divided into two spheres, the church and the state, the former being ruled by the Spirit of Christ and the latter by the sword. Some have concluded from such a division that Luther was indifferent to the wider culture, except that it did need some ordering by the magistrate, and that the Christian ought to put all of his eggs in the basket of the church, and spiritual life. This is a gross misunderstanding of his two kingdoms approach, as many Luther scholars have pointed out. Luther in fact developed a good bit of social theory using the theology of calling and the priesthood of all believers as his foundation.[37]

There are all kinds of versions of the two kingdoms approach, and all kinds of advocates, some which would not be comfortable using the expression. Some advocate natural law while others do not. Some would have ties to the Anabaptist tradition while others do not. This is not the place to explore this vast field. Suffice it to say here that a common thread among the many who hold to this theory is that God's primary work since the Fall is the redemption of his people through the ministry of the Church (the preaching of the word, the sacraments, prayer, ministries of mercy, missions, and so forth). While these advocates come at it with different emphases, they all would affirm that God's work in the world, though history, politics, culture, and the like, is at best secondary. Meredith Kline for example advocates a significant distinction between "cult" and "culture;" the former referring to holy activities, principally worship, Sabbath practice and the like, whereas the latter refers to "profane" activities performed outside the church. Cultural activities on the whole are practiced in a world characterized by "common curse," tempered by "common grace."[38] For David VanDrunen, living in two kingdoms means we are sojourners in the world, with only natural law to help us interact with unbelievers in the institutions of this world.[39]

But wait. Are things so black and white? The apostle Paul's teaching should alert us to be wary of all such dichotomies. Romans 12:1–2 tells us not to be conformed to this world, but to be transformed, testing God's will to find out how effective it is in the world. He even uses terms such as presenting our bodies "a living sacrifice," and "spiritual worship." Apparently for him, worship is not restricted to Sunday morning activity but to all of life. 1 Corinthians 10:31 tells us, *"So, whether you eat or drink, or whatever you do, do all to the glory of God."* His application is comprehensive, yet it's interesting that he should begin with such "ordinary" activities as sitting at a table. The reason he can say this, without imposing dichotomies such as "sacred" and "secular" or "holy" and "profane" is that Jesus Christ is preeminent in all things (Col. 1:15–23). There is a seamless transition for him between Christ the mediator of all of the creation, and his Lordship over the church.

That is Paul. What about Genesis and the rest of the Old Testament? While the contrast in Gen. 1–4 is certainly between the original goodness of creation, including God's special blessing upon humanity, and the curse upon our first parents and their roles, yet as we can see, all was not lost. In the very first expression of the Gospel, God tells the serpent he will be the enemy of the woman's seed until the day his head is bruised (Gen. 3:15). Thus, Satan, represented by this strange crawling voice piece, would eventually be crushed under foot. God, our refuge, will enable us to tread on the lion and the adder (Ps. 91:13). Jesus gave his disciples authority to tread on serpents and scorpions (Luke 10:19). In the end Jesus' death and resurrection was his own bruising and the powers of darkness' ultimate defeat (Col. 2:14–5; Rev. 20:2). So the mandate to have dominion still holds, but now it must include reversing the effects of sin through the one who gained the power over sin, Jesus Christ. Through death he destroyed the one who has the power of death, that is, the devil. Now, we too, through him have that power (Heb. 2:14–15).

So we still have dominion over the earth, but it now must include eradicating the cancer of sin, and proclaiming the glories of God's redeeming love. Childbearing has been made hard. That great human privilege of motherhood is challenged by pain and hardship. Yet by his grace, God allows mothers to bear children and fathers to see their image-bearing offspring (Gen. 4:1–2; 5:3). The beauty of marriage has been mitigated, often becoming a power struggle (Gen. 3:16). And yet marriage is restored and now can even image the relation of Christ to his church (Eph. 5:22–33). Human labor is cursed and made hard. But still, it goes on. Cain brought fruit from the ground. Abel raised livestock (Gen. 4:2). At best, work can lead to building cities and producing beauty (Gen. 3:17–19; 4:17–22). The city in the Old Testament can be a place of corruption, as was Babylon. Yet it can also be a place of hope. Indeed, the new heavens and the new earth are portrayed as a city, the heavenly Jerusalem from above (Rev. 21:2) on Zion's hill (Heb. 12:18–24). Much of Israel's life was spent in cultural pursuits, whether in buildings, poetry and music, political organization and the pursuit of justice, in agriculture and the like.

Worship has also become idolatry. Presumably God's refusal to accept Cain's offering was not because there was something wrong with bringing fruit out of the ground, and we should not make too much of the contrast between Cain's descendants and Seth's. Certainly there is a contrast between the Cainites who build cities and boast to their wives and the Sethites who worship.

But the expression "call upon the name of the Lord" should not be narrowly defined to mean Sabbath worship. Rather, the phrase is comprehensive. 1 Chronicles 16:8 and many other portions of Scripture relate calling upon the Lord to the telling of all his deeds. Calling upon the Lord is equivalent to seeking him by faith (Ps. 14:2; Rom. 10:12–13). When we do, he gives us our desires (Ps. 145:18). Neither can worship be isolated from culture. Nor can culture be developed without religion, which is a form of worship. Just at the factual level this is clear. We don't worship on the Sabbath without a number of cultural elements: the style of music, the language we use, a preaching style, the building we worship in, the dress code, etc. And when we engage in culture, be it science or politics or art, or even marriage and procreation, there is always a fundamental spiritual orientation involved.

Reiterations

A striking feature of biblical revelation is the recurrence of the theme of the Cultural Mandate in various versions. We will not have time to look at all of them, but we may pause over a few. What they all have in common is a reference, however indistinct at times, to the Cultural Mandate of Genesis 1:26–30. Each has a particular significance in the history of redemption. Yet each has a reference to the whole.

One of the first important manifestations of this mandate is the Noahic covenant. When the great flood subsided, Noah was told to go out of the ark with his family. God told him, *"Bring out with you every living thing that is with you of all flesh—birds and animals and every creeping thing that creeps on the earth—that they may swarm on the earth, and be fruitful and multiply on the earth"* (Gen. 8:17). Again in 9:1 God blessed mankind. This is the third time this blessing is given (1:28; 5:2). He was told to be fruitful and multiply and fill the earth, also for the third time (1:28; 8:17). This time the covenant blessing is with the entire creation, and it is signified by the rainbow (9:9–17). So we have a reiteration of the Cultural Mandate. However, several new features can be found here. For example, there follows a special legislation about the relation of man to beast, using military terminology. From now on animals will fear and dread human beings (9:2). So, while the blessing and filling reflect the Creation Mandate, this fear reflects the new relationship of the animals to man, because of the fall (3:15). At the same time, every moving thing can be for food, on condition that animals be drained of their blood, the neglect of which is sanctioned severely.[40]

The punishment is more severe for any man that sheds another man's blood, because *"God made man in his own image."* This is a significant statement. As in Genesis 1, there is a connection between the *imago* and the mandate that follows. God reiterates, *"And you, be fruitful and multiply, teem on the earth and multiply in it"* (9:6–8). Whereas 8:15–17 constitute so many hints in this story "that the post-flood era represents the start of a new creation," 9:1–7 actually "repeats almost verbatim [God's] blessing on the old pre-flood humanity.[41] Only here we have the addition of the capital sanction for murder, something that did not need spelling out in the pre-lapsarian era.

There is considerable debate among commentators about whether we have here the foundation of the state or something else. John Frame believes the state only became a reality gradually, and that here we simply have family discipline described. He then argues that an evolution took place in government, through a tribal system, royalty, and eventually the Roman state.[42] I think this can work, although I would be more inclined to see an application of societal order beyond simply Noah's family or the family in general.[43] Whichever the case we clearly have an advance over the Cultural Mandate as given before the fall, both in the positive developments of culinary practice, the beginning of social order, and in the more negative provision for the protection of human life against assaults. The three components are there:

1. God's covenant blessing is at the center (9:1, 8, 13).

2. The children of Noah were to begin populating the earth again (9:1, 7).

3. They were to have dominion over the creation and govern human society (9:2–6)

A second crucial step is in the Abrahamic covenant. The special call to Abraham and then the other patriarchs also contains strong reminders of the Cultural Mandate. Like Adam's descendants, Abram and his family had to leave his country. But unlike the earliest people who wandered east until they settled in various places, Abram was directed to a land that God would show him (Gen. 12:1). That would be the land which became the main location for the unfolding history of redemption. Again, the center of God's call to Abram is the blessing. Not only would he and his descendants be blessed, but they would become a blessing to others. Abram's descendants would become a great nation, refocusing the "be fruitful and multiply" in a redemptive direction. We have here not only a revisiting of the Cultural Mandate, but now it is cast in a missionary direction. Chapters 15–22 present a particularly important episode in the history of redemption. Abram wondered how God's promises could be fulfilled since he had no offspring of his own. God nevertheless promises that he will have a son and that his descendants will be as numerous as the stars in the heavens. He will give this land, not yet owned by this family, to Abram's offspring. Only in the fourth generation after the "iniquity of the Amorites" is full would they come to populate the promised land. This promise is confirmed by an oath, ratified by the fire passing between the pieces of sacrificed flesh (Gen. 15). Then the narrative develops. Abram's name is changed to Abraham (father of many nations) in 17:5.

Finally Isaac the miracle child is born (Gen. 21). This son of the promise was to be sacrificed by his father in a test of faith. In a display of the biblical principle of "the devoted thing," Abraham was willing to surrender his son, the only human hope for the future of the covenant people, believing that God would provide.[44]

As in much of Scripture, a promise is made and then tested in such a way that the fulfillment would seem impossible, and then God finds a way. Here the promise relates to the central theme of the Cultural Mandate—God's blessing and the procreation of children to fill the earth. Similarly, in the dark story of Jacob, the treacherous son whom God loved more than Esau, it would seem impossible for the promises to be fulfilled. As a low point in his life, nevertheless, God blesses him and renames him Israel, "wrestler with God." He then reiterates the earlier mandate: *"I am God Almighty: be fruitful and multiply"* (Gen. 35:11). He adds that a whole company of nations would emerge from his own body. This occasioned erecting a pillar and naming the place *Bethel* (the house of God).

Again, in view of the Fall, the application of the Cultural Mandate is corrective as well as redemptive. Despite the sinful behavior of Jacob and his flawed character, yet God meets him and wrestles him to the ground by his grace. God prevails against this unsavory son of his, and out of Jacob's family would indeed come a great people who would live in God's house, a theme that continues throughout the Old Testament becoming more and more localized, culminating in the temple. And then on into the New, when even the Gentiles would be included in the household of God (Eph. 2:19–22). Again, the three components are represented:

1. God's covenant blessing, this time for the people destined to become the Jews, is confirmed by an oath and a sign of atonement (Gen. 12:2–3; 22:17–18; 26:3; and 15:17–18; 17:2, 7).

2. Abraham's descendants were to multiply until they become as numerous as the stars in the sky, even though for a while they must endure persecution (13:16; 15:5; 16:10; 17:2; 22:17; 26:4; and 15:13).

3. Abraham and his descendants would rule the promised land (Gen. 13:15; 15:14, 18; 17:6).

Third, one of the clearest restatements of the Cultural Mandate is in Psalm 8. It is a royal psalm, written by David the great king of Israel. The terms of the beginning are typically militaristic, contrasting the majestic name of God in the earth to the enemies of Israel. David's sense of God's majesty stems from the contemplation of the glory of his vast creation. As he looks up to the heavens, he not only sees the strength and handiwork of God, but he also sees, by comparison. the finitude of man. This leads to the famous question, *"What is man that you are mindful of him, and the son of man that you care for him?"* (v. 4). There is some debate about the meaning of man (*'enosh*) and the son of man (*ben 'adam*) in this psalm. Traditionally interpreters consider these terms to refer to generic or democratic man. Indeed, at the dawn of creation, God creates man (mankind, *'adam*) in his image. Yet in the second version of the creation story, God creates Adam, the first man, the husband of Eve.

As we know, Adam was designated to be our covenantal head. However, he failed the probation. This has led some interpreters to consider that it is David himself, leading the new humanity, whom God has provided to accomplish what Adam had failed to do. Ultimately Jesus Christ would be the true last Adam or second man, or the man from heaven, who would lead his people into his resurrected image (1 Cor. 15:47).[45] I am more comfortable with the traditional view, that the psalm is pointing to mankind.

Resolving the issue is not fundamental to our thesis. The psalmist goes on to answer his own question in terms very close to the Cultural Mandate:

Yet you have made him a little lower than the heavenly beings
And crowned him with glory and honor.
You have given him dominion over the works of your hands;

You have put all things under his feet,
All sheep and oxen,
And also the beasts of the field,
The birds of the heavens, and the fish of the sea,
Whatever passes along the paths of the seas. Ps. 8:4–8

Quite a bit is going on here. God has made man a little lower than the heavenly beings. The Hebrew word here is *'elohim* which is usually translated "God." But it can also signify angels, as does the LXX, which is quoted in Hebrews 2:7. The NIV and ESV both translate "heavenly beings," which may be closer to the author's intent. If this psalm is a lyric reflection on Genesis 1, then David's calling humanity "a little lower than the *'elohim*" could well be a reference to the plural of God's self-deliberation in Gen. 1:26. In any case, David here remarks on the glory of God's image-bearer, glory like unto a crowned king. The Scriptures often compare man, even fallen man who is being redeemed, to a king (see Ps. 21:1–7). We are a "royal priesthood," the Bible tells us (Ex. 19:6; 1 Pet. 2:9).

As has been the case in the different occurrences of the Cultural Mandate, it is clear that as ruler, man exercises his dominion over God's works, including the animals, the birds, and the sea creatures (Ps. 8:6–8). This rule, as we have seen, is but a subset of God's greater rule, for which he is worthy of high praise (vv. 1, 8).

The fascinating thing is the New Testament application of this psalm to Jesus Christ (Heb. 2:5–9). The author uses the Septuagint translation, which suits his purposes in adapting the man of the psalm to Jesus. The "great salvation" should not be neglected, for it has come through Christ's testimony, confirmed by his witnesses and by miracles, as well as the gifts of the Holy Spirit (Heb. 2:3–4). This salvation, the already-not-yet of the world to come, was not subjected to angels, but to Jesus (v. 5).

Psalm 8 is appropriated as a sure prophecy of the rule of Christ but with an important twist. In order to subject the world to himself, Jesus had to suffer and be humiliated, to be made for a little while lower than the angels (Heb. 2:9). By his death he destroyed the one who had the power of death (Heb. 2: 9, 14). This way he can help the offspring of Abraham to become fully members of the family of God (Heb. 2:16). Indeed the pattern of Abraham, whose descendants waited under oppression for four hundred years before possessing the promised land, is fulfilled in Jesus, who suffered before he came into resurrection glory.

Today we do not yet see everything in subjection to Jesus (Heb. 2:8). There is a "not-yet" to this great salvation. But we do see Jesus himself, through the testimony of the witnesses and through the illumination of the Holy Spirit. This is the "already." As our Lord himself told the disciples, his followers will receive *"a hundredfold now in this time, houses and brothers and sisters and mothers and children and lands, with persecutions, and in the age to come eternal life"* (Mark 10:30). So here the Cultural Mandate takes on vast proportions. Not only our enemies are subdued, but death itself and its bondage are vanquished (Ps. 8:2, Heb. 2:14–15). Not only is man crowned with glory to rule over God's creation, but Jesus Christ is crowned after much suffering so that sons can be brought to glory (Ps. 8:5; Heb. 2:10). And now our rule is preserved, but not only over the world, but over our very trials and temptations (Ps. 8:6-8; Heb. 2:18). The three features of the Cultural Mandate are clearly reiterated in Psalm 8:

1. The blessing of the majestic God who makes man with great glory and establishes strength for his people (8:5, 1–2).

2. Who evokes praise from king David as well as from babes and infants (8:1, 9; 8:2).

3. Who gives dominion over all the works of his hands (8:6–8).

Fourth, one of the most significant restatements of the Cultural Mandate is in Jeremiah 29, the prophet's letter to the exiles. The setting for his message is the seventy-year captivity of Judah. The southern kingdom fell when most of its people were deported around 605 BC, followed by two major invasions by Nebuchadnezzar, king of Babylon, in 597 and 586 BC. Jeremiah had often prophesied this exile, but he also foretold the return to the land. The people would return and "be fruitful and multiply" (Jer. 23:3). But first, the land would become a ruin and a waste. Then after seventy years, the Lord would punish his people's enemies, destroying their own lands (Jer. 25:8–14). The destruction of Judah included silencing any joyful song, the happiness of newlyweds, the productive work of grinding at the mill, and feasts held in the light (v. 10). Early in the reign of Zedekiah, Hananiah, a false prophet, emerged, and he asserted that God would break the yoke of Babylon and would bring the people back within two years (28:1–4). Jeremiah disagreed. The Lord had told him the exile would be long and hard, and Hananiah would die because of his prevarication.

At this point Jeremiah wrote and sent a letter from Jerusalem to the elders of the Judahites, a message which is nothing if not astonishing and counter-intuitive:

> *Thus says the Lord of hosts, the God of Israel, to all the exiles whom I have sent into exile from Jerusalem to Babylon:* "*Build houses and live in them; plant gardens and eat their produce. Take wives and have sons and daughters; take wives for your sons and give your daughters in marriage, that they may bear sons and daughters; multiply there, and do not decrease. But seek the welfare of the city where I have sent you into exile, and pray to the Lord on its behalf, for in its welfare you will find your welfare....*" Jer. 29:4–7

These words are a paraphrase of the Cultural Mandate. One finds an important parallel in Ezekiel 36:8–15 where it is the Lord who returns to Israel. In the subsequent portions of Jeremiah's letter, the Lord tells them their fortune and hopes will indeed be restored. When they call upon him he will hear, and when they seek him they shall find him (vv. 11–14). In short, God will bless them beyond measure.

But the blessings of God's presence begins now even in the hard place of captivity. Houses were to be built. They were to begin new families and have children: *"multiply there, do not decrease"* (Jer. 29:6). Perhaps most surprising of all is God's call for the Judahites to seek the welfare of the city (Jer. 29:7). The word translated "welfare" is the wonderful Hebrew word *shalom*, which means peace, concord, and justice.

Why would God's people suddenly love their enemies? This attitude is not-so-sudden. Job said he should be condemned if ever he rejoiced over the misfortunes of his enemy (Job 31:29). David affirms that when his enemies were sick he prayed and grieved for them as though they were family (Ps. 35:13–14). Darius insisted that the people of Israel have all they need for their worship, so that their prayers for him and his sons may be heard (Ezra 6:10). Indeed, the very existence of Israel was to benefit outsiders, a light to the nations (Isa. 42:6; Luke 2:32). But here more is at play than good motives and good example; Judah was actually to work intentionally for the welfare of the city. Where there was a need, they should help, where there was injustice, strive for justice. Here we see the close connection between "evangelism" (the sharing of blessing) and doing good (bringing peace and welfare to the city).[46]

And in the bargain, *shalom* will come to the Jews as well (Jer. 29:7). This is not so much a pragmatic strategy as one that expresses the remarkable principle that blessings overflow not only to those who are being evangelized but to the evangelists, when they are reaching out. This is a common theme in the Bible. If we are blessed and bring blessings to others, then they in turn will bless God and that in turn will bring more blessing to us. Notice for example how Psalm 67 combines these notions and makes reference to the earth yielding its increase:

May God be gracious to us and bless us
and make his face to shine upon us,
that your way may be known on earth,
your saving power among all nations.
Let the peoples praise you, O God;
let all the peoples praise you!
Let the nations be glad and sing for joy,
for you judge the peoples with equity
and guide the peoples upon earth.
Let the peoples praise you, O God;
let all the peoples praise you!
The earth has yielded its increase;
God, our God shall bless us;
God shall bless us;
let all the ends of the earth fear him!

Joining Babylon, rather than staying outside of it, does not mean losing one's identity. There were likely practices and attitudes by the Jews which would have annoyed the Babylonians. Nevertheless they are told to enter the city and work towards its betterment. Such love for enemies actually becomes a source of power for the Jews themselves.

Timothy Keller argues for Christians inhabiting the city for the same reason. He notes that today, as yesterday, the city is a center for power and influence. This is the reason the apostle Paul primarily evangelized urban centers. The effect of this approach was (and is) to increase the spread of the Gospel throughout the wider world.

Keller writes:

Through [the Christians'] service to the city they will become attractive. Their ideas will matter. Their God will be honored. And whatever influences the city influences the whole culture. God here lays down an important principle: the way to power and influence is not to seek power and influence, but to seek to serve.[47]

Again the three elements of the Cultural Mandate are here:

1. God blesses, bringing welfare (*shalom*) and restoration, but in his own way and in his own timing, not like that of the false prophet (Jer. 29:7, 11–4).

2. Multiplying and being fruitful, even in exile, are at the heart of this letter (Jer. 29:6).

3. Proper dominion, building, intercession, still can be exercised under oppression (Jer. 29:5, 7)

Fifth, we finally arrive at the Great Commission. The most-often cited version of it is from Matthew 28:18–20. This commandment of Jesus to his disciples is perhaps the most often quoted at missions conferences. Indeed, it does contain everything important about missions:

> *And Jesus came and said to them, "All authority in heaven and on earth has been given to me. Go therefore and make disciples of all nations, baptizing them I the name of the Father and of the Son and of the Holy Spirit, teaching them to observe all that I have commanded you. And behold, I am with you always, to the end of the age.*

The version of the Great Commission found at the end of Mark is likely not in the original. So we shall leave it unexplored. Mark's gospel does allude to going to the nations (*ethnos*) in the Olivet discourse on the end of times: *"and the gospel must first be proclaimed to all nations"* (Mark 13:10).

Luke's version is interesting. This gospel connects the Great Commission with Jesus opening the disciples' minds to understand the Scripture, particularly all that is prophesied about him, from every portion of the Bible (Luke 24:8, 25, 44–45). It also says more than Matthew about the way power to fulfill this commission will be conferred upon them. Here are the words of the command (Luke 24:45–49):

> *Then he opened their minds to understand the Scriptures, and said to them, "Thus it is written, that the Christ should suffer and on the third day rise from the dead, and that repentance and forgiveness of sins should be proclaimed in his name to all nations (ethnos), beginning from Jerusalem. You are witnesses of these things. And behold, I am sending the promise of my Father upon you. But stay in the city until you are clothed with power on high."*

The conditions for this empowerment and strategy are further elaborated by Luke in Acts 1, when Jesus ascends to heaven in order to pour out the gift of the Holy Spirit.

John's version is unique. It connects the missions mandate to the authority of the Holy Spirit to preach the forgiveness of sins. John 20:21–23 is spoken to the assembled disciples (with the notable exception of Thomas):

> *Jesus said to them again, "Peace be with you. As the Father has sent me, even so I am sending you." And when he had said this, he breathed on them and said to them, "Receive the Holy Spirit. If you forgive the sins of anyone, they are forgiven; if you withhold forgiveness from anyone, it is withheld."*[48]

John also illustrates the missions mandate in several ways in his post-resurrection appearances. First, he deals with Thomas, who is invited to verify that Jesus is really there in front of him, but who is told that those who have not seen and yet believe are blessed. Second, there is the episode where Jesus tells the empty-handed disciples to cast their net on the right side of their boat, where they will find a catch so great it should have broken the net. This is a clear metaphorical foretelling of their success as catchers of men (see Luke 5:1–11). Finally, there is the poignant story of Peter's restoration. Every time (three in fact, paralleling his denial) he asks Peter if he loves him, and he answers in the affirmative, Jesus replies: *"Feed my lambs."*

Each of the examples we have cited share the three themes. The Great Commission according to Mathew stresses the authority of the risen Jesus over all of creation and all of history. While this parallels Genesis 1, where God tells the first humans as well as the animal creation that *I have given you* the produce of the earth as food, Matthew records that Jesus tells his disciples to make disciples of the *ethne*, to baptize them in the Trinitarian baptism and to teach them to observe everything he has commanded. These are comprehensive directives. Grammatically, there is only one straight imperative, and three participles, thus: Make disciples by going, baptizing and teaching.

Making disciples (*matheteo*) is thus the center of the commandment. The only other verbal form of discipleship is a chapter earlier, in Matthew 27:57, where Joseph of Aramathea is referred to as a "disciple" of Jesus. However, the term "disciple" is used throughout the New Testament. And the only English translation of it in the old Testament is in Isaiah 8:16. However, the concept of discipleship runs throughout the entire Bible. It basically means to te taught by a master or a sage. The King James translates Matthew 28:19 as to *teach* all nations.

The practice of gathering disciples, or students, was widely observed in the ancient world. It was still practiced in various cultures well after the time of Christ. Augustine, for example, had disciples, or tutees, who learned rhetoric from him, and generally were to follow his example as a man of virtue.

Discipleship is identified numerous times in the gospels. John the Baptist had his tutees, as did the Pharisees. Jesus based his ministry, for the present and the future, on the work and teaching of his disciples. Here in the Great Commission, the concept is transferred from the narrow group of his followers to the nations (the *ethne* were the Gentiles, primarily). Preaching the Gospel as such is not mentioned here, although making disciples surely includes preaching the Gospel of salvation unto eternal life. Whereas baptism signifies the initiation into the community of the saved, washed clean in the name of the Father, Son and Holy Spirit, teaching them to observe *all* that Christ has commanded goes far beyond the initial conversion and into the life of adopting an entire worldview.

Luke's and John's mandates focus on slightly different aspects of the missionary command. The parallel is Luke. It is clear that at the heart of discipleship is *"repentance and forgiveness of sins should be proclaimed in his name to all nations"* (Luke 24:47). John's stresses the need to empower the disciples to proclaim the forgiveness of sins and the care of the sheep. We thus understand from all of these versions that "salvation" is comprehensive. In each instance of the Great Commission, we see the three basic elements at work:

1. The rich covenant blessing of God as he gathers his people together into his kingdom through the agency of the preached word and the appropriate social action.

2. The fruit-bearing and spreading of the good news to all the nations in anticipation of populating the New Jerusalem from above.

3. Dominion over all the forces that oppose God's purposes, human guilt, idols, and death itself.

Lastly then, the final installment of the Cultural Mandate is in the new heavens and the new earth. The book of Revelation makes it clear that God will replace the first heaven and earth with the new one, centering on the holy city, the new Jerusalem (Rev. 21:2). This does not mean an absence of continuity between the old and the new. John writes, *"By its light will the nations walk, and the kings of the earth will bring their glory into it"* (Rev. 21:24). This is an astonishing statement. What glories do the kings bring in? All that has been gathered here on earth. Richard Mouw has dedicated a powerful book elucidating these verses in the light of the prophet Isaiah.[49] A careful comparison of Isaiah 60 and Revelation 21, the book argues that while there is a discontinuity in the old and new worlds, especially because sin will be gone, yet there will be a good deal in common, including the engagement in cultural pursuits. His thesis is:

But the Holy City is not wholly discontinuous with present conditions. The biblical glimpses of this City give us reason to think that its contents will not be completely unfamiliar to people like us. In fact, the content of the City will be more akin to our present cultural patterns than is usually acknowledged in discussions of the afterlife.[50]

Space prohibits going into the meticulous details which brings Mouw to his conclusions, but they build a strong case for our own view that shows continuity in the different versions of the Cultural Mandate.

In any case, in this final installment we have, once again, the three themes that thread these iterations together, albeit with important differences because much of the purpose of the original mandate has now been fulfilled:

1. The full blessing of God in his covenant presence: *"Behold, the dwelling place of God is with man. He will dwell with them, and they will be his people, and God himself will be with them as their God."* No more suffering, no more death, all of that now gives way to the full redemption we have in the revealing of the children of God (Rev. 21:3–4; Rom. 8:19).

2. While there is no longer marrying and giving in marriage, the multiplication of God's disciples is now complete, and all his children will be in that great number, worshiping the savior and enjoying his banquet table (Rev. 7:9; 19:9).

3. Now at last the end of the age has come, and we do see everything in subjection to Jesus Christ, and the glory of the nations are brought into the New Jerusalem and the other cities over which Jesus' people will rule (Matt. 28:20; Heb. 2:8; Rev. 21:22–27; Luke 19:15–19).

Final Connections

I hope it is clear to the reader that, as Harvie Conn put it, "The so-called 'missionary mandate' is the covenant mandate's anticipated fulfillment in redemptive grace."[51] So then there is continuity and discontinuity. In a form appropriate to the era of revelation in which it is given, the different versions of the Cultural Mandate indicate the three overarching purposes of God's work among human beings. Theologically speaking, we could inscribe each of them within the worldview of creation-fall-redemption. We could also show how they fit into the covenant of creation and the covenant of redemption (the one covenant of grace, in its two basic administrations, the Old and the New Testaments).

The Cultural Mandate of Genesis thus has its ultimate accomplishment in the new heavens and new earth by way of the fulfillment of the great commission. While finding the continuity and discontinuity in the different versions of the Cultural Mandate may not settle all the questions about the relation of spiritual growth and cultural activity, it goes a long way toward understanding God's plan for the whole person in the whole of human society, and argues persuasively against any worldview that dichotomizes between the holy and the profane.

---

1. Gary R. Corwin, A. Scott Moreau, and Gary B. McGee, *Introducing World Missions: A Biblical, Historical, and Practical Survey* (Grand Rapids, MI: Baker, 2004), 153.
2. Timothy Keller, *Generous Justice: How God's Grace Makes Us Just* (New York: Dutton, 2010), 162.
3. John Gladwin, "Evangelism and Social Action," *International Review of Mission* 69/274, 194. Emphasis mine.
4. John R. W. Stott, *Christian Mission in the Present World* (Downers Grove, IL: InterVarsity Press, 1976), 41.
5. H. Richard Niebuhr, *Christ and Culture* (New York: Harper Colophon, 1951).
6. Ibid, 32.
7. Harvie M. Conn, *Evangelism: Doing justice and Preaching Grace* (Grand Rapids, MI: Zondervan, 1982). The specific comparison of the two mandates is found on p. 63.
8. Bruce Waltke, with Charles Yu, *An Old Testament Theology* (Grand Rapids, MI: Zondervan, 2007), 221.
9. This was the view held by various church fathers, including Justin Martyr. Sara Parvis, Paul Foster, *Justin Martyr and his Worlds* (Minneapolis, MN: Fortress Press, 2007), 140.
10. Meredith Kline, "Review of H. Blocher's *In the Beginning*," *Christian Scholar's Review* 14, 1985, 398.
11. See Umberto Cassuto, *A Commentary on the Book of Genesis*, part I, "From Adam to Noah," (Jerusalem: The Magnes Press, 1978), 55.
12. Joüon Paul, S. J. *A Grammar of Biblical Hebrew* (Rome, 1996), ad loc.
13. David J. A. Clines, "The Image of God in Man," in *Tyndale Bulletin* 19, 1968, 68.
14. Gordon J. Wenham, *Word Biblical Commentary*, vol 1, Genesis 1–15 (Waco, TX: Word Books, 1987), 28.
15. Cassuto, Op. cit., 55–56.
16. Bruce Waltke with Cathi J. Fredricks, *Genesis: A Commentary* (Grand Rapids, MI: Zondervan, 2001), 65.
17. See A. Abou-Assaf, P. Bordreuil, & A. R. Millard, *La statue de Tell Fekherye* (Paris: Eds.) Recherche sur les civilisations, 1982.

18. C. John Collins, *Genesis 1-4: A Linguistic, Literary* and *Theological Commentary* (Phillipsburg, NJ: P&R Publishing, 2006), 66.
19. Francis A. Schaeffer, *Basic Bible Studies*, in *The Complete Works*, vol. 2 (Westchester, IL, Crossway, 1982), 329.
20. J. Douma, *The Ten Commandments: Manual for the Christian Life* (Phillipsburg, NJ: P&R Publishing, 1996), 211, 53.
21. Waltke, *Genesis*, op. cit., 71.
22. What follows is from his *An Old Testament Theology*, Op. cit., 215ff.
23. While there is no dualism, there is certainly a sort of duality of body and soul. But Waltke is at pains to avoid Platonism. Space forbids a detailed exploration of anthropology here. See Hans Walter Wolff's *Anthropology of the Old Testament* (London: SCM Press, 2011).
24. See Lynn White, Jr., "Historical Roots of Our Ecological Crisis," *Science* 155, 1967, 1203–7; Colin Russell, *The Earth, Humanity and God* (Boston, MA: Routledge, 1994); Richard Bauckham, *The Bible and Ecology: Rediscovering the Community of Creation* (Waco, TX: Baylor University Press, 2010), esp. 2–12.
25. C. John Collins, *Genesis 1-4: A Linguistic, Literary, and Theological Commentary* (Phillipsburg, NJ: P&R Publishing, 2006), 69.
26. Richard Bauckham, Op. cit., 30.
27. Ibid., 31.
28. Actually, there were several trees, on either side of the river, drawing on Ezekiel 41:18–26. "The one tree of life in the first garden has become many trees of life in the escalated paradisal state of the second garden (Gregory K. Beale, *The Book of Revelation: The New International Greek Testament Commentary* (Grand Rapids, MI: Eerdmans, 1999), 1106.)
29. As Raymond Williams once put it, "Culture is one of the two or three most complicated words in the English language." This is partly because the word has a long history in the English, and partly because it has been appropriated by different disciplines and worldviews in ways that are not quite analogous." *Key Words*, rev. ed. (New York: Oxford University Press, 1983), 87–93.
30. Marquis de Mirabeau, *Précis de l'Organisation, ou Mémoire sur les Etats provinciaux*, 2e ed., tome III (Hambourg: Chrétien Hérold, 1758), 23.
31. It is important not to confuse the art product with the beautiful. The two can overlap. But art can serve to portray the ugly and the cruel, as it must do if it aiming at truth.
32. See Jeanne A. Schuler, "Reasonable Hope: Kant as Critical Theorist," *History of European Ideas* 1995 21(4): 527–533.
33. Although many still do. We often hear about politicians, "history will judge his administration," and the like, meaning that history is progressive, so that later generations will have better judgment than the present one.
34. Schilder did use the term culture, and, unlike Kuyper, was convinced that the Christian community could produce culture because it benefitted from God's special grace to do so. See N. H. Gootjes, "Schilder on Christ and Culture," in *Always Obedient: Essays on the Teachings of Dr. Klaas Schilder*, ed. J. Geertsema (Phillipsburg, NJ: P&R Publishing, 1995), 35.
35. Abraham Kuyper, *Wisdom and Wonder: Common Grace in Science and Art*, Nelson D. Kloosterman, transl. (Grand Rapids, MI: Christian's Library Press, 2011), 96–7.
36. John Murray, "Common Grace," *Collective Writings of John Murray*, vol. 2 (Edinburgh, Carlisle: The Banner of Truth Trust, 1977), 113.
37. For example, Roland Bainton, *Here I Stand: A Life of Martin Luther* (New York: Mentor, 1950), 184-190; William J. Wright, *Martin Luther's Understanding of God's Two Kingdoms* (Grand Rapids, MI: Baker, 2010); Robert Kolb & Charles Arard, *The Genius of Luther's Theology* (Grand Rapids, MI: Baker, 2007).
38. Meredith G. Kline, *Kingdom Prologue* (Eugene, OR: Wipf & Stock, 2006), 67, 154, ad loc.

39. David VanDrunen, *Living in God's Two Kingdoms: A Biblical Vision for Christianity and Culture* (Wheaton, IL: Crossway, 2010), esp. 161ff.
40. The reasons for this prohibition have partly to do with kindness to animals and surely also a preview of the ritual animal sacrifices legislated in the rest of the Pentateuch.
41. Gordon J. Wenham, Op. cit., 187, 192.
42. John Frame, *Doctrine of the Christian Life* (Phillipsburg, NJ: P&R Publishing, 2008).
43. See C. F. Keil & F. Delitzsch, *Biblical Commentary of the Old Testament, vol. 1 The Pentateuch* (Grand Rapids, MI: Eerdmans, 2006), 151–153.
44. See Jon Levenson, *The Death and Resurrection of the Beloved Son* (New Haven, CT: Yale University Press, 1993).
45. Thus Douglas Green, in http://www.wts.edu/resources/articles/green.html.
46. This duality runs through the history of redemption, right up into the New Testament as we shall see.
47. See, for example [http://www.redeemer2.com/visioncampaign/index.cfm?page=keller_blog]
48. The Protestant understanding of this statement, which parallels Jesus saying on the keys of the kingdom (Matt. 16:19 and Rev. 1:18) is that church discipline is spiritual and declarative, that is, no human being has the power to send people to heaven or hell, only God himself, operating through the preached word by a duly authorized church, can have such power.
49. Richard J. Mouw, *When the Kings Come Marching in: Isaiah and the New Jerusalem* (Grand Rapids, MI: Eerdmans, 2002).
50. Ibid., 20.
51. Harvie M. Conn, Op. cit., 63.

APOLOGETIC COMMUNICATION

HOW SOMEONE WHO ISN'T A CHRISTIAN IS MEANT TO EXPERIENCE SOMEONE WHO IS

Zack Eswine

PhD, Regent University
Senior Pastor, Riverside Community Church
St. Louis, MO
Director of Homiletics & Scholar in Residence, Francis A. Schaeffer Institute,
Covenant Theological Seminary
St. Louis, MO

As followers of Jesus, we can become frightened, anxious, or even rebellious when somebody questions, dislikes, or disagrees with us. Our palms begin to sweat; our hearts pound; our thoughts race. Some of us boil over in anger. Others of us freeze up with fear. Others of us become hollowed-out performers, shedding any resemblance of ourselves, in order to get the other person to speak well of us at any cost.

The Apostle Peter warns of three temptations Christians face when other-than-Christian people try to figure us out. First, we are tempted to let our fears and anxieties get the best of us. Peter writes, *"Have no fear, nor be troubled"* (1 Pet. 3:14). Second, we are tempted to pay no mind to the questions our other-than-Christian neighbors might ask us. Peters counters that we should always be *"prepared to make a defense to anyone who asks you for a reason for the hope that is in you"* (1 Pet. 3:15). Third, we are tempted to betray the character of Jesus with our ways while trying to commend the Gospel of Jesus with our words. According to Peter, this cannot be. When you defend the hope you have in Jesus, he says, *"do it with gentleness and respect"* (1 Pet. 3:15). This gentleness and respect is even for those who might slander you. He writes, *"It is better to suffer for doing good, if that should be God's will, than for doing evil"* (1 Pet. 3:17).[1]

This third temptation forms the focus for our present discussion. Every apologetic communicator must study to thoughtfully engage art, reason, and worldviews, and to answer them with articulate sense-making of Jesus for persons and cultures. Some of us dismiss this kind of attentiveness, but Peter's teaching corrects us.

But others of us who do study to be prepared often need Peter's other correction regarding our way of being with other-than-Christian persons. Every Jesus-follower must likewise ask this question: "Do my relational ways with my neighbors commend Jesus' manner while I attempt with my words to commend Jesus' message?" Peter assumes that we must answer "Yes" to this question.

Let's look first at how someone who isn't a Christian is meant to experience someone who is. Then let's look at three basic objections often raised against our attention to gentleness and respect when talking about apologetics and communication.

Tears as a Spark of Fire

The first "sermon" I heard Jerram Barrs "preach" was in an apologetics class. It was this apologist's way of *being*, as much as what he said, that broke through to my young and judgmental heart. Jerram was telling students about two of his neighbors. One was the victim of murder; the other was the perpetrator. Jerram began to read Psalm 10:

He sits in ambush in the villages;
in hiding places he murders the innocent.
His eyes stealthily watch for the helpless...
The helpless are crushed, sink down,
and fall by his might....
Arise, O Lord;
O God, lift up your hand;

forget not the afflicted.

At this moment, Jerram's voice faltered. He looked out above his glasses but away from us. He searched the wall with his eyes and heaved a deep breath. He could read no further. Then he looked down, pulled off his glasses, and set them on the lectern. He pulled both hands up and spread them flat upon his face, covering his cheeks, forehead, and eyes.

All of us paused. Everything stopped. I think back now, and words from poet Sylvia Plath come to mind: "I could feel the tears brimming and sloshing in me like water in a glass that is unsteady and too full."[2]

Without warning, the glass could no longer hold. It was as if Jerram's head and torso collapsed into a heap and pounded down hard into the lectern. His shoulders shook amid the rubble. Then his voice found its breath. The waters splashed over.

I look back and realize Jerram must have been near the age I am now. In his mid-forties, Jerram *cried like a man* as if none of us were there. I'm not sure I had ever seen a grown man cry like this. But there it was.

The biblical text and love for God and neighbor led the apologist to weep. Reread that last sentence if you don't mind. Class was in session. The sermon thundered. As a minister in training, all semester, I learned a great deal about the -isms and idols that create barriers to the Gospel in our hearts and in our culture. I learned what an apologist is meant to say. But that day, I was introduced to *who* an apologist is meant to *be*.

Jerram's mentor was Francis Schaeffer, and many have suggested that the most crucial legacy of Schaeffer as an apologist is his tears.[3] "L'Abri taught a person how to cry in light of our fragmentation with God, with each other, and ourselves."[4] I see now that Jerram was living what he had learned, teaching what had been taught. The love which drove the tears was like a baton and he was holding it out for us.

These tears were neither fraudulent nor sentimental. This apologist's "drops of tears turned to sparks of fire."[5] The weeping bore a tenacious message. Love is "the mark of a Christian."[6]

I took note. I still remember. With others, I'm holding out my hand to Jerram's baton, seeking to take hold and pass it on.

What if apologetics addresses our sorrows and not just our skepticism? What if doubt and faith, our questions and objections, arise not only because we sin, but also because of the wretched ways in which we are, all of us, sinned against? After all, it was Jesus' defense of hope against death that included tears. *"See how he loved,"* the mourners said of Jesus when he wept (John 11:35–36). Jesus taught that love is how they will know you are Christians (John 13:35).

Love cries. Compassion makes visible. Tears give voice. Truth feels.

If the goal of Christian apologetics "is to defend and commend the truthfulness of Christian belief,"[7] an apologist's way of being with other people is itself part of what defends and commends the Christian faith.

Biblical Foundations: A Jesus Way of Being

The Apostle Peter assumes that a Christian's demeanor and practice will leave a certain kind of impression upon others. In this case, "gentleness and respect" describe the desired impact of a Christian's presence upon their neighbors and place (1 Pet. 3:15). In fact Peter states emphatically the kind of imprint a Christian is forbidden to create in the life of another human being. Dislike or rejection of a Christian must arise because of the content of that Christian's faith *not* because that Christian acts like a jerk or perpetrates a damaging way of relating to themselves or to others (1 Pet. 4:15–16).

Paul agrees. When doing life with other-than-Christian persons we are to *"walk wisely"* and be *"always gracious,"* (Col. 4:5–6). Moreover, *"The Lord's servant must not be quarrelsome,"* Paul clarifies, *"but kind to everyone... patiently enduring evil... correcting his opponents with gentleness"* (2 Tim. 2:24–25).

Jude too urges us to *"show mercy on those who doubt"* (Jude 1:22).

John likewise pulls no punches. He wrote, *"Anyone who does not love does not know God"* (1 John 4:8).

Paul tears our masks off. If anyone speaks, teaches, expresses faith, sacrificially gives, or dies at the hands of others for their faith, none of it means anything apart from love (1 Cor. 13:1–3).

When those who aren't Jesus-followers hear us reason about Christian faith, they are meant to encounter a genuine face of:

- hope
- wisdom
- gentleness
- respect
- nothing quarrelsome
- kindness
- mercy
- love

- patience
- kindness
- no envy
- no boasting
- no arrogance
- no demanding
- no rudeness
- no irritability
- no resentment
- an ability to bear with all
- belief in all things
- endurance
- hope

Can you imagine what it would feel like for someone to treat you in these ways? Be humble toward you, kind to you, patient with you, with no envy of you, no boasting over you, no quitting on you, no desire to quarrel, and every desire to respect you? This describes the way Jesus defends and commends himself to you.

Jesus is not only the truth, he is also the way. A Christian is meant to defend and commend the faith in such a way that the listener is given a front-row seat to that rarest of divine-goods, called *love*.

This is why, Schaeffer, would say:

> If I have only an hour with someone, I will spend the first 55 minutes asking questions and finding out what is troubling their heart and mind, and then in the last 5 minutes I will share something of the truth.[8]

First Objection: What About Boldness?

"But what about boldness?" someone asks.

Before we answer this good question, may I suggest that we make sure we've lingered long enough with Jesus amid the plain teaching of the Bible which has just been set in front of us? Sometimes we raise a question, even an important one, too quickly, or more dangerously, in order to avoid being teachable toward what was just made plain. Only after such lingering can we rightly keep such things as gentleness, kindness, and no impatient desire to quarrel in the picture as we answer this important question of boldness. In brief, when we object to gentleness and call for boldness, we often make four mistakes.

First, we assume gentleness or respect isn't bold. But one mustn't shout in order to show courage. Whether you have a loud or quiet personality isn't the question. Biblically speaking, loud words are more often associated with folly than with wisdom (Eccl. 9:13–17).

Second, we are prone to assume that one must show anger or intimidation in order to speak boldly. But whatever boldness is, it cannot sidestep, but must surrender to and uphold, what Jesus' command to love requires of us. We find ourselves struggling to trust Jesus' way if we believe we must turn to the fruits of the flesh, rather than the fruit of the Spirit, in order to courageously commend and defend the faith.

Third, we tend to mistake how the word "bold" is used biblically. As one example, when Paul says, *"We were bold in our God,"* he tells us the way in which he expressed this boldness: *"We were gentle among you, like a nursing mother taking care of her own children.... For you know how, like a father with his children, we exhorted each one of you and encouraged you and charged you..."* (1 Thess. 2:2, 7, 11–12).

Likewise when the rulers, elders, and scribes perceived the boldness of Peter and John (Acts 4:13), it was because of what Peter *"said"* to them (Acts 4:8), not because of his tone.

We commend and defend with earnest zeal and love. We might raise our voice or lower it in our appeal, but loud anger doesn't make one courageous. We experience such easy oratory and fleshly strategies every day in public and private. What remains rare, and requires far more courage, is to boldly state one's claim with no hedging and with all quality of love, whether or not those who listen agree with or disregard us.

Fourth, on rare occasions when Jesus and the prophets before him shouted *"Woe!"* it was not their normal mode of speech. It was almost always reserved for those who claimed to be part of God's covenant people, and not for those who were outside and did not follow God.[9]

Many of us refer to Jerram as a quiet lion. Time and again he has boldly declared the truth according to the Bible, regardless of his audience, conservative or liberal, Christian or otherwise, regardless of politics, constituency, power, or rank. I have often thought, "Wait a minute, did he just say what I think he said?"

Seventeen years after the apologetics class of tears, I visited with Jerram in his study. I was a local pastor. I noticed the small statue of a dragon on his desk. It represented a story that he recounted to me: Apparently a student in class continued to challenge Jerram, not with honest questions, but with accusations regarding his motive and character and the motive and character of the class.

Jerram reportedly said, "If I were a dragon I would breathe fire and consume you!"

A bold thing can be said firmly and without a shout. Immediately afterward, Jerram felt his wrong and asked this student and the class to forgive him, which is its own kind of demonstration of who an apologist is meant to be. Someone had given him a dragon to memorialize the moment. Jerram kept the dragon as a reminder of his own need for grace. I think it reminds each of us student apologists of our need as well.

The point is that there are many louder and angrier apologists who speak with less courage. We commend and defend the faith "boldly," but many of us need to take greater care when regarding what biblical boldness requires of us.

Second Objection: Cynical About Love

Others of us encounter talk of love and apologetics with cynicism.

Such critics suggest first, that the apologist hasn't applied to his own life what he proposes to teach to others. For example, when Jesus cried, some saw this as love for a neighbor, but others hardened toward Jesus. They challenged his compassion with a question: *"Could not he who opened the eyes of the blind man also have kept this man from dying?"* (John 11:37).

In other words, "What is this teacher crying about? Hasn't he said that his message about God, life, all of us, and himself is the only true truth? If he is so smart, divine, and powerful, why all of this human fuss?"

Other critics say that compassion reveals not just a misapplication of truth, but a dangerously soft stance toward truth altogether. So when Jesus healed a man on the Sabbath, many watching hardened their hearts toward Jesus—seeing him as one who disregarded biblical truth in the name of compassion toward a crippled man (Mark 3:1–6). Tears, it is supposed, reveal a liberal weakness which threatens sound theology with a slippery slope. But our Lord's compassion fulfilled rather than denied the truth.

In a seminary class on apologetics, a similar kind of cynicism declares that such tears reveal a soft and weak academic program. "I thought this was supposed to be an apologetics class! Why are you reading Psalm 10, telling us about your personal neighbors, and crying about them? Instead you should lecture on the cosmological arguments for God's existence or untangle how presuppositional vs. evidentialist approaches differ."

Others simply cannot believe that the love offered is real. Those who have known pain and what it means to be used or manipulated, suspect that such love and welcome must be false; either a game designed to trap us or a public show that hides a private hypocrisy. Such hypocrisy exists, but not always. And this is cynicism's problem.

Cynicism has a prejudice against Good. Cynicism profiles Wholesomeness. If Genuineness or Joy walks into the store, Cynicism follows it. Cynicism keeps an eye on it because it doesn't trust it. Cynicism stereotypes Joy. Cynicism is an all or nothing thing. Either everything is beautiful or nothing is. Either everything goes well or nothing does.

Cynicism trusts darkness, but not light. It gets real about pain but has no capacity to get real about beauty. The cynical trust brokenness, but not healing. If hypocrisy stood in front of him, the cynic would believe it. But if true wholesomeness were to visit, the real thing—the real thing that he longs for—he would dismiss it.

Cynicism can never embrace Joy. It can never embrace goodness. It might be an illusion after all. Because one thing might trick you in life, all things everywhere are without trust.

Cynicism can help us for a while. It has its place. But cynicism will never save us or bring us home because we would doubt any remedy that would come our way. The one thing in life that a cynic trusts is doubt. The cynic ultimately says to the rest of us, you can't trust anything, except my cynicism, to get through life. Jerram writes, "Cynicism is corrosive—it works like a cancer taking over all that is healthy and hopeful, and we are all impacted by it."[10]

Cynicism doesn't know how to stand, feisty with hope, staring at a tomb, or a leprous hand, or a Jesus apologist collapsing into a heap of tears out of love for neighbors and the longing for redemption. We are helpless to cure without God.

Apologetics Amid the Dishes

Those years ago, when I was a student, about to graduate from seminary, I had lunch with Jerram in his study on campus. As our conversation came to a close, and as our plates sat barren of all but crumbs, we rose to go. We walked toward the door into the hallway of the old Rayburn house and I made an offer, wanting to prove helpful.

"Shall I take our plates to your secretary?"

Jerram kept walking but slowed his pace. Concern grabbed onto the contours of his brows. He looked out over his glasses and into my eyes. Gently, but quite firmly, he said, "Zack, my secretary is not our maid. She is not paid to do our dishes. We mustn't treat her as such. We can take our own dishes to the sink and wash them ourselves." The Apologist was the first to defend the dignity of a secretary and then to sink his hands into the dirty dish-water and scrub.

Years and years later, when I was a fellow professor, a trauma had burst the pipes within the walls and beneath the floors of my life. Jerram had always invited folks to stop by his home unannounced. I finally ventured to take him up on his unusual invitation. I knocked at the door. His dear wife answered and warmly welcomed me. Just inside the door, the landing allowed one to either go upstairs or downstairs. Jerram was downstairs. Unbeknownst to me, Jerram had just come in from his garden and was downstairs changing out of his work clothes and toweling off the sweat from the balmy summer morning. Unbeknownst to him, I was standing there on the landing.

So, sweaty and dressed quite differently from what an occasion of receiving a visitor normally requires, Jerram started up the stairs and there I was. A bit red in the face but with a smile and warmth, he reached out to welcome me. We sat on the couch in the living room, sipping tea, having sandwiches. The Apologist didn't look his best. There was no "show." What he offered was himself; a place of welcome for my quiet ache of tears.

Amid the welcome of compassion and gentleness and a listening presence, true truth was not compromised. After noticing a rising bitterness in my voice he said, "You are rightly hurt and you have every reason to feel as you do. As you hurt, remember, be angry but do not sin in your anger for our anger cannot bring about the kingdom of God" (Jas. 1:20).

When an apologist commends Jesus, not only by the content of his talk, but also by the Jesus-manner of his ways, it can confound us. The eye contact alone is among the most authentic, restful, and welcoming eye contact we've ever experienced. It is so rare to encounter someone who listens to us this truly that we can put up our defenses, just because this kind of welcome feels so foreign.

And yet, apologetics at its core has to do with giving a reason for the hope that we personally have in Jesus. This hope includes argument and defense, commendation and reasoning, but it also reveals our personal experience of what it means to look to Jesus to find hope for our own life.

So, when you ask the apologist (as I did), "if there is a heaven, what is it that you look forward to?" He just might surprise you. He might say something about the beauty of Jesus and how, in his presence, he looks forward to learning how to play the flute. "I've never had time in this life because of other responsibilities. But I've always wanted to learn."

This way of hope has its own kind of defense and commendation to it. We not only defend and commend by giving reasons for our hope, but by the hope itself, the One in whom we hope changes our way of being in the world.

Third Objection: What about Speaking the Truth in Love?

If we are not careful, we tend to use this phrase in such a way that "speaking truth" means saying hard and confrontational things to people, and we therefore define "in love" as making sure we have a nice tone to our voice or that we begin our sentence with "no offense but…."

I hope, however, that you can see that Jesus' actions of love, along with the clear statements above regarding how Peter, James, John, and Paul, defined love, will expose how anemic and trite equating love with a nice tone is, and how sad it is that "truth" is only equated with hard or frowning things.

To speak of our hope is to defend what is true. To do so with all the resources of gentleness and respect undercuts trite smiles or polite tones.

After Paul calls upon us to speak the truth in love, he qualifies and expands upon what he actually means. When we speak and do life with one another, we are meant to resist sinful anger, dismiss stealing from others, stop using our words to tear down others, and reveal grace for them (Eph. 4:25–30). In fact, to speak the truth in love requires that we Christians: *"Let all bitterness and wrath and anger and clamor and slander be put away from you, along with all malice. Be kind to one another, tenderhearted, forgiving one another, as God in Christ forgave you."* (Eph. 4:31–32)

Seeing love as merely being nice or using an emoji reveals that we remain amateur in our biblical understanding of truth. Social media distance, up-close and personal coldness, or avoidance reveals our strangeness to love. True love costs us. It bends us into patience, humility, kindness, and tenderhearted esteem for the persons we encounter. They experience us as patient, kind, and tender people of deep conviction.

No wonder we often want to reduce what love actually requires of us. After all, when Paul describes love as kind, patient, etc, he is ultimately describing who Jesus is! The height, depth, width, and breadth of Jesus' love is an ocean. The smallness, shallowness, slimness, and narrowness of our views and expressions of love are tiny drops on the smallest tip of just one of his waves.

Furthermore, love and truth are not as easily separated into separate categories as we would let on. Notice how Jesus' follower named John puts these two together:

Whoever says he is in the light and hates his brother is still in darkness. 1 John 2:9

If anyone says, "I love God," and hates his brother, he is a liar; for he who does not love his brother whom he has seen cannot love God whom he has not seen. 1 John 4:20

Perhaps you, as an evangelical reader, see the word "brother" in these verses. You think to yourself, "He isn't calling us to love other-than-Christians. He is calling us to love Christians." I offer three brief statements for you to consider:

1. At minimum, by our own reasoning, many of us will still have to admit that our love for fellow followers of Jesus is amateur compared to what Jesus and his apostles say that love is, especially with those who disagree with or differ from us.
2. We are saying that we only need to love those who are like us, so we receive Jesus' strong correction (Luke 6:32–36) because we have severely reduced "neighbor love."
3. We are like those who fall short on both counts in Jesus' teaching, *"You have heard that it was said, 'You shall love your neighbor and hate your enemy'"* (Matt. 5:43). We've become those who no longer say "love your neighbor," and we've become those who say "we can hate those who aren't our brothers and are enemies to us."

No wonder Francis Schaeffer remarked that, "Biblical orthodoxy without compassion is surely the ugliest thing in the world." It proposes to uphold truth by using false ways of relating in order to do it.

In her novel, *Death Comes to the Archbishop,* Willa Cather describes the rare gift of a face that isn't false in its welcome toward another human being, especially when that other human being differs culturally and spiritually:

> Jacinto liked the Bishop's way of meeting people.... In his experience, white people, when they addressed Indians, always put on a false face. There were many kinds of false faces.... The Bishop put on none at all... Jacinto thought this remarkable. [11]

Cather describes what a person who wasn't a follower of Jesus experienced in the presence of one who was.

As I think back on Jerram the Apologist, I realize that what strikes me most is not the deep intellectual capacity which he possessed for addressing perplexing questions, or the history of thought in which he was well-versed, but rather, the absence of false faces when he did so and the hospitable room given to others because they are human beings. It gives me hope that gentleness toward and respect for others can become a way of life in Jesus. A life of grace-dependence gradually joins the solidity of our reasoning and builds its case for Christ to those who ask.

So, the boy who asked his father after my first sermon, "Daddy, why did that man yell so much?" was right! He instinctively recognized my need for a closer embodiment in my being to what I was proposing to teach. After all, to burn red-in-the-face and to yell with a pointing finger about grace exposed a profound split in me. Grace, by its very nature, isn't a red-faced yeller.

No wonder what Jacinto observed in the Archbishop pleasantly startled him. Disconnected preaching and preachers, where the thing spoken of finds little resemblance to the way one speaks or wears it, is commonplace. But it is truly remarkable, by which I mean, it is truly a work of Jesus' grace, when in some incomplete but substantive measure, a person is actually in the world among his neighbors as Jesus was with his (1 John 2:6).

---

1. Peter applies here what Jesus taught him and us regarding what it means to love a neighbor, including our enemy (Matthew 6).

2. Sylvia Plath, *The Bell Jar* (Portsmouth, NH: Heinemann, 1963), 82.
3. John Fischer, "Learning to Cry for the Culture," *Christianity Today*, March 19, 2007, http://www.christianitytoday.com/ct/2007/april/13.40.html.
4. William Edgar, *Schaeffer on the Christian Life: Counter Cultural Spirituality* (Wheaton, IL: Crossway, 2013), Kindle Location 3712.
5. William Shakespeare, *Henry VIII.*
6. Francis Schaeffer, *The Mark of the Christian* (Downers Grove, IL: IVP Press, 1970).
7. James K. Beilby, *Thinking About Christian Apologetics: What It Is and Why We Do It* (Downers Grove, IL: Intervarsity Press, 2011), 20.
8. Jerram Barrs, "Francis Schaeffer: The Man and His Message" (2006) quoted in Michael Poore, "The Virtue of Listening—Because there are no Little People," The Humanitas Forum on Christianity and Culture, February 3, 2015, accessed December 14, 2017, ttp://humanitas.org/?p=3229.
9. For more on this subject, see Zack Eswine, *Preaching to a Post-Everything World: Crafting Biblical Sermons that Connect with our Culture* (Chicago: Baker, 2008).
10. Jerram Barrs, "The Saturation of Cynicism," Covenant Theological Seminary, February 28, 2007, accessed May 7, 2019, https://www.covenantseminary.edu/the-saturation-of-cynicism/.
11. Willa Cather, *Death Comes to the Archbishop* (New York: Vintage Classics, 1990), 93–94.

SHORT STORIES ABOUT JERRAM FROM HIS STUDENTS

You would never see Jerram peeved about anything, except Pharisaical Christians. He had exceeding kindness to everyone, but a sharper edge would emerge when he heard something proud or harsh coming from those who should truly know better. Having said that, I used to drive Jerram and prospective students on admissions lunches. One day driving back to Covenant Seminary he stopped his conversation with the student and said to me, "Do watch your speed at this intersection. The police love to give tickets there. Don't they have criminals to arrest or something?!"
I smiled on the inside.
Even Jerram gets peeved by speed traps.
Stu Kerns

As an RUF intern, I had read *The Heart of Evangelism* before seminary, and many of the teachers in my life highly valued Jerram and what Jerram had to say. So, when I arrived at Covenant Seminary as a student after my internship was completed, I have to admit I was a bit starstruck. I had this false notion that someone so accomplished would likely be ostentatious in someway. However at a student orientation event, I heard another respected professor say that Jerram Barrs was the kind of person that you *wanted* to repent to. "Wanted to repent to!" That hit my heart so hard, as being wrong, repenting, and apologizing were (and still are) very hard for me. But, in that moment realized that I wanted to exude that goodness to others. I wanted it to be true of me one day that I would be the kind of person that someone wanted to repent to. I wanted to be the kind of person that people knew would handle shame with grace, kindness, and understanding, while returning them to Jesus.

Jerram always took time to talk with his students. During my time at Covenant, Jerram regularly wore noise-canceling headphones because an outbreak of shingles inside his ear made any sound above a whisper incredibly painful. But rather than avoid the pain, he was regularly in conversations with others. I imagine at a great cost to himself. I also really appreciate his love, care, and ability to see the dignity in non-Christians. Having come from a predominantly non-Christian family, I could never quite relate to the demonization of those outside of Christianity. However, personal story after story, Jerram expounded on the beauties of all people, including those who have been marginalized and neglected by the Church.

Jerram's heart and care for other people is so amazing—the way he and Vicki have constantly been focused on ministering to and loving others! As one of the only women in the Masters of Divinity program, I felt a special sense of care from him. Before I was married, he always made a point to engage my questions, encourage my curiosities, and demonstrate before my brothers that he valued my contribution. When I was engaged to my husband Lee, who was also a student, we met with Jerram. Toward the end of our conversation with Jerram, he was encouraging us as we were about to embark on a life of ministry together, and he encouraged us to allow ourselves to be seen as a "two-for-one." He said that churches will see two gifted people and two people willing to serve, and it is honoring and fair for both for us to be compensated for our work. I felt so seen, cared for, and valued, and I was humbled by his encouragement for Lee and I to expect others to treat me similarly. He is truly a man of greatness and humility, and he is constantly thinking of others! I am truly grateful for all that he has done for us, and I love him for teaching me how to love more sincerely.

Sarah Viggiano Wright

In the fall of 2016, I walked into Jerram's office to pitch an idea for an

independent study. I was working toward my MDiv. I wanted to study the modern horror film and the historical development of horror. My biblical basis for the study was grounded in Romans 8:22. I was asking the question if the artist could inform the groans of creation, give some measure of definition to that which is difficult to discern—what is the world groping at to understand its fallen reality? Jerram approved it, and I enjoyed various affirming conversations with Jerram, and he even encourage me to not exclude various types of horror films which I had pre-judged as not being worthy of study. I included those films in the end. When I was working toward my MAC, I referenced horror films all the time. The independent study with Jerram, and his relational presence helped shaped my choice of vocational ministry. I'm a counselor.
Scott Jones

Jerram was answering a question in regard to legalism as it relates to evangelism. It was about a pool party and swimsuit policy for a high school youth group. A youth pastor was asking his advice and someone in class, after he shared the story, said that Jerram was encouraging kids to have sex with each other by allowing girls to just wear the swimsuit they chose rather than having a legalistic policy. That's when he said, "If I were a dragon, I'd consume you with my fire breath!"
Jerram still tells this story in class as a teaching moment, and it is hilarious. My favorite part of this is when he recounts this moment, he has that Jerram side-eye looking down at the ground lightly laughing with pause. Then quickly turns to the class and adds, "And of course after class I sought him out to ask his forgiveness." Yep. That's the man.
Ben Sinnard
Jason Pogue
Jim Pullizi

In my first year of seminary, at an FSI ministry lunch, Jerram asked each of the students in attendance what we had done before coming to seminary. I shared that I had been a carpenter. After the lunch, Jerram approached me and asked if I could rebuild the deck at his house.

Beginning with that project, I had the distinct honor of being Jerram's carpenter for the next four years.

During my second year of seminary, I was in the middle of installing a greenhouse in Jerram's garden. I had gotten to the point in the semester where I had papers and projects due in nearly all of my classes. In addition, I was also working as the youth director in a local church.

The greenhouse was halfway installed. I was overwhelmed and didn't have time to come work on it. I felt ashamed because I thought I was letting Jerram down. For three weeks, I avoided him on campus.

On day I was walking towards the chapel, and I didn't see him coming towards me. Before I knew it, he was standing right in front of me, and he asked me how I was doing. I immediately started to apologize for not finishing the greenhouse. I told him I knew he must be disappointed in me, and I would try to finish it as soon as possible.

Jerram wrapped his arms around me. He hugged me and told me he wasn't disappointed in me at all. He said, "I know how hard you're working. I'm not concerned about the greenhouse. I'm concerned for you." And then he told me he loved me.

In that moment, Jerram taught me something that he would reiterate time after time as I worked on other projects around his house. While he was always grateful for the work that I did for him, that wasn't where my value comes from, and wasn't why he loved me. He loved (and still does) me because of Jesus. My value and my worth are rooted in Christ. Jerram's value and worth are rooted in Christ. Because Jerram knows how greatly he has been loved by Jesus, he loves others greatly in the name of Jesus.

Jerram taught me that I can do work that is valuable, but my value never comes from what I do.

Todd Crusey

At graduation, Jerram approached me and told me he wept when he read my final paper because he was so moved. It was a research paper. I was so humbled in that moment and figured that if Covenant Seminary equipped me to write a research paper that resulted in Jerram weeping, it had truly been a worthwhile experience.

Blythe Sizemore

During my first semester of seminary, I was a knucklehead and thought I knew how to do stuff. I took this internship at a smaller church and just immediately made a mess of it. I was fired after six weeks (and I should have been). I was completely convinced I wasn't cut out for ministry and I was thinking about being done with seminary after the first semester.

I was taking several of Jerram's classes, and one of the other students told Jerram what was going on and encouraged me to go talk with him about it. Jerram finally caught me after class one night and told me he'd heard what was going on. I started crying and telling Jerram that I didn't think I was cut out for ministry. He told me that what I needed to do wasn't quit the ministry, but learn from what had happened, repent of my sin, and let it make me a better pastor. If it weren't for Jerram, I don't think I would have finished seminary or entered ministry. It was Jerram's classes, stories, and wisdom that kept me going every semester. I owe my ministry, and certainly the way I think about evangelism, to Jerram.

Wes Martin

My wife and I told ourselves we would wait until after seminary to have children because we couldn't afford it, but the Lord had other plans halfway through the MDiv program. We couldn't find childcare during Jerram's "Theology of Ministry" course when Courtney needed to work. It was a stressful day. I hesitated to sit in the back with our infant's stroller with my welcoming friends, but I left the room of sixty students multiple times when a few students would stare (after all, they spent thousands of dollars to be here).

During class Jerram quipped with a smile, "Her cries are the amen to my lesson" and people laughed, which helped my self-consciousness a bit.

But after class, he approached me in the hall and these words brought me to tears: "Cody, this covenant child is ALWAYS welcome in my classroom, and don't you dare feel like you need to keep her out. Please, bring her. It is a good lesson for the other students, and I love getting to see little Rebekah." I brought her to class the rest of the semester. Nobody will know how much this made a mark on this first-time dad (especially given that another professor asked me to not bring her to

class—though most Covenant profs were receptive to her). I can't tell this story years later without getting choked up. Talk about a theology of ministry! That covenant attitude I carry to my pastorate as much as anything else I learned in that class. God bless Jerram.
Cody Brobst

I remember a story Jerram told us in class about when he worked at L'Abri. He was sitting at his desk one afternoon when he said he had a sudden, strong urge to go out to the road. He got up and ran, and he found a woman who had been staying at L'Abri who was a few seconds away from throwing herself in front of a truck. He stopped her. He used this as an example of the Holy Spirit working through his people in the here and now to push back the curse of death and destruction. Here was a professor at the denominational seminary teaching us to listen to the Holy Spirit in an extremely practical way. Never forgot it. In addition, when we had to write our letters to an unbeliever in Apologetics and Outreach, the man I was writing actually came to faith while my letter was in the mail. Jerram not only stopped class to announce it, but we all publicly thanked God for his conversion. It was one more place where we saw that this was not an academic exercise for Jerram or for his students. This was kingdom work.
Christine Burkley Gordon

I often tell the story of my first Francis Schaeffer Institute public engagement event at Borders bookstore where Jerram talked about Lewis and Narnia. During the Q & A, a lady with tears in her eyes genuinely asked/commented, "Prof Barrs, I feel guilty. What if I want to go to Narnia more than I want to go to heaven?" In return Jerram, with tears in his eyes said, "My dear, that's not your fault. That's our fault in the church for not adequately proclaiming the glory and majesty of the New Heaven and Earth."
Eric Mitchell Ashley

Jerram allowed me, at the age of fourteen, to sit in on a few night

classes while my dad was studying for his MDiv. Jerram patiently and thoroughly answered my questions even when I (as I realize in hindsight) monopolized his class, and other's tuition, with comments and "clarifications" that could have been left unsaid. But those conversations were not wasted. As I started to have serious doubts about the faith or painful church experiences over the next decade, much of what Jerram said on those evenings resounded and kept me reading my Bible. I highly doubt I would have ever gone to seminary or work in ministry today without someone like Jerram taking the time to listen.
Caleb Miller

Hands down, Jerram is the meekest man I know and have ever known! When my husband, Eric, and I were engaged, we were in a small Bible Study he was teaching. One thing that stuck with me was his definition of meekness verses being a doormat for someone. He taught that the biggest difference is a doormat is weak and unhappy but meanness is strong and willing to serve others. Being meek is what Jesus modeled for us when he overturned the moneychangers in the temple. He was angry yet meek in his response to them. Jesus was always kingdom focused and that is how we need to be as well. Jerram's love and care for others is immeasurable!
Hope Burch

When Jerram officiated my wedding, we told him that there would be a lot of non- and nominal Christians there, so he should say and preach whatever he felt he needed. He preached one of the most beautiful sermons I've ever heard.
Then, in classic Jerram form, he spent nearly the entire reception speaking with an atheistic Jew who was so drawn to his graciousness that he had to talk to him.
After the reception, that person (the atheist) came up to me and said, "I have never, ever met a Christian like that man."
I'm so thankful for Jerram.
Jeremy McNeill

My seminary experience was not easy. I quit half way through when my wife and I had our first child. I'm not very academic, I actually failed one of my classes. Which means I have an F on my Covenant Seminary transcripts. I eventually came back to finish seminary part time just so my first two years weren't a waste of money but I switched out of the MDiv program and wasn't sure what vocation I would head into. During my time in seminary, I worked in Jerram's gardens and mowed his lawn so I had gotten to know him very well and he was well aware of all my struggles. Toward the end of my time at Covenant, he called me into his office and sat me down and said, "Brad, I would be honored to be a member in any church where you were my pastor." That conversation changed my life. I would not be in ministry as a vocation if not for Jerram.

And one of the most profound impacts on my view of my marriage is when Jerram called me to tell me about how God had healed his hearing condition. He said that one of the greatest joys about it was that he could sit and listen to Vicki play the piano once again. His love for his wife was profound.

Brad Lucht

I'm sure Jerram was late to class that day, and I'm sure his class had no idea the healing work from which he had just walked away. I arrived at Covenant Seminary in January, 2007. My husband and I both decided to work full time while we attended seminary.

A month after we arrived, I was hired as Jerram's assistant. I was so afraid to talk to him at first because of his Tinnitus, so we mostly communicated through email. He was warm and kind. I always felt valued by him which made it a joy to serve him. One day I was making copies for his Apologetics and Outreach class which was to start in fifteen minutes.

When he came to retrieve them from me at the copier, I apologized profusely for not having them completed yet. He looked into my face and said, "I get the impression you have not been treated well by men." I was stunned! How could he know that? Was it so obvious?

I began to cry right there at the copier. He asked questions and listened with kind eyes. I shed ears as I shared with him several stories over the prior ten years in ministry.

I didn't realize how wounded I was. I just thought the way I had been treated was normal.

He told me he was sorry! He hadn't done anything wrong with regard to me, and yet he asked for forgiveness—on behalf of all the men who had said hurtful things, shunned me, or made me feel like my opinion as a woman in ministry was not important. God used Jerram in my life over the next two years to redeem my view of men in ministry and to give me a renewed sense of hope that God could and would use me as a woman in his kingdom work.

April Barber

7:30 am on my first day of seminary (I started in a Spring term), Jerram opens his apologetics class with what I felt was a gross over-generalization of something. I let bitterness fester for weeks and finally decided I had to talk to him. I expressed my concern. He listened attentively. I readied myself to argue it out. And then he said, "I'm sorry." I sat speechless, completely blindsided. I had been the jerk, ignorant of the log in my own eye, and he showed me humility. Every one of his words after that carried the weight of gold.

Michael McBride

Jerram gave us an assignment of writing a letter to someone who wasn't a Christian to explain the Gospel. But the most important part was first to show grace and understanding for the other person's worldview. I've worked in cross-cultural ministry and as a missionary all these years. The one simple assignment of learning to show grace and appreciation of another person's worldview has been one of the most useful ministry tool besides learning the language.

Paul Fox

While I was a student at Covenant, I was blessed to have office hours with Jerram a few times. In one of those, he asked me what my hobbies were, and I shared that I really loved superhero movies. I told him that in one particular movie, there was a conversation between two characters about there being grace for the failures of humanity, which surprised me because it was written by a staunch atheist. It was a clear sign of common grace.

When I finished, Jerram shared that he had been praying for one particular movie director for many years, and that when we see beauty in something, we should pray for the person that created it. He then proceeded to ask me the name of the director of the movie I had just talked about and then wrote it down. I have never forgotten that moment. It showed me how oriented towards loving and praying for others Jerram was, and that he truly believed that God is moving in the hearts of people today.

Alvin Lin

I first heard of Professor Barrs in 1997 while listening to taped lectures for an apologetics course I was taking by extension. Other than Jack Miller, I had never heard another person speak so powerfully, so truthfully, and so boldly at the same time.

One might underestimate Professor Barrs and consider him soft on sin because he is so loving and gentle. Not so!

I personally experienced his bold correction when I said something in a second class I took from him, a comment that unbiblically blurred a line between Christians and non-Christians in need of the Gospel.

In any case, I took another correspondence class taught by Barrs in the summer of 2000, the run up to my last year at Covenant Seminary, while I was interning with World Harvest Mission in Ireland. As I listened to those lectures, I determined that before I graduated from Covenant I wanted to spend one-on-one time with him.

For a bit of context, because of my deeply broken relationship with my earthly father and those attendant insecurities and longing for love, I took advantage of all the free counseling I could get while in seminary. Those counseling times with grad students getting their practicum hours and counseling professors were a great blessing to me personally. However, it was Professor Barrs who held me in the arms of Christ more than anyone else. When I finally set up the meeting with him, he was so willing and eager to give me time in his busy schedule. I was afraid of presuming upon him (and other faculty members too), but he had this gentle joy about him that caused me to let down all my self-protective strategies for living and engaging others, including my naturally hard demeanor.

It felt a bit surreal as we talked freely about my relationship with my dad. As one who has a hard time crying, seeing tears welling up in his eyes as I talked was unnerving as he gently probed and asked discerning questions. His tears brought tears to my eyes as our time continued. As we came to the end of our meeting, he shocked me when he stood and wrapped his arms around me and said "I love you."

I'm fairly skeptical when people say those words around lightly. There was no cynicism from me that day. I had never had another man love me the way he did. And the good ol' hard person that I am melted in his embrace.

No one has ever taught me more about the love of my Heavenly Father than Jack Miller, whom I never actually met personally.

That said, no one has ever brought me to actually experience the embrace of my Heavenly Father more than Jerram Barrs. One of the joys of my life has been to write a biography of the life, ministry, and teaching of Jack Miller. As I think about next writing projects, I would greatly enjoy writing a biography of the life, ministry, and teaching of Jerram Barrs.

Mike Graham

In his well-known letter to a non-Christian assignment, I chose to write to my grandfather. Spending a semester intentionally remembering and processing through our relationship helped me begin to understand some of the heartbreaking pain in his life. My grandfather died suddenly the week before our final exam. My view of his life and death were deeply impacted by the months I had spent drafting the letter. I believe I was free to grieve his loss in ways I could not have done without Jerram's guidance. When the semester started I had no idea the Lord could work such amazing healing through one assignment. But he did.

Among many other things, Jerram taught me that God's love is offered for both the offended and the offender. That was over ten years ago, but as I have worked through the various griefs of life, those I am ministering too and my own, this lesson has continually guided me.

Becky Kiern

ABOUT WHITE BLACKBIRD BOOKS

White blackbirds are extremely rare, but they are real. They are blackbirds that have turned white over the years as their feathers have come in and out over and over again. They are a redemptive picture of something you would never expect to see but that has slowly come into existence over time.

There is plenty of hurt and brokenness in the world. There is the hopelessness that comes in the midst of lost jobs, lost health, lost homes, lost marriages, lost children, lost parents, lost dreams, loss.

But there also are many white blackbirds. There are healed marriages, children who come home, friends who are reconciled. There are hurts healed, children fostered and adopted, communities restored. Some would call these events entirely natural, but really they are unexpected miracles.

The books in this series are not commentaries, nor are they meant to be the final word. Rather, they are a collage of biblical truth applied to current times and places. The authors share their poverty and trust the Lord to use their words to strengthen and encourage his people. Consider these books as entries into the discussion.

May this series help you in your quest to know Christ as he is found in the Gospel through the Scriptures. May you look for and even expect the rare white blackbirds of God's redemption through Christ in your midst. May you be thankful when you look down and see your feathers have turned. May you also rejoice when you see that others have been unexpectedly transformed by Jesus.

www.ingramcontent.com/pod-product-compliance
Lightning Source LLC
Chambersburg PA
CBHW020150090426
42734CB00008B/764